The Predicament of Privilege

NEW DIRECTIONS IN SCANDINAVIAN STUDIES

ANDY NESTINGEN, SERIES EDITOR

This series offers interdisciplinary approaches to the study of the Nordic region of Scandinavia and the Baltic States and their cultural connections in North America. By redefining the boundaries of Scandinavian studies to include the Baltic States and Scandinavian America, the series presents books that focus on the study of the culture, history, literature, and politics of the North.

The Predicament of Privilege

Inequality and Ambivalence in
Contemporary Scandinavian Culture

DEVIKA SHARMA

UNIVERSITY OF WASHINGTON PRESS
Seattle

The Predicament of Privilege was made possible in part by grants from the Independent Research Fund Denmark, the New Carlsberg Foundation, the Scandinavian Studies Department at the University of Washington, and the Samuel and Althea Stroum Endowed Book Fund.

Design by Katrina Noble   Composed in Adobe Caslon Pro

UNIVERSITY OF WASHINGTON PRESS   uwapress.uw.edu

Cataloging information available from the Library of Congress
Library of Congress Control Number: 2025038042
ISBN 9780295754109 (hardcover)
ISBN 9780295754116 (paperback)
ISBN 9780295754123 (ebook)

For EU product safety concerns, please contact Easy Access System Europe Oü 16879218, Mustamäe tee 50, 10621, Tallinn, Estonia, gpsr.requests@easproject.com, +372 56 98939.

∞ This paper meets the requirements of ANSI/NISO Z39.48-1992 (Permanence of Paper).

Contents

Preface and Acknowledgments

AFTER SUBMITTING THE manuscript for this book, I read Thomas Piketty's *Capital and Ideology* (2020) and *A Brief History of Equality* (2022). I had long wanted to read these impressive and imaginative books, and I should have done so earlier—not least because Piketty's studies provide a helpful framework and vocabulary for thinking through some of the bearings of *The Predicament of Privilege* outside its most immediate contexts. That is why I shall say a few words about the connections between this study and Piketty's work in this preface and then return to them again in the coda.

Both *The Predicament of Privilege* and Piketty's work deal with inequality, and this book shares Piketty's overall interest in public expressions of disapproval of the inequality regimes under which we live.[1] My study is about a crisis in one dominant framework for making sense of the inequalities between the global South and the global North: modern sentimental humanitarianism. Piketty would describe such a crisis as an ideological conflict.[2] I describe it instead as a crisis in sensibility, as a critical mutation in humanitarian sensibility. To the public culture I examine—the sources on which this book builds its argument are not economic statistics but cultural artifacts—humanitarian sentiments and attitudes have become morally suspect. They no longer seem right. This modification of the historically sedimented ethos of sentimental humanitarian sensibility I term *skeptimentality*.

I examine this crisis in humanitarian sensibility not as it is viewed by a local or global "underclass" but, rather, as it is lived and navigated by a relatively privileged collective subject: the Scandinavian middle classes. My study demonstrates that as an established moral, cultural, and political framework for comprehending and responding to inequality and privilege in a global context, modern humanitarianism has become suspect and thus, in a sense, interrupted. Put simply: the well-established modern narrative that explains to the globally privileged Nordic publics that humanitarian aid is a way, perhaps the only way, to repair the world has come to seem false, syrupy, unsustainable, imperialistic, and above all embarrassingly sentimental to these same globally well-to-do publics. "No human society can live," Piketty argues, "without an ideology to make sense of its inequalities" (2020, 1034). This is, in essence, the cultural work carried out by what I call *skeptimental privilege sensibility*: trying to make sense of disparity in a global context. In this manner, the skeptimental sensibility of privilege is a response to the global inequality regime in which we live now.

Portions of this book have appeared in different form in *The Nordic Journal of Aesthetics, Konsthistorisk tidskrift / Journal of Art History, Comparative Literature Studies, K&K, Journal of Aesthetics and Culture*, and *Discursive Framings of Human Rights*, edited by J. R. Kjærgård & K-M. Simonsen. I am grateful to Penn State University Press, Taylor & Francis, and the journal editors for permission to reuse those portions here. Financial support for the project was given in the form of network funding from Independent Research Fund Denmark and a grant from the New Carlsberg Foundation.

The Predicament of Privilege has greatly benefited from a number of collective efforts, including rewarding editorial collaborations with Elisabeth Oxfeldt, Mikkel Bolt Rasmussen, Christian Dahl, Jonas Ross Kjærgård, and Tue Andersen Nexø on special issues of the Nordic journal *K&K* on, respectively, guilt and shame in Scandinavia, cultural critique, affectivity, and sentimentality. The Interventions Research Network on Humanitarian Politics and Culture (funded by Independent Research Fund Denmark), which I led from 2017 to 2021, provided a timely infrastructure for initiating a host of transdisciplinary collaborations on our shared topic; I would especially like to thank my co-conveners Anne Vestergaard and Sine Plambech for the expertise and organizational effort they put into it. A special thanks to Miriam Ticktin, Bruce Robbins, Iain Wilkinson, Wendy Hesford, Michaël Neuman, Lynn Festa, Didier Fassin, Thomas Keenan, and Jasbir Puar for contributing to our network conversations in Copenhagen, and in profound ways to this study.

The Predicament of Privilege has been further enriched by enduring conversations with my colleagues at the Department of Arts and Cultural Studies, UCPH, and the Comparative Literature and Modern Culture Section in particular. I owe special thanks to Isak Winkel Holm, Lilian Munk Rösing, and Mathias Danbolt for their characteristically clever and helpful responses to early drafts. The book is indebted also to the participants of the research cluster "Nordic Models" at the Department of Arts and Cultural Studies, which has proven to be a highly relevant forum for debates about the cultural politics of the region we call Norden. Thanks to my department chair Helle Munkholm Davidsen for unwavering support when I needed it. Outside UCPH, I would like to thank Lasse Horne Kjældgaard, Bruce Robbins, and Jonas Ross Kjærgård for excellent feedback on chapter drafts. I am very grateful also to Larin McLaughlin and Andrew Nestingen at University of Washington Press and to my anonymous readers at the press. Thanks to Neil Bennun and Elizabeth Mathews for perceptive copyediting.

Friends and family have been mercifully forgetful about exactly how many years I've been working on this book. Adda and Leo added abundant measures of joy and distraction to those years, and I wish to thank them for, among many other things, their tender patience with me. I owe by far the most to Rasmus Øhlenschlæger Madsen, whose support I have relied on heavily while writing this book (and beyond), not least in terms of countless meticulous readings and agile family-managing in pressed time binds. His tireless encouragement is an unearned, and cherished, privilege of my own.

The Predicament of Privilege

Is This Okay?

THE PREDICAMENT OF privilege is the awkward yet ordinary experience, or accusation, that one's global privilege is a problem. In the Scandinavian societies, this predicament raises variants of the same fundamental question: Is this okay? Is it okay, for instance, to go on holiday to Greece in the middle of a refugee crisis? Is it okay to buy fair trade products? Is it okay, or is it hypocritical, to support a humanitarian organization with 100 Norwegian kroner a month? Is it okay to hire a Romanian cleaner? Is my compassion for poor populations elsewhere okay, or is it a sign of my sense of moral superiority? Is it okay to donate your old clothes, or are you then just using the global South as the "garbage bin for the bad conscience of the rich countries," as suggested by the Ghanian beach monitor Joe Ayesu (Jensen 2023, 12)? Is it even okay to ask questions like these, or is it indulgent navel-gazing?

In Scandinavian public discourse, the predicament of privilege takes up a lot of space, not least in the ways in which market actors and popular culture simultaneously address it and try to soothe the experience of it. For instance, when a Danish sustainable clothing brand that manufactures in India employs the slogan "This is okay. Certified okay!" it seeks to assure its customers that the commodities it produces and the lifestyle to which they may add up are virtually guilt-free.[1] Today, in Scandinavian publics, this kind of reassurance resonates in many places and in many different tonalities. However, the continuing reassurance that this or that product or lifestyle choice is perfectly okay also points to a shared reality where some things are, in fact, not okay.

In this study, I argue that the predicament of privilege is a sensibility central to contemporary Scandinavian cultural life. We live in a historical moment where the Nordic middle classes have gotten a sense of living at the expense of others. I want to emphasize, however, that the predicament of privilege is not exclusively a Scandinavian problematic. It is, rather, a broader Western phenomenon, registering as it does a sense of living off economically and politically exploitative systems and their histories, a sense that came to the fore as a historical matter with the postwar decoloniza- tion movements. While this historical sensibility is thus not confined to the Scandinavian region alone, it has gained relevance in twenty-first-century Scandinavian societies where the postwar development of a Nordic welfare state has fostered a popular egalitarian imaginary according to which socio- economic privilege is not perfectly okay.

What makes the Scandinavian case special is that, here, the issue of privilege takes on a pressing character due to the presence of a historically sedimented welfare-statist preoccupation with equality and a discourse on benevolent Nordic internationalism, both of which play a constitutive part in the Nordic senses of self. The predicament of privilege is urgent in contem- porary Scandinavian societies because it is ordinary, so to speak, insofar as it organizes public discourse and shared cultural practices rather than being mainly a topic of intellectual concern or limited to certain political and class demographics (as would seem to be the case with the UK and US contexts, for instance). That is why I focus mainly on this region. I shall say more about the specificity of the Scandinavian case in the latter part of this introduction; for now, let me just note in passing that the egalitarian imaginary—by which I refer also to the idea that Scandinavian countries are exceptionally egalitar- ian societies—is simultaneously a precondition for and at stake in the Nordic sensibility of privilege with which *The Predicament of Privilege* is concerned.

Pivotal to the predicament of privilege is the experience of benefiting from an unjust world order. This is an order considered unjust to the extent that it exploits some populations while conferring benefits upon others—"me and others like me."The moral philosopher Sandra Lee Bartky offers a useful description of the meaning of *privilege*, as I use the term in this study:

> "Privilege" in this context is a special advantage, or favor that is granted to some individual or group of individuals and not to others; the term also carries the connotation of an exemption from some duty or burden. The guilt that emerges from my recognition that I occupy a privileged position in the social totality has to do not only with the benefits I enjoy that I have not earned but also and equally with the fact that others have been excluded from their enjoyment unjustly by a mere accident of birth.

Here is a double consciousness: the recognition of my unearned privilege and the concomitant recognition that the unjust denial of privilege to others is the result of the "normal" workings of the social order. (Bartky 2002, 136)

When speaking of privilege as something someone *enjoys,* in the active sense that pleasure may be derived from its possession, we miss the central trait of privilege sensibility, according to which privilege is not so much an object of enjoyment but a condition provoking feelings of embarrassment, guilt, indignation, sadness, entitlement, resignation, defensiveness, or apathy.

Considering one's privilege to be a problem implies intuiting an exploitative global infrastructure with complex histories and lasting effects. There are various labels for this historically sedimented infrastructure: capitalism, imperialism, racism, neocolonial violence, the capitalocene, neoliberal hegemony, white supremacy, or simply what Ruth Wilson Gilmore, referencing Stuart Hall, calls the "global maldistribution of symbolic and material resources" (Gilroy and Gilmore 2020). In Scandinavian public culture, however, this world order figures not so much as a clearly demarcated political system or a mode of government but, rather, as a conglomerate of diffuse and unfinished histories of injustice. Diffuse, distracted, or disavowed, a sense of profound global inequality is key to what I call *the predicament of privilege.* To subjects who sense their privilege to be a problem, the problem is also that the tools they employ to try remedy the injustice—say, humanitarian donations, fair trade products, or socially engaged art—all seem to spring from that same exploitative infrastructure.

In his book *If You're an Egalitarian, How Come You're So Rich?,* the philosopher G. A. Cohen examines the moral disposition of people who believe in equality, think of themselves as egalitarian, do not "give a relevant amount of [their] money away," and yet still believe their behavior to be in line with their egalitarian principles (Cohen 2000, 156). I mention Cohen's work here in order to distinguish this particular problem in moral philosophy—which is related to the "shallow pond" argument offered most prominently by the moral philosopher Peter Singer—from the predicament of privilege. Cohen asks, "If you hate inequality because you think it is unjust, how can you *qualmlessly* accept and retain money your retention of which embodies that injustice—money which you could give to others, or donate to an egalitarian cause, and thereby diminish, or hope to diminish, the amount of injustice that prevails, by benefiting sufferers of that injustice?" (Cohen 2000, 159). By contrast, I describe the predicament of privilege as the qualms people *do* have about retaining money, possessions, and opportunities, the retention of which embodies an injustice, and as the qualms they *do* have about finding no good-enough solutions. The Scandinavian protagonists described in this book have notably less faith in the charitable ways out of such qualms suggested by Cohen—"giving" and "donating"—and they may very likely doubt even the political *relevance* of their own such qualms. Nevertheless, these qualms are commonplace, and their ramifications can be observed in Nordic art, literature, cinema, volunteerism, ethical consumption, public discourse, and the cultures of feeling articulated in the course of recent decades.

The predicament of privilege and its basic question, Is this okay? are the animating force of the collective Scandinavian sensibility, what I call *the sensibility of privilege*. Identifying a collective sensibility, as I do in this study, does not mean that all Scandinavians feel the same about their relative global privilege. Rather, tracking the sensibility of privilege involves identifying a recurring pattern of moral, emotional, aesthetic, and political articulations in the ways in which Scandinavian culture deals with glaring global inequalities. Historically, the term *sensibility* indicated subjective tenderness and virtue, "innate sensitivity," and "delicate emotional and physical susceptibility" (Todd 1986, 7). Here I use the term to refer to a sensorial and affective form of common sense, a visceral imaginary or collective "historical sensorium" (Berlant 2011, 3).[2] I argue that the Scandinavian sensibility of privilege is a collective sensibility not because all Scandinavians see themselves as unjustly privileged (they do not) but because even very diverse experiences and utterances must relate to this sensibility, this visceral kind of common sense, in order to be meaningful and acceptable *as* experiences or utterances. Scandinavian privilege sensibility gives rise to a wide repertoire of opinions and affective attitudes permeated by political beliefs, class positions, and generational dispositions. It instigates a variety of investments. But to be affected by the predicament of privilege is not the prerogative of, say, guilt-tripping left-leaning elites: The suspicion that "we" live at the expense of "others," the global poor and other others, runs, rather, like a discomforting undercurrent in Scandinavian culture at large. The reassuring response to this suspicion, Don't worry, this is okay! is a soothing response at certain times but profoundly unsettling at others.

Privilege Genres

Analyzing the predicament of privilege as a collective sensibility rather than, say, a problem in moral philosophy or political theory, which it also is, is consequential to my archive and my method. The theories, concepts, and modes of analysis employed in the chapters to follow derive from the traditions of cultural studies, literary studies, and critical theory as these traditions have taken shape mainly within the humanities. Rather than offering a coherent critique of Scandinavian privilege sensibility, however, *The Predicament of Privilege* aims to provide an interpretation of the affective claims, moral-political stakes, aesthetic forms, and theoretical dilemmas called up by this sensibility. Its mode of analysis focuses on the cultural mediation of a historical space of time, present-day Scandinavia, characterized by privilege sensibility: In-depth study of cultural objects registering the predicament of privilege and its private and public reverberations is my method of unearthing what is at stake in this historically specific sensibility.

Art and culture are hardly the only strata of the social real in which to analyze the collective interpretation of privilege. However, our cultural archives are rich locations for tracing the ways in which older fantasies of a better world unravel while new fantasies acquire form and rhythm, if only slowly. The archive of this study includes cultural texts—in the broad sense of cultural objects inviting our "reading"—from domains such as contemporary art, literary fiction, cinema, humanitarian appeals, and other areas of Scandinavian popular and public culture. The cultural texts that compose my archive all engage with some form of humanitarian crisis inciting the sensibility of privilege with questions of responsibility, agency, complicity, indifference, and the (ir)relevance of the privileged subject's feelings of sympathy. I pay attention to the complex and contradictory interpretation conveyed by these cultural texts of global economic inequality, of Nordic privilege, and of conventional humanitarian responses to "what is intolerable about the state of the contemporary world" (Fassin 2012, 252).

Is this okay? is the fundamental question structuring Scandinavian privilege sensibility. In explicating this question, this book is divided into four parts, each of which engages with one subfield of the okay and the not okay: Is it okay *to feel* like this? Is it okay *to look* at this? Is it okay *to (ac)count* like this? Is it okay *to critique* in this way? These four subfields—ways of feeling, seeing, (ac)counting, and critiquing—are significant cultural practices.

They are also critical topics in modern cultural theory, with which this study engages deeply. By studying storylines in Scandinavian cinema that expose well-intentioned and morally good characters, we may come to understand how the predicament of privilege transforms the cultural status and feel of moral sentiments such as compassion and sympathy. By analyzing objects of visual culture that mock the white saviorism of humanitarian iconography, we may grasp how the problematic of what Susan Sontag discusses in *Regarding the Pain of Others* is, in Scandinavian publics, increasingly sensed to be racialized (Sontag 2003). To understand the difficulty of knowing the difference between a benevolent gift and an installment in the repayment of imperial debt, we may study artworks and humanitarian products that complicate notions of "benefactors" and "beneficiaries." Similarly, we also have to analyze the literary fiction and poetry employing an aesthetic of complicity in order to understand the impasse in cultural critique in those scenarios in which the critical subject discovers herself to be in some way complicit.

To a cultural text meditating upon the issue of privilege, the predicament invariably also bears upon the text's own terms of production: the cultural artifact will have to somehow address its own conditions of possibility, checking its privilege, as it were. In literature and works of art, such quandaries of production (and representation) may affect existing notions of the autonomy, authority, and general okayness of art. Take for example the Norwegian poet Cathrine Grøndahl's "Prisen for et dikt" (The price of a poem) from her 2008 collection *Jeg satte mitt håp til verden* (I set my hopes on the world). This poem asks how to write, and exist as, poetry after recognizing one's own entanglement in global inequality.

This poem employs
a daycare provider from Morocco
and a cleaning lady from Poland
It talks for 350 kroner per hour
at the expense of
small children and poor women
who do not know the language
If this poem really appreciates words that much
It ought to pass them on to others, I suppose?
Not just stand there talking
but give the Norwegian child a children's poem

take care of the Moroccan one
so that the mother may learn Norwegian
and pay the cleaning lady
for reading Wislawa Szymborska
out loud in Polish.[3]

This is the suspicion at the heart of the predicament: We, including our poetry, exist at the expense of less affluent others. The poem-subject may employ female care workers for a wage, but the wage does not dissolve the subject's disturbing sense of debt.[4] The poem asks, What is the cost of me, and who pays it? Subjects preoccupied with the predicament of their privilege ask such questions. Experiencing one's privilege as a problem gives rise to all sorts of messy, yet patterned, thoughts and feelings and a range of shared gestures and rhetorics for navigating them.

This study regards Scandinavian privilege sensibility as a sensibility mediated by a repertoire of cultural forms for processing and responding to a present organized by the predicament of privilege and the reality of global economic inequality to which it refers. I call these shared forms *privilege genres*. A privilege genre might be an artistic genre—as we shall see in the chapters in part 4 on what I call *hypocrisy literature*, a genre to which we may assign Grøndahl's "Prisen for et dikt." Most often, however, privilege genres are structured ways of negotiating the predicament. As such, they traverse aesthetic, cultural, and social domains. For instance, the privilege genre I call *privilege montage* is a visual and discursive technique for juxtaposing and integrating signs and images signifying poverty, vulnerability, violence, war, and disaster with signs and images signifying Nordic welfare ordinariness. Privilege montage is a simple, and in contemporary Scandinavian culture ubiquitous, genre for conveying knowledge about the radically different and yet interconnected conditions of life in "the safe world" and "the unsafe world" respectively. In an age of privilege sensibility, however, privilege montage is also an ordinary way of seeing, a gaze structure that organizes what is seen *into* a privilege montage. In this manner, privilege montage is an established way of representing an unequal world *and* a common way of seeing, permitting the privileged observer to catch a glimpse of the pain of others in his or her own conditions of living. In chapter 9, I discuss the privilege genre I call *the artful guilt trip* and argue that guilt trips cunningly executed in art or public culture constitute a common mode of making (sometimes morally disputable) responses to humanitarian claims on a subject. Other genres for responding to the sense of unjust privilege examined in this book are donation hesitation, aid satire, and humanitarian gifts.

In some instances, then, what I call privilege genres are best understood as discursive or artistic genres, while in other cases particular privilege genres should be regarded more as "styles of managing" or "modes of responsivity" (Berlant 2011, 4–6).[5] I mobilize the concept of privilege genre in order to pinpoint the ways of feeling, modes of seeing, methods of (ac)counting, and styles of critiquing enabled by the sensibility of privilege, rather than, say, specific emotions or visual sensations called forth by the experience of unearned privilege. I will be saying more about this structural approach to sensibility in the chapters to come. Taken together, privilege genres mediate and mark out the contours of the Scandinavian sensibility of privilege; I tend to the conventions of each of these genres and to what I call the *aesthetic of complicity* fundamental to them all. This aesthetic of complicity is, I will be arguing, a critical mutation in the aesthetic of sympathy with which we typically associate sentimental cultural texts. I shall return to the issue of sentimentality and what I refer to as its *skeptimental* mutation momentarily.

Late Humanitarianism

In his 2012 landmark study *Humanitarian Reason: A Moral History of the Present*, the moral anthropologist Didier Fassin remarks that humanitarian reason had become so morally unassailable that critique amounted to an intellectual taboo (Fassin 2012, 244). In this book, Fassin describes humanitarianism as "a mode of governing" occupying a key position in the contemporary moral order of Western societies. He coins the term *humanitarian reason* to designate the distinct moral and emotional logic prompting Western publics to save lives and reduce the suffering of vulnerable subjects and populations, notably in the global South.[6] According to Fassin, the politics of humanitarianism employ "the terms of suffering to speak of inequality," thus giving emphasis to the condition of victimhood over and above the political life of precarious subjects and populations (Fassin 2012, 8). To this humanitarian vocabulary of human suffering, moral sentiments—care, compassion, sympathy—are the self-evident frame of reference for acting on what seems not right in the world.[7] Whereas the presence of moral sentiments in political life is not itself a recent phenomenon, by the end of the twentieth century, Fassin argues, we saw a stronger articulation of moral sentiments in public space and political action, encompassing both the proliferation of humanitarian organizations and the regular description of political conflict as humanitarian crisis.[8] In the age of "humanitarian government," Fassin writes, moral sentiments have effectively reconfigured politics into a politics of precarious lives (2012, 5).

Today we have to look again at Fassin's important insight that critique of humanitarianism had become an intellectual and political taboo. Firstly, we have, in recent years, witnessed a remarkable scholarly interest in humanitarianism from within law, the social sciences, and the humanities.[9] While critical engagement with "the politics of compassion," like this politics itself, has a much longer history including the historical critiques of the eighteenth-century French and US declarations of rights, the last two decades have provided us with an especially rich scholarship engaging the historical, ideological, legal, moral, and affective foundations of contemporary humanitarianism.

Responding to the humanitarian expansionism of the 1990s and the frequent employment of the moral vocabularies of humanitarianism for making sense of conflict and military intervention, this scholarship generally regards current forms of humanitarianism as deriving from the depoliticization and neoliberalization of the 1970s and onward. Legal scholar Samuel Moyn's *The Last Utopia* (2012) greatly contributed to the recognition that contemporary humanitarianism and human rights discourse originated not in the revolutions of the eighteenth century, nor in the collective shock of the 1940s, but in the "postideological" political landscape of the 1970s.[10] The anthropologist Miriam Ticktin's work on the "antipolitics" of the politics of compassion voiced a widely shared critique of how, by hoping to be beyond politics, exceptional humanitarian measures based on the moral imperative to relieve suffering likely end up reinforcing the extant inequalities responsible for the suffering in the first place.[11] Rather than contravening some intellectual taboo, then, critique of the politics of humanitarianism now constitute a thriving interdisciplinary field of study.

Second, the humanitarian politics of care themselves seem to be undergoing a sea change, inasmuch as criminalizing humanitarian aid and rescue is in several charged places now a common response to patterns of migration. As *The New Humanitarian* put it in a 2019 newsletter, "Aid organisations have long faced suspensions in difficult operating environments due to geopolitical or domestic political concerns—from Pakistan to Sudan to Burundi—but they now face a new criminalisation challenge from Western governments, whether it's rescue missions in the Mediterranean or toeing the US counterterror line in the Middle East."[12] In October 2024, Israel banned the United Nations Relief and Works Agency for Palestine Refugees from operating within Israel and occupied East Jerusalem, in effect obstructing the distribution of humanitarian aid in Gaza. In Europe, we have witnessed how the EU member states, assisted by the governments of Turkey, Libya, and Tunisia, work to deter humanitarian search-and-rescue operations both at sea and on the ground with the aim of preventing refugees from having safe and legal ways to seek asylum in Europe. In the United States, the Immigration and Customs Enforcement agency has in recent years "detained and deported record numbers of people from the United States"; this militarization of the border region has produced "rampant abuses" of immigrants and regularly includes harassment and prosecution of human rights activists.[13]

Noticeably, the deterrence in these border areas of humanitarian assistance provided by NGOs and civil society actors is often justified by a mixture of humanitarian and security discourse. States evoke the safety of immigrants as motivation for criminalizing humanitarian work, and humanitarian actors are accordingly prosecuted for facilitating illegal entry—that is, for human smuggling. This is what the political scientist Paolo Cuttitta calls "humanitarian exclusion": the governmental humanitarian discourse on, for instance, the EU's maritime border, which prescribes that "migrants should be prevented from attempting the sea crossing because this protects their rights to life" (Cuttitta 2019, 19). It is important to note that what is new in this development is not that the humanitarian discourse and practice of states risk reinforcing restrictive immigration and border policies. On the contrary, this has often been the effect of humanitarian exceptions to closed-doors immigration policies: The humanitarian politics of care are, Ticktin reminds us, "about the exception rather than the rule," and their measures of compassion thus run the risk of acting as "a form of policing, choosing a few exceptional individuals and excluding the rest" (Ticktin 2011, 127).[14] What *is* new, however, is that the exclusionary effects of humanitarian discourse and humanitarianized border regimes, rather than the inclusionary effects, are now becoming evident to Western publics. The governmental criminalization, on humanitarian grounds, of humanitarian work has made it all too plain that contemporary humanitarian reason is not so much "morally untouchable" as it is a zone of significant political conflict.

The Nordic region is not exempt from these reconfigurations of humanitarian government. While Scandinavia is, according to observers, a "humanitarian brand" with liberal asylum legislations, the 2015 asylum crisis in Europe prompted both new restrictive measures on asylum and immigration and an intensification of those already existing, some of which have made international headlines (Bengy Puyvallée and Bjørkdahl 2021). In 2015, the Danish Ministry of Immigration, Integration, and Housing published an official advertisement in Lebanese newspapers, announcing the recent tightening of asylum regulations in Denmark (Gormsen 2015).[15] In 2016, the so-called jewelry law was passed, stipulating that asylum seekers' valuables could be seized by Danish authorities (Gormsen 2016). In 2021, Denmark, not unlike the United Kingdom, began a collaboration with Rwanda, which resulted in a joint statement in 2022 to establish "a mechanism for the transfer of asylum seekers from Denmark to Rwanda."[16] Yet while Denmark is often highlighted as the region's hardliner on immigration and asylum, since 2015 similar policies have been adopted in Sweden and Norway (Browning 2021; Gammeltoft-Hansen 2021). As the human rights scholar Thomas Gammeltoft-Hansen argues, such "indirect deterrence policies" constitute a form of "negative nation branding" that seek to render the region as unattractive as possible for asylum seekers and refugees (Gammeltoft-Hansen 2021). This deterrence strategy is often legitimized on the moral grounds of saving lives—that is, as "a particular form of humanitarianism" (Gammeltoft-Hansen 2021, 50). With the special laws of 2022 for refugees from the war in Ukraine, discussions about the differential, and racially marked, distribution of humanitarian hospitality erupted in Nordic publics.

Third, and this is the argument I develop in this study, humanitarian sensibility in Scandinavia is at odds with the twenty-first-century sensibility of privilege. In *Humanitarian Reason*, Fassin suggests that humanitarian government is "the response made by our societies to what is intolerable about the state of the contemporary world" (2012, 252). So is the sensibility of privilege, I contend—if a "response" of another kind. While humanitarian reason calls on its constituencies to relieve suffering and save lives, it does not, in any immediate way, invite "us" to make causal connections between our own affluence and the vulnerable existence of others.[17] But, as we shall see, this is exactly the type of causal relationship articulated over and over again in the archive of *The Predicament of Privilege*. As I mentioned above, the cultural texts composing my archive all engage with some form of humanitarian crisis. But these texts also tell of a crisis *in* humanitarianism. From the archive of this book we thus get an impression of a collective subject not being able to connect with or endorse the humanitarian cause (but also not yet having any developed idea of a better alternative). I take this to signify that to a historical sensibility concerned—distractedly, reluctantly, defensively, or fiercely—with global hierarchy and privilege, humanitarianism and its devices are not necessarily okay.

The wager of *The Predicament*, then, is that to Nordic publics, humanitarianism is no longer a satisfying framework for imagining and contributing to a better world. I therefore use the term *late humanitarianism* to designate an extended present in which humanitarian reason has come under pressure not solely from nationalism and its politics of security but also from the common sensation of being in fact not, or not merely, the humanitarian benefactors of "the global poor" but, rather, the beneficiaries of global structural inequality. Within the Nordic middle classes, we can trace the familiar suspicion of living at the expense of others, and this experience is, I suggest, part of what today disturbs the fantasies of shared humanity, progress, charity, and the equal value of human lives that buttress humanitarian interpretations of the world and its future.

To be sure, the resistance in Scandinavian publics to humanitarian reason is at times triggered by nationalism, security, class conflict, and joblessness. My focus, however, is the incongruity of humanitarian sensibility and the sensibility of privilege. *The Predicament of Privilege* does go some way to critically evaluate contemporary forms of humanitarianism, but what interests me more is the cultural reasoning that goes on at this juncture where humanitarianism meets the predicament: How does Scandinavian privilege sensibility modify and alter the humanitarian imaginary? Whereas humanitarian organizations typically respond in an optimistic tone to the pressure exerted by the predicament of privilege, affirming that this is okay! and hoping that innovative humanitarian campaigns will mend the half-broken faith in charity as a way to rectify the world, we find far less assured responses when looking to the broader cultural archive of art, literature, and cinema. The historical situation interpreted by the cultural archive of this book is, I argue, a situation in which humanitarian reason has reached a threshold.

Skeptimentality

Let me return to the issue of sentimentality flagged above. One striking common denominator of recent scholarship on humanitarianism is that the humanitarianism under study is by and large a *sentimental* humanitarianism. Certainly, while it does occasionally point explicitly to the importance of, for instance, the eighteenth-century cult of sensibility in Europe or nineteenth-century American sentimentalism to the genealogy of humanitarianism, sentimentality is not a tag employed consistently throughout this extensive literature. Yet the assessment this scholarship makes of humanitarianism and its culture of feeling corresponds to the assessment of sentimentality to be found in scholarship on sentimental culture, broadly perceived, and the role of sympathy and its aesthetic in race, gender, and class relations.[18]

Inasmuch as sentimentality and humanitarian reform movements form part of the same eighteenth-century genealogy comprising the emergence of moral sentiments in literary fiction, moral philosophy, and common sense, this correspondence is unsurprising (Haskell 1992; Ashworth 1992; Festa 2006; Hunt 2007). Yet in pointing out that the literature on humanitarianism takes its object of study to be a sentimental one, I wish to emphasize the special, yet underexamined, relevance of the study of sentimental politics—a field of study thriving particularly in American(ist) feminist scholarship—to the ongoing study of humanitarianism. And, by forging in the chapters to come a conversation from a Nordic vantage point between the study of humanitarianism and the study of sentimentality, I hope *The Predicament of Privilege* may contribute to both these fields.

In both fields of study it is generally assumed that the moral sentiments so decisive to humanitarianism and sentimentalism alike—the "noble" feelings of sympathy, care, and compassion for the plight of others—operate according to a sentimental logic. By contrast, I argue that in privilege-sensitive publics such as the Nordics, moral sentiments operate instead according to what I call a *skeptimental* logic. The sentimental is frequently described as a structure of feeling in which a "positive" basic feeling of care generates a "positive" metaresponse that says, for example, It's so heartening that I feel sympathy for people who are less fortunate than me.[19] Thus, according to both expert and vernacular description, feeling for the plight of others incites moral and affective uplift in the feeling subject, this amplification of charitable affect being one of the reasons why sentimentality, as emotional, aesthetic, and political mode, is typically negatively assessed (Knight 1999; Solomon 2004, 10–13). Insofar as "we," the "sympathizers" feeling for the "sufferers," are emotionally rewarded for feeling morally right, sympathetic emotion (so the general understanding goes) gives us cause to feel good about ourselves. A vast repertoire of critical insights on humanitarianism and sentimentalism hinges on this assumption of a particular affective dynamic of the moral sentiments.

As evidenced by this book's archive, however, in Scandinavian contemporary culture, moral sentiments are experienced as fundamentally ambivalent. Here, the "noble" moral sentiments may at any time change sign and appear instead to be a symptom of something *im*moral in the feeling subject, whether individual or collective. To a skeptimental sensibility, a basic feeling of care will habitually spur a "negative" metaresponse.[20] Therefore, in scenarios and experiences marked by skeptimentality, the reflexive moment in the perception of a tear-jerking object manifests itself not as an affective and moral boost but, rather, as a shudder of suspicion. This shudder might query, Why am I being touched by my own impulse to goodness? Or, I'm not sure I like the implications of this touching object in front of me, but I feel moved by it nonetheless. In contrast to the positive metaresponse we associate with the sentimental, the skeptimental metaresponse to the moral sentiments basically says, How morally embarrassing that I (or we, you, or they) feel morally good! In this manner, the skeptimental manifests a critical mutation in the sentimental.

Skeptimentality, then, is my term for the sense that there is something morally embarrassing in "virtuous" moral sentiments and in the sentimental aesthetic we associate with them. Skeptimental publics are marked by a chronic doubt concerning the appropriateness of humanitarian sentiments: These moral sentiments are experienced, in part, as symptoms of the feeling subject's structurally privileged position in a social ensemble—even, at times, as signs of this subject's complicity with an unjust "system." Moral sentiments, I suggest, simply operate according to a different logic in skeptimental, privilege-sensitive publics than they do in sentimental ones. In the former, they always risk being complemented by negative evaluation, from within or from without.

Privilege sensibility is about how we relate to global relations of inequality and to our own position in these relationships. Central to this sensibility is a skeptimental structure of feeling, in which conventionally good feelings might very well turn "ugly," to invoke the vocabulary of the cultural theorist Sianne Ngai, while conventionally ugly feelings might, conversely, prove useful and legitimate (Ngai 2005). In this manner, the predicament of privilege transmutes moral sentiments into potentially immoral sentiments; it inhibits the humanitarian sentiments that have mobilized modern humanitarianism, its culture, and its politics. *The Predicament of Privilege* explores the skeptimental habits of Scandinavian culture by trailing the skeptimental modification of sentimental humanitarianism as it plays itself out in a range of contemporary cultural artifacts. Just as what Lauren Berlant calls "sentimental publics" are mediated by cultural objects such as novels, magazines, and cinema employing a repertoire of sentimental visual and narrative tropes, skeptimental publics are mediated by skeptimental cultural objects, some of which make up the archive of this book. While we associate sentimentality with an aesthetic of sympathy, skeptimentality is, conversely, characterized by a skeptimental mutation in the aesthetic of sympathy. I call the resulting modified aesthetic an aesthetic of complicity.

Plenty of the decried features of a politics and aesthetics of sentimentality are left intact by the skeptimental mutation that serves as my focus in this study. For instance, critics of sentimental politics have emphasized the fundamentally asymmetrical structure of the noble moral sentiments, in their being emotions directed downward in social and geopolitical hierarchies (Ellison 2012; Wexler 2000; Schuller 2018; Badiou 2001; Rai 2002): "In operation," Berlant writes, "compassion is a term denoting privilege: the sufferer is *over there*. You, the compassionate one, have a resource that would alleviate someone else's suffering" (Berlant 2004, 2). This observation holds true also for the skeptimental logic of moral sentiments, which *cannot not* denote privilege, hierarchies, and asymmetrical power relations, the recognition of which the skeptimental mutation is, precisely, registering. Similarly, if sentimentality is marked historically by its whiteness, so is skeptimentality, although the latter tends to grapple somewhat less optimistically with this fact.

For several reasons, then, this study's attention to the skeptimentalization of sentimentality induced by the predicament of privilege is not aimed at recuperating the moral sentiments, now skeptimentalized, for a newborn criticality or progressive agency—one such reason being the fact that the skeptimental also records, as we shall see, a certain scandalizing of the moral sentiments. Rather, with the concept of skeptimentality I wish to engage critically with the assumption, prevailing within academic and public discourse alike, that the moral sentiments operate according to a self-charitable sentimental logic. In the distinct conjuncture of twenty-first-century Scandinavia, this assumption is imprecise and ill-suited to make sense of the predicament that privilege poses here.

What I want to emphasize in particular is that many of the assumptions we routinely make with regard to self-ennobling sentimentality, and hence with regard to sentimental humanitarianism, are no longer accurate in twenty-first-century Nordic publics. The skeptimental suspicion of the moral sentiments bears significance for the public endorsement of the politics and culture of humanitarianism, inasmuch as certain features of sentimental humanitarianism that are often taken for granted—its "salutary power for us" (Fassin 2012, 252), for example, and its bestowal of moral superiority on the Western responsible subject capable of sympathetic agency (Badiou 2001)—are exposed to some unanticipated developments provoked by the skeptimental impulses arising from the predicament of privilege.[21] Skeptimental sensibility marks, I argue, an interruption in humanitarian sensibility and its forms of care, whose contingent nature is thus intuited. This is, in my opinion, one of several reasons why the sensibility of privilege deserves our attention: The skeptimental modification of contemporary sentimental politics leaves this politics open to change. Yet the skeptimental hesitation before the sentimental politics of humanitarianism does not in itself instigate a more robust politics of egalitarianism. Rather, the mistrust in the sentimental register brings out a vacuum in which the skeptimental public seems to be lacking a "positive" affective, moral, and political grammar for responding to political and economic inequality.

In her study *The Need to Help: The Domestic Arts of International Humanitarianism* (2015), the anthropologist Liisa H. Malkki took on the tendency in studies of humanitarianism to consign domestic humanitarian practices to the realm of "the mere"—that which we feel inclined to belittle and diminish, rendering it merely sentimental, inefficient, and somehow unreal.[22] *The Predicament of Privilege* shares with Malkki's study the interest in what is actually at stake in the humanitarian imaginary for northern donor publics. By paying closer attention to those objects of late-humanitarian culture that, in actual fact, exhibit great ambivalence toward the politics of humanitarian sentiments and toward the sentimental aesthetic of sympathy, and by taking into account that at least in privilege-sensitive contexts such as the Nordics sympathy is rarely a purifying moral sentiment, the study of humanitarianism can perhaps move into terrains where sympathy and compassion need not be quite so maligned as affective-political attitudes, as they can sometimes be in scholarly study. Surely, hard questions are to be asked about the politics of sympathy. Yet my archive also prompts us to reconsider, I suggest, whether humanitarian forms of care are unsatisfactory because they are based on the moral sentiments of compassion and sympathy or, rather, because they fail to challenge the political principles of inequality that lie behind the dispossession, poverty, violence, and crises that animate humanitarian response.

Nordic Interpretations of Privilege

The predicament of privilege is not an exclusively Scandinavian phenomenon, but it does come in a particularly Scandinavian configuration. This configuration, I suggest, results from a fundamental misalliance between two different interpretations of privilege, both of which play a constitutive role for prevailing collective self-images of Scandinavian societies. According to the first interpretation, Nordic prosperity and global privilege are not a problem for the good done in the world by the Nordics. This implicit understanding that Nordic material privilege is okay is characteristic not least of the widespread idea that the Scandinavian countries are "benevolent actors on the world stage" (Browning 2021, 14). Both internally and externally, the Nordic countries are described as representatives of a particularly progressive internationalism, which is expressed in the region's historical solidarity work in the Third World, its unmatched contributions to international development and humanitarian assistance, its promotion of human rights, its peace-brokering, and its prominent role in international bodies such as the UN and WHO.[23]

To be sure, behind this discourse on benevolent Nordic internationalism lie a number of very diverse political statements, actions, and interventions of the twentieth and twenty-first centuries by changing foreign-policy-making communities of the region. There is a long way from, say, the Swedish Social Democratic Prime Minister Oluf Palme's repeated critique in the 1960s of the US involvement in the Vietnam War or the Swedish Social Democratic economist Gunnar Myrdal's ideas for a "Welfare World" to the twenty-first-century military adventurism of Denmark and Norway. Nevertheless, the overall impression of the region as "the conscience of international society" seems durable enough both as self-image and as foreign-policy brand (Inge-britsen 2006, 13). Both Norway and Sweden are continuously described as exceptionally peaceful nations, and more generally the Scandinavian coun-tries have been labeled as "humanitarian superpowers," "moral superpowers," and "global good Samaritans" (Tvedt 2002; Brysk 2009; Vik et al. 2018).

I suggest we call this interpretative framework *the discourse of benevolent internationalism.* According to this framing, privileges and the asymmetric relationships to which they refer are *unproblematic.* Indeed, Nordic privilege is perceived as a prerequisite for being capable of doing good around the world (as we shall see in the discussion in chapter 1 of *Danmarks indsamling* [Denmark collects], it is not exceptional to think that the better off you are, the more you are able to help). According to such (self-generated) narratives, the Nordic countries are especially fit for helping out globally *because* they have a material (and moral) surplus to draw on; benevolent Nordic interna-tionalism is, accordingly, based on the Nordic "way of life," its affluence, its domestic democratic norms, and its technologies of care. This wide-ranging interpretive framework is active also in the perception that Scandinavian colonial projects were marginal enterprises in distinction to those of its European counterparts.[24]

The second interpretation of privilege playing a part in Nordic senses of self relates to the Nordic welfare state's preoccupation with equality. Accord-ing to this welfare state framing, privileges are *not* unproblematic. By contrast, with this interpretive framework comes a willingness or obligation to prob-lematize socioeconomic privileges: Where do they come from, how did the community contribute to them, and how should they be taxed and redistrib-uted so that they may benefit the community at large? I suggest we call this framework *the discourse of the Nordic welfare model.* The political scientist Gøsta Esping-Andersen's description of the Nordic countries as paradigmatic for a certain type of social democratic welfare state has been important to accounts of a "Nordic model" based on core values of social security, redistribution of wealth, gender equality, public service, and generalized trust.[25] After World War II, this Nordic welfare model emerged as an attractive alternative to the more "liberal" welfare model of the Anglo-American nations with its prefer-ence for market solutions and a residual statist role of targeting benefits only to the demonstrably needy. With more weight on egalitarian redistributionist measures and social welfare than its European and North American coun-terparts, the Nordic model remains a point of reference, idealized or demonized, in domestic and international political discourse alike. In this narrative, the Scandinavian countries are exceptionally egalitarian societies because of their social democratic tradition of advanced welfare, universal benefits, and high ambitions regarding socioeconomic leveling. According to observers, the Scandinavian societies thus "have the welfare state as a central part of their self-understanding" (Brochmann and Hagelund 2012, 8).[26]

Let us hone in for a moment on a common assumption in the literature on the Nordic welfare model—an assumption that, albeit in modified form, also informs my study of Scandinavian privilege sensibility: that the Nordic countries, in the words of historian Stephen Graubard, paraphrasing Tocqueville, seem to show a "true passion for equality" (Graubard 1986a, 8–9). Whereas this idea of a pronounced regional desire for equality on which the Nordic welfare states purportedly rest is prominent in the literature, explanations as to the origins of this desire tend to vary. The Nordic passion for equality "was present long before the welfare state began," suggests the political scientist Bent Rold Andersen; "it is in our blood" (1986, 114). The historian Hans Fredrik Dahl connects the "Nordic equity syndrome" to a "rural radicalism" of the small-scale farms "that dominated the Scandinavian landscape since the early nineteenth century"; accordingly, the "pervasive egalitarianism in the Nordic countries" rests on "core values of Nordic agrarian culture as they have been mediated through religious, political, and economic institutions" (Dahl 1986, 103–4). The historians Henrik Berggren and Lars Trägårdh, to whose argument I shall return in chapter 2, suggest that the passion for equality is a function of a deep-seated Scandinavian desire for freedom. In their book *The Swedish Theory of Love* ([2006] 2022), they describe how the Swedish social contract responds to the fundamental belief that human beings can be truly *free* only if they are *independent* of each other, and they can be truly independent only if they are *equal*. This equation is what Berggren and Trägårdh call the Swedish "theory of love."

Whatever the genealogy of such existential and political egalitarianism, the trade union movement and the region's social-democratic parties are most often credited with its political institutionalization. This is what the historian Peter Baldwin calls the "laborist interpretation" of the genealogy of a solidaristic welfare state: the idea of "working-class pressure confronting middle-class resistance." In his classic study *The Politics of Social Solidarity: Class Bases of the European Welfare State 1875–1975*, Baldwin, however, critically reassessed this laborist interpretation. Not contesting the notion of a strong egalitarian impetus in the Scandinavian welfare states, he views it as resulting from the history of political institutions and the battles surrounding their legislative actions. More specifically, Baldwin argued that the "solidaristic social policy in the North" sports "a pedigree older than the left" (1990, 25). The cornerstones of the "unparalleled solidarity" of the social policy of the Scandinavian welfare state, that is, were not decided "in the 1930s or after the Second World War, during the tenure of Social Democratic power, but already with the first legislative initiatives at the end of the nineteenth century" (Baldwin 1990, 62–63). Here Baldwin refers, among other initiatives, to the introduction in Denmark in 1891 of all-inclusive, noncontributory tax-financed pensions, catapulting Denmark "into the welfare vanguard" (1990, 63). Rather than a socialist victory by "a coalition of the downtrodden," this and similar legislations were the outcome of battles "between a rising agrarian bourgeoisie and entrenched, but declining, bureaucratic and urban elites" (63). Therefore, to explain egalitarian Nordic attitudes we need not, Baldwin maintained, resort to "unique Scandinavian virtues or to the anachronism of socialism's forward march in these heavily petty bourgeois European nations. The origins of virtue turn out to be mundane" (94).

Emphasizing the egalitarian ethos of the region, two observations on this literature have been important to *The Predicament of Privilege*. First, my study corroborates the idea that the history of the welfare state and the societies' profound self-understanding as extraordinarily egalitarian together serve to firmly legitimize a keen preoccupation in Scandinavian public culture with unequal social formations. Second, I note that the literature unanimously identifying a Nordic "passion for equality" tends not to weigh this critically against, for instance, the missionary work and colonial and imperial enterprises within and of the region. Nor does this literature, in general, try to counterbalance any desire for equal relations with the interventionist international role played by the Scandinavian countries in the late twentieth and early twenty-first centuries as "benevolent actors on the world stage" (Browning 2021, 14). Coming back to my own argument, I suggest that the particular Scandinavian configuration of the predicament of privilege is the result of a conflict in the collective sensorium between two understandings of self. One communicates equality; the other communicates privilege and entitlement. Another way of putting this is to suggest, as I do in the coda, that Scandinavian skeptimental culture is a response to the failure of social-democratic societies to update their egalitarian narratives.

I am thus identifying two different ways of thinking and feeling about privilege, both of which organize Scandinavian senses of self and collective agency: a nonproblematizing and a problematizing mode of interpretation, respectively. It is important to note that I am not naming actual historical and political practices or the intentions behind them. However, to the extent that these distinct senses of self—benevolent Nordic internationalism and Nordic domestic welfare—*are* in fact based upon political government, they stand, conversely, to be imperiled by ongoing developments such as the increasing commodification of welfare services, rising domestic inequalities, the emergence of asylum and immigration as a primary matter of welfare policy, and the region's recent turn toward military adventurism. Current reinterpretations of the history of the Nordic welfare states stressing the colonial and imperial past and present of the Nordic region further contribute to a sense of the fragility of regional self-perceptions.[27] Yet the fact that each of the two interpretive frameworks is noticeably contested does not make the question of the meaning of privilege raised by their coexistence any less pressing.

It is common to consider these two discursive and ideational formations, and the real and imagined practices to which they refer, as two strands in one coherent discourse of Nordic exceptionalism. I am suggesting not that they are unconnected in Nordic self-images but that they can be usefully separated analytically; in this way we come to recognize the important difference in their respective interpretations of privilege. It is this difference, I contend, that shapes the particular Nordic configuration of the predicament of privilege. Certainly, experiencing one's systemic privilege as a disturbing sign of injustice is not an experience reserved for Scandinavians, but because Nordic self-understandings rely, broadly speaking, on two central narratives in which privileges are interpreted in conflicting ways, the predicament of privilege takes on a remarkably urgent character here. While in the latter half of the twentieth century we seemed to witness a collaboration between the two frameworks for imagining Nordic privilege—benevolent internationalism and the welfare state—in the twenty-first century, they clash more loudly. As both the benevolent internationalism and the Nordic welfare model encounter opposition as self-narratives, the relationship between them also appears less clear. Are the Scandinavian countries behaving like "humanitarian superpowers" *because* they have material and symbolic surpluses created by the welfare state—privileges, that is—to distribute? Or is the current international engagement rather about protecting such national positions, surpluses, and privileges? These basic, but in terms of self-understanding eruptive, questions run like radiant nerve fibers in the Scandinavian sensibility of privilege. The important thing for my study is that at the heart of the collective sense of self lies an unresolved question about what it means to be privileged.

Thus far I have used the terms *Nordic* and *Scandinavian* somewhat interchangeably. In practice, however, I will be referring to the public culture of twenty-first-century Norway, Sweden, and Denmark, the three "Scandinavian" nation-states according to most regional delineations, thus leaving out of my picture Finland, Iceland, and the three self-governing areas Greenland, the Faroe Islands, and Åland, the polities represented in the Nordic Council, not to mention transecting regions such as the North Atlantic or the Arctic. This rather traditionalist delimitation is based on the assumption that in this postimperial region the predicament of privilege comes most significantly to the fore in the former imperial states rather than in the former colonies, whose political subjectivity, internationalist orientations, and senses of self have had to include relations to their former metropoles (Adler-Nissen and Gad 2014).[28] Firstly, the discourse of Nordic benevolent internationalism is linked in part to the idea of the "innocent colonialism" of Denmark(-Norway) and Sweden. Secondly, the discourse of the Nordic welfare model is intimately associated with social democracy, which has had a particularly strong foothold in Sweden, Norway, and Denmark rather than in Iceland and Finland (Arter 2016, 7–12). While some aspects of the predicament of privilege figure prominently in the public culture of Iceland and Finland, the force of collusion in the public mind of the two dominant interpretations of privilege identified above is more intense in Sweden, Denmark, and Norway. Therefore, the sensibility of privilege I am outlining in this study is first and foremost a Scandinavian sensibility. Some of its features are certainly shared by other Nordic polities, while occasionally these other polities, former colonies and current self-governed areas, figure as *objects* of the Scandinavian privilege imaginary—albeit this imaginary orients itself primarily toward ideas of a global South rather than toward intraregional practices of subordination and domination of indigenous peoples and ethnic minorities.

A few words are in order about the relation of *The Predicament of Privilege* to the Norwegian collective research project *ScanGuilt* (2014–19), led by the literary scholar Elisabeth Oxfeldt.[29] In a series of important publications, *ScanGuilt* (short for *Scandinavian Narratives of Guilt and Privilege in an Age of Globalization*) demonstrated that Scandinavians are not just "counting themselves lucky for their unusual privileges," as the project website puts it; "they also feel uncomfortable and suffer from what we call 'Scandinavian guilt feelings.'" Based on the assumption that guilt is today a central component of Scandinavian cultural identity, the members of the project analyzed a number of artistic and political narratives about Scandinavian feelings of guilt, as a central task in the project was to "understand the role of art, aesthetics, and rhetoric in conveying the feelings of guilt" (Oxfeldt 2016a, 9).[30]

The Predicament of Privilege shares with *ScanGuilt* the presupposition that a sense of unjust privilege permeates Scandinavian public culture and its affective setup. My study submits, however, that this predicament of privilege manifests itself not only in feelings of guilt but also in a more encompassing sensibility of privilege modifying a range of sensory and cultural practices including ways of feeling, seeing, (ac)counting, and critiquing. Mine is a more "formalist" study, by which I also mean structural, in the sense that I focus on privilege *genres* and their aesthetic of complicity, rather than on narratives and representations of guilty feelings. As suggested by the pertinence to the *ScanGuilt* project of the social critic and documentary filmmaker Shelby Steele's distinction between positive and negative versions of white guilt, *ScanGuilt* has been drawn to evaluating expressions of guilt as either prosocial or self-preoccupied and narcissistic (Oxfeldt 2016b; Oxfeldt 2018). By contrast, my study makes no claims about which emotional states—or which ways of representing them—are more prosocial or progressive than others. I attempt, rather, an *a*moral reevaluation of the predicament of privilege and the privilege-qualms at its heart. Thus, I offer the notion of skeptimentality to designate an affective structure: an emotional interpretation of a perceived or implied guilty relationship not necessarily entailing feelings of guilt. I elaborate on this structural aspect of skeptimentality in chapter 1.

Is This Book Okay?

The strength of this study is the close readings it offers of cultural texts circulating in contemporary Scandinavian publics and the attention paid in these readings to how the predicament of privilege transfigures a specific historical sensorium and a range of intimate cultural practices significant to it, most notably ways of feeling, ways of seeing, ways of (ac)counting, and ways of critiquing. In this manner, the book does not outline a cultural history of the Nordic region, nor does it pay a great deal of attention to intraregional comparisons. My interest in the predicament of privilege, hardly an emergent popular resistance movement, has to do with the resistance it *does* pose to older ways of thinking, or not-thinking, about the okayness of economic privilege in an unequal world. By detecting a certain immorality in the status quo of Nordic living, the predicament of privilege comprises, as visceral common sense, a moral critique of economic privilege and the principles of inequality behind it. In particular, I am interested in the resistance it poses to the sentimental politics and aesthetic of conventional humanitarian ways of responding to an unequal world, because this resistance registers, I claim, an impetus to imagine and build new forms of egalitarian relations transnationally—although in this study, the impetus to cultivate more egalitarian relations between the region and others is admittedly manifested most evidently in the skeptimental suspicion of those already existing. While a more radical side of skeptimentality could be brought to the fore by focusing primarily on cultural texts signaling that this is *not* okay, my aim is to identify the broader collective sensibility that includes a wide range of responses to the central question, Is this okay? If this skeptimental question signals in fact a new phase of Nordic popular egalitarian imagination, it is because it weighs up not only what "we" thought Nordic egalitarianism to be, what it was not, or what it is now (if anything), but what it could be, too. The optimism of *The Predicament of Privilege* lies in the attention it pays to this opening.

Not surprisingly, given its Scandinavian origin, *The Predicament of Privilege* is, however, a book very much *of* Scandinavian privilege sensibility. Am I okay? it asks anxiously when treading on theoretically charged matters, checking its privilege as would any skeptimental object. More specifically, two fundamental questions about the relevance of this book's project are perceptible as a recurring vacillation in the following chapters. The first query asks about the *political* relevance of studying the Scandinavian sensibility of privilege. Is not, one could ask, the predicament of privilege first and foremost an ideology offering purifying effects to the Nordic conscience and sense of self?

The argument that it may well prove cathartic to attend to one's own privilege guilt plays a certain role in the study of Nordic privilege (Browning 2021; Nestingen 2017; and Dancus, Hyvönen, and Karlsson 2020). It sometimes relies on the cultural theorist Sara Ahmed's work on the cultural politics of emotions and, more specifically, what Ahmed calls "the politics of bad feeling," according to which "bad" feeling may in fact confirm that the feeling subject, which may be a national community, is a "good" subject (Ahmed 2005, 72). For instance, Ahmed suggests, declarations of national shame may wind up merely confirming that "we," the shameful ones, are indeed well-meaning subjects (Ahmed 2005, 77). Versions of this reservation are ubiquitous in discussions of the political relevance of the "negative" moral feelings of complicity, shame, and guilt and their public exposition. And so if what I call the predicament of privilege is, in this manner, primarily a way for Scandinavians to hold on to their "virtuous difference," if it is indeed a new "Nordic distinction," then where would that leave *The Predicament of Privilege*, which is not chiefly a critique of it (Browning 2021, 224)? Reservations about the political relevance of studying Scandinavian privilege sensibility might also be about the fact that this sensibility mobilizes only awkwardly, if at all, and that it, unlike humanitarianism, does not set out any useful action instructions for governments, citizens, activists, donors, or consumers. All that affect to no material effect, one could argue, and one would not be wrong.

I do not think the predicament of privilege is only a matter of ideology in the form of virtuous distinction. Rather, experiencing one's privilege as a problem hinges on a perception of distributive injustice and forms of trans-national power asymmetries, a perception that only rarely surfaces as explic-itly political matters of concern in Nordic public discourse—and therefore needs interpretation to be unearthed as such. At any rate, these questions of political relevance are at the very heart of Scandinavian privilege sensibil-ity and the cultural artifacts responding to it. Rather than trying to decide on them, this study therefore asserts their persistent cultural productivity *for* the sensibility of privilege. For instance, in part 3 and 4, I pay atten-tion to how the common suspicion that guilt and shame are backhandedly self-ennobling feelings manifests as a skeptimental distrust of the "negative" moral sentiments (feelings of complicity, shame, guilt) for being in fact *as* sentimental, and thus as self-charitable, as the "positive" moral sentiments (feelings of sympathy, compassion, care). This skeptimental suspicion shapes in particular the privilege genres I call, respectively, the artful guilt trip and hypocrisy literature. Similarly, if sentimental traditions are characterized by a faith in the transformative power of sympathy and its aesthetic, as epito-mized by the legends of the abolitionist activism sparked by Harriet Beecher Stowe's sentimental novel *Uncle Tom's Cabin* (1852), skeptimental objects and subjects are, as we shall see, fully aware of the limitations of their agency. In other words, rather than settling these doubts about the political relevance of the predicament of privilege, I uncover the work they do in the cultural texts under study.

Second, reservations are to be had about the *historical* relevance of the predicament of privilege. The Scandinavians don't seem to mind their privileges at all, one could object; by contrast, it seems as if they are doing everything imaginable to hold on to them. In other words, Do privileges actually figure as a problem in contemporary Scandinavian culture?

I argue that they do, yet the evidence in public discourse to the contrary is ample. For instance, the deep-seated "sense of entitlement" identified by the philosopher Aaron James manifests itself in the Nordic societies as the experience of having the moral right to consume, enjoy, own, and speak on the basis of a sense of national entitlement that immunizes the collective subject "against the complaints of other people" (James 2014, 5; Danbolt 2017). In particular, scholars such as Lene Myong and Mathias Danbolt have emphasized the "entitlement racism"—racism legitimized by invoking rights of freedom such as the freedom of speech and artistic freedom (Essed 2013)—operating in the everyday culture of the Scandinavian publics. Analyzing a certain will to reproduce racist words, images, and narratives forming part of Nordic cultural history, Myong ponders, "Why is it the racist provocation, precisely, through which 'freedom' is most effectively affirmed in recent years?" (Myong 2014).[31] Exploring in a similar way why Danes "demand their right to consume" racialized commodities, Danbolt points to "fear of change" being part of the reason, in particular "fear of changes in habitual patterns of consumption and pleasure" (Danbolt 2017, 109). This fear should be set, Danbolt argues, against the backdrop of a Nordic racial exceptionalism that has succeeded in casting the Nordics as societies practically free from racism.[32] Hence, the change feared is, we could say, the loss of a sense of innocence, including what the historian Robin Bernstein calls "racial innocence" (Bernstein 2011). In other words, the changes feared are the ones springing from the charge that everything is not okay.

In this manner, a sense of entitlement and a sense of unjust privilege are both distinct presences in contemporary Scandinavia. I regard them as opposing orientations in the collective sensibility of privilege. If the question Is this okay? is indeed the animating pull of the Scandinavian sensibility of privilege, as I suggest it is, zealously affirming one's right to feel good, benevolent, and (racially) innocent is one of several conflicting ways of responding to it. This is why the predicament of privilege registers not only asymmetrical power relations on a global scale but multiple domestic social antagonisms as well. Senses of entitlement, therefore, also figure in this study, although when I use the phrase *the predicament of privilege* I am almost always referring to the sense that privilege, and the economic inequalities it names, *is* in fact a problem. Importantly, however, both dispositions, the sense of entitlement and the sense of unjust privilege, are always open to all sorts of private or public bargaining. In privilege-sensitive publics, I believe, no one is immune from this form of negotiation.

Structure

For a sense of what bargaining with entitlement and privilege can look like in contemporary humanitarian communication, consider the "Donor uden grænser" (Donor without borders, 2014) appeal by Læger uden Grænser, the Danish branch of MSF, Médecins Sans Frontières. This particular video forms part of a push by MSF Denmark to assure the Nordic donor publics that they are indeed as vital a part of the humanitarian community as the doctors carrying out aid work in faraway places (Læger uden Grænser 2014a). Like much current humanitarian communication, the "Donor Without Borders" appeal builds on a contrast between safe and unsafe global zones: In the Scandinavian "safe world," a white dad unpacks wholesome groceries, his fresh-faced kids playing in a garden bathed in a soft, dreamy light, while the "unsafe world" is represented by a scene of war, presumably, in which we follow a white MSF female doctor saving a young black child from what seems to be a collapsed building. When an explosion occurs in this unsafe world, the doctor runs with the child in her arms, covering the distance from there to here in a split second, arriving at the Scandinavian domestic space, where dad and kids hurry to make room for the patient and doctor, converting their dining room into an emergency room. The video proceeds to inform us that the humanitarian organization needs donors without borders, people who will not shut the door on the outside world.

What I wish to attend to here, rather than the video itself, is the explanation given by MSF Denmark for launching the campaign: "With this campaign, we also wish to tell Danes that *it is okay* to enjoy a good and safe life in this country, with a clear conscience. As long as one also looks up from time to time and does not shut the door on those who live in a world that is neither safe nor good" (Læger uden Grænser 2014b; emphasis added).[33] This is a striking formulation, and a specifically late-humanitarian way of bargaining with privilege and entitlement. I take it to suggest that humanitarian organizations such as MSF Denmark recognize that the predicament of privilege poses a real challenge to humanitarian mobilization, given that the organization is aware of a need to reassure the donor public of the okayness of enjoying a good life. In contrast to the general contention that humanitarian interpellation comes with the benefit of moral and affective elevation, "Donor Without Borders" attests to a sense that enjoying "a good and safe life" is in fact not absolutely okay, and to a need on behalf of the humanitarian organization to navigate that collective sensation.

"Donor Without Borders" is an example of the privilege genre I call privilege montage, a genre in which images signifying poverty and vulnerability are juxtaposed with images signifying the good life of Nordic welfare; I return to this particular campaign in part 1, "On Feeling," as an example of the use of privilege montage in late-humanitarian culture. The bulk of part 1 develops the notion of a skeptimental structure of feeling and of skeptimental publics through readings of the Swedish director Ruben Östlund's award-winning feature film *The Square* (2017), examples from the cinema of the Swedish filmmaker Roy Andersson, and the recurring Danish televised fundraising show *Danmarks indsamling* (Denmark collects, 2007–). I think through the range of hesitant responses to humanitarian imperatives presented in these bodies of work in order to come up with a fuller picture of the ongoing, incoherent activity in contemporary Scandinavia of bargaining with structural privilege. This part of my study engages theoretically with the literature on moral sentiments and their political (ir)relevance.

Each of the book's four parts is divided into three chapters, beginning with a shorter chapter introducing the central problematic and outlining its theoretical implications. The two chapters following are more analytically engaged.

Part 2, "On Seeing," gives an account of humanitarian spectatorship in the skeptimental mode and proposes an alternative to the assumptions in visual cultural studies on the maladies of "spectating man," more specifically the maladies of the humanitarian spectator (Rancière 2011b, 6). Glimpsing or detecting pain, injustice, extraction, and exploitation in the everyday objects and environments surrounding him or her is, I argue, a way of seeing common to the subjects of skeptimental publics. The bodies of work under study are explicitly about self-implicatory ways of seeing as much as they are about "the pain of others" (Sontag 2003): a selection of outputs from the fictitious Norwegian humanitarian organization Radi-Aid (2012–22) and the Dutch visual artist Renzo Martens's classic art documentary *Episode III: Enjoy Poverty* (2008). As the predicament of privilege always testifies to the global context of its emergence, cultural texts of various (if not any) origin can indeed be in the skeptimental mode. Thus, I hope readers will find relevant the concepts my study offers—privilege sensibility, privilege genres, skeptimentality, and the aesthetics of complicity—when engaging cultural phenomena in privilege-sensitive contexts in and outside of the Nordic region. At any rate, the fact that the sensibility of privilege is not confined to the Nordic region alone is amply evidenced by Martens's documentary, which I consider to be a film in the skeptimental mode; including *Enjoy Poverty* in this study offers me an opportunity to forge a dialogue between the Scandinavian archive and the distinct predicaments of humanitarian spectatorship so meticulously put on view by this celebrated documentary film. Radi-Aid and *Enjoy Poverty* are visual productions that display their own visual implication, thus registering aesthetically what I take to be an ordinary skeptimental way of seeing. I focus in particular on the ways in which these visual productions make the conventional correlation of humanitarian subject positions with racialized identities stand out.

Part 3, "On (Ac)Counting," demonstrates that the predicament of privilege is always also a predicament of accounting, rationalities of exchange, and methods of calculation. I discuss economic privilege genres such as humanitarian gifts and microloans, both of which belong to the economies of humanitarianism. I also examine the meaning of *sentimental economy* and discuss how such economies are responding to the issues of debt and guilt raised by the predicament of privilege. This part of my study also thinks about distinct forms of debtor subjectivity in conversation with the work of thinkers such as Maurizio Lazzarato and Ananya Roy. The final chapter of part 3 discusses the art projects *Hornsleth Village Project Uganda* (2006) by the Danish artist Kristian von Hornsleth and *European Attraction Limited* (2014) by the Swedish artist Lars Cuzner and the Norwegian-Sudanese artist Mohamed Ali Fadlabi. I propose we recognize both art projects as belonging to the privilege genre of the artful guilt trip in the mode of scandalous skeptimentality.

Part 4, "On Critique," investigates critique under conditions of complicity. The type of critique I am here aiming to pin down is generally criticized for being pseudocritical or downright uncritical—and it also criticizes itself. A central question for the meditation in skeptimental publics on the conditions of possibility for critical speech, is, I suggest, How can you throw stones when you live in a glass house and are acutely aware of it? In order to flesh out and respond to this question, the chapters examine the works of writers such as Peter Højrup, Lone Aburas, Negar Naseh, Kirsten Hammann, and Victor Boy Lindholm as examples of what I call Scandinavian hypocrisy literature. Characteristic of this literary genre is the emergence of a moral consciousness looking with apathy, impotence, or abhorrence at its own immoral conditions of possibility—"hypocrisy" being the critical verdict passed by this consciousness on its own moral inconsistency. In discussing hypocrisy literature, these chapters draw upon thinkers such as Sandra Lee Bartky, Bruce Robbins, and Sara Ahmed, all of whom have dwelled meticulously on variants of the question, When and how is self-criticism by the unjustly privileged critically relevant—and when is it not?

Part 1

On Feeling

I.

Skeptimentality

IN THIS CHAPTER, I shall describe the structure of feeling central to the Scandinavian sensibility of privilege. The predicament of privilege is always, also, an emotional predicament, entailing anxious reflection on, or dispute about, the value of the "noble," moral sentiments—what the philosopher Robert C. Solomon refers to as "the family of fine sentiment": sympathy, empathy, benevolence, compassion, care, and pity (Solomon 2004, 52). In contemporary Scandinavian societies, I suggest, mistrust of these virtuous sentiments has become an emotional habit: They are typically perceived and represented as morally embarrassing. This does not mean that all Scandinavians will exhibit identical emotional patterns. Nor does it mean that Scandinavian publics are emotionally temperate; indeed, feelings, and moral discourses on feelings, are ever-present in Nordic public arenas. It does mean, however, that the moral sentiments are susceptible to change sign and become indicative of something *im*moral in the feeling subject, be this subject an individual or a collective. The sensibility of privilege is a register of how we relate to global inequality and to our own place and part in this unequal world. Central to this sensibility is a structure of feeling in which conventionally good feelings might turn ugly while, conversely, conventionally ugly feelings might prove useful and legitimate (Ngai 2005).

Let us consider an example of the former. In the Danish author Kirsten Hammann's novel *En dråbe i havet* (A drop in the ocean, 2008), to which I shall return in part 4, the portrait of the female protagonist is a depiction also of the predicament of privilege as an emotional predicament. *En dråbe i havet* is about an author, Mette Mæt (Mette Satiated), who wants to change the world by writing a touching novel on the topic of the global South. Media images of emaciated children make Mette angry: "Enough is damn well enough! Just redistribute the world's wealth so everyone can have a share!"

(Hammann 2008, 35), and she regularly asks herself and her world, "Why, exactly, should people fortunate to be born on the rich soil be allowed to stay living there?" (Hammann 2008, 22).[1] But alongside this desire to cast off her global privileges, Mette is quick to ridicule her own moral indignation and the actions into which it leads her. So when she makes a personal attempt to create a drop of equality in the world by moving an Ethiopian family into her apartment in Copenhagen while she and her daughter sleep on an Indian garbage dump, the third-person narrator voicing Mette's self-critical evaluation can but conclude, "She knows it's ridiculous and just an attempt to buy absolution, but, even so, it was important for her to prove to herself that she would match words with deeds" (Hammann 2008, 305).[2] This is, then, a central element in the sensibility of privilege: Something seems morally important while simultaneously appearing morally embarrassing and ridiculous. I use the term *skeptimentality* to identify this structure of ambivalent feeling and its aesthetic forms.

Skeptimentality differs from sentimentality, often described as an aesthetic mode and structure of feeling in which a positive "basic feeling" gives rise to a positive metaresponse that says, for example, It's so life-affirming that I feel empathy with people who are less fortunate than me. This twofold charitable response is one reason for the frequently negative assessment of sentimentality as emotional and aesthetic mode: We commonly interpret sentimental emotional response as self-satisfied because in the sentimental mode, charity seems to be, in part, self-charity. In his book *In Defense of Sentimentality*, Solomon (2004) refers to the writer Milan Kundera as representative of the prevalent negative evaluations of sentimental constellations of feeling and their aesthetic.[3] In Kundera's *The Unbearable Lightness of Being* (1984), sentimentality is designated "kitsch." Sentimentality and kitsch are both aesthetic-affective registers indicating nostalgia, cheap conventionality, melodrama, and links between bad art and bad morality. As Solomon points out, to Kundera *kitsch* is a term for the aesthetic and emotional profile of a totalitarian politics; yet even without this explicitly political element, the novel's description of kitsch logic is valid as an example of the general understanding of the sentimental logic of moral sentiments I wish to feature here: "Kitsch," the narrator of *The Unbearable Lightness of Being* explains, "causes two tears to flow in quick succession. The first tear says: How nice to see children running on the grass! The second tear says: How nice to be moved, together with all mankind, by children running on the grass! It is the second tear that makes kitsch kitsch" (Kundera qtd. in Solomon 2004, 12). If we substitute *sentimentality* for *kitsch*, we could say that it is the self-perpetuating, reflexive moment that makes the sentimental mode sentimental.

In the case of the skeptimental mode, the moral sentiments are fundamentally ambivalent inasmuch as in this mode a "positive" feeling of benevolence generally incites a "negative" metaresponse. In scenarios and experiences characterized by skeptimentality, the reflexive moment in the experience of a touching object manifests itself not as a warming tear but rather as a frisson of suspiciousness. This frisson is perhaps asking, Why do I fall for this object's cheap convention? Or, Why am I moved by my own impulse to goodness? Or expressing, more hesitantly, I'm not sure I like the implications of this object in front of me, but I nonetheless feel moved by it. Unlike the "positive" metaresponse we associate with the sentimental mode, in skeptimentality the reflexive metaresponse is basically saying, Actually, it's morally embarrassing that I feel morally good. In this manner, the skeptimental is a critical mutation in the sentimental logic of moral sentiments and their aesthetics.

Sianne Ngai's study of "ugly feelings" (2005) and their noncathartic aesthetic is instructive for the further pinning-down of the skeptimental structure of feeling I am describing. Examining the cultural work done by negative emotions, Ngai tracks a range of petty, morally tainted feelings such as envy, irritation, and anxiety, which, she shows, register situations of suspended agency. The "morally degraded and seemingly unjustifiable status" of these ugly feelings, Ngai argues, "tends to produce an unpleasurable feeling *about* the feeling (a reflexive response taking the form of 'I feel ashamed about feeling envious' or 'I feel anxious about my enviousness')" (Ngai 2005, 10).

The skeptimental structure of feeling that I am identifying shares such uglifying metaresponses with the negative feelings in Ngai's inventory. Yet, the "negative" aspect of skeptimentality is, significantly, a response to a "positive," rather than an "ugly," feeling, as is the case with Ngai's repertoire. Thus, while Ngai considers the moral feelings to *be* in fact ennobling and potentially beatific (she contrasts the ugly feelings with the moral feelings and their sentimental aesthetic of sympathy), I focus instead on the ugly mutations, caused by the predicament of privilege, *in* the "virtuous" sentiments. Hence, the skeptimental mutation in the sentimental politics of moral sentiments gives rise to reflexive responses taking the form of "I feel embarrassed about my compassion."

In this manner, it is important to note that the negative metaresponse pivotal to skeptimentality is a function of the subject's embodied awareness of being somehow positively involved in the affecting object in front of her. The negative evaluation does not cancel the positive attachment. Rather, in the skeptimental mode, the moral feelings move restlessly between something the subject experiences as morally proper and something she experiences as morally improper.[4] This profound uncertainty also concerns exactly *what* it is the subject is so hesitantly passing judgment on: Is it the touching object itself (a humanitarian appeal, for instance) or the subject's own moved response thereof?

It is also important to note that this predisposition for critically evaluating something that, on the face of it, seems morally good is not a disposition reserved for intellectual or academic antisentimentalism. Paul Gilroy, arguing for the need for sympathy and compassion at a historical moment where Europe is haunted by new forms of racism and fascism, suggests that the current "hostility to sympathy" among "radicals and what is left of the Left" is a trend that "seems to be particularly evident among academics" (Gilroy 2019, 10). Looking to the Scandinavian publics, however, it is evident that the distrust of moral sentiments and their cultural forms—what I call skeptimentality—is not predominantly a radical leftist or academic phenomenon. On the contrary, skeptimentality is utterly ordinary. The impression that the moral sentiments are complicit in a system of domination, whatever we think of as the system, is a commonplace across the political spectrum.

In other words, as in the case of the sentimental, there is something distinctly communal and commonplace about skeptimental scenarios, even though skeptimentality is, of course, not a term we use. However, identifying a collective sensibility, as I do in this study, is not to postulate that everyone feels the same in relation to global economic inequality and entitlement to privilege. Rather, it implies the identification of a recurrent pattern of articulations in the ongoing cultural interpretation of the issue of global privilege. As an aesthetic mode, the skeptimental has its own tropes, which often take an explicitly critical position on sentimental ones. The skeptimental aesthetic is an aesthetic not of sympathy but of complicity. The privilege genres I tend to in this book—the cultural forms for processing and responding to the predicament of privilege—include emergency aid satire, donation hesitation, humanitarian gifts, artful guilt trips, production-sensitive artforms, hypocrisy literature, and privilege montage. These privilege genres all have a propensity for the skeptimental mode, although they may also call up the sentimental.

Ambivalence

Skeptimentality, then, is my term for the sense that there is something morally embarrassing about the moral sentiments and the sentimental aesthetic we associate with them. Exactly *what* is taken to be morally embarrassing about the moral feelings may vary significantly. Generally speaking, however, the immorality perceived by the feeling subject is linked to an impression of either guilt or shame, or a combination of the two. I can, for instance, evaluate my compassion for poor people in the global South as being morally embarrassing because a part of me is also feeling guilty about the object of my compassion: that is, their poverty. Or I can evaluate my compassion for poor people as being morally embarrassing because part of me simultaneously regards compassion as a sign of self-righteous and syrupy humanism, and that part is consequently ashamed of my self-righteous and syrupy humanistic sensorium. And, finally, moral sentiments are regularly thought to be most embarrassing when expressed by others. In this manner, the skeptimental encompasses quite diverse ideological positions and political attitudes. The skeptimental structure of feeling could be said to display elements of the Nordic "Law of Jante" and Protestantism alike.[5] I suggest, however, that skeptimentality is a better interpretative framework because this concept links, as I use it, more directly to our contemporary concern about privilege and the aesthetic-cultural forms assumed by its predicament.

While I employ Raymond Williams's term *structure of feeling* in this study, I do not take the term to mean exactly the same thing Williams did. Like Williams—and like most recent discussions of affectivity, too—I wish to bring into focus aspects of emotionality that should be understood as "social experience, rather than as 'personal' experience." That is, my interest is in the "affective elements of consciousness and relationships," which, instead of being purely personal and subjective, can be said to be shared, collective, and thus historically significant, or, in a word, *cultural* (Williams 1977, 131–32).[6] While my investigation of a skeptimental structure of feeling attends more closely to actual emotional content than Williams did, I nonetheless follow Williams's structural approach to affectivity by approaching skeptimentality as a structure of affective elements, "a set, with specific internal relations, at once interlocking and in tension" (Williams 1977, 132).[7] Hence, when arguing that it is often an impression of guilt or shame that causes a skeptimental modification in a sentimental structure of feeling, I do not mean to imply that the subject necessarily experiences a sharp pang of guilt or a sting of shame; I mean, rather, that the subject has a sense of *being in a guilty relation* to something.[8] This sense of guilty relationality might well feel like guilt, and often does, but it can also feel like indignation, triumph, sadness, cleverness, irritation, or embarrassment. In this, I follow Berlant's distinction between a "structure of relationality" and the *feel* of that relation. For instance, the optimistic attachment, always invested in continuity, as Berlant writes in *Cruel Optimism*, "might feel any number of ways, from the romantic to the fatalistic to the numb to the nothing" (2011, 13).

While sentimental reason differentiates itself clearly from what the philosopher Peter Sloterdijk ([1983] 2001) calls cynical reason, certain incidences of the skeptimental are likely to be confused with "modern cynicism," given that the skeptimental, when teamed with the scandalous, might evolve into a form of "open immorality," as we shall see (Sloterdijk 2001, 4). Sloterdijk famously classified modern cynicism as "enlightened false consciousness," a state of consciousness that "follows after naive ideologies and their enlightenment" (2001, 3). He generally describes neocynicism as an "enlightened" response to—in the form of conscious dissociation from—what appears naive and stupid. Hence, cynicism is "the stance of people who realize that the times of naiveté are gone," and it is "the universally widespread way in which enlightened people see to it that they are not taken for suckers" (2001, 5).

This *drive* toward illusionlessness, which according to Sloterdijk is linked to a kind of disappointment and the "mourning for a 'lost innocence,'" is also to be found in some instantiations of the skeptimental structure of feeling (2001, 5). Skeptimentality is not, however, a response to a diffuse collective intelligence test the way cynicism, in Sloterdijk's analysis, seems to be. Rather, the skeptimental is a response to a diffuse, but historically specific, experience of being a global problem. Nor, therefore, is skeptimentality "detached negativity" (Sloterdijk 2001, 6). Negativity, in the skeptimental structure of feeling, is instead a function of the subject experiencing positive involvement too. Therefore, one reason that skeptimentality cannot be reduced to cynicism is its fundamental ambivalence; skeptimentality is not coupled with clear-sightedness or moral authority but with moral unrest. I also differentiate between cynicism and skeptimentality on the grounds that we typically use *cynicism* in everyday speech as a critical evaluation—of others. Conversely, skeptimentality is relevant as a description of a structure of feeling only to the extent that a collective subject actually experiences itself as caught up in the predicament of privilege and its cultural mode.

One aim of part 1 is to emphasize the special relevance of the study of sentimental culture to the ongoing formation of critical humanitarianism studies. The study of sentimental politics usually lives its life within the arts and literature, while humanitarianism studies are most often grounded in the social sciences. Whereas *sentimentality* is thus not a keyword employed consistently, or even typically, in the scholarship on humanitarianism, this scholarship broadly treats its object of study as sentimental.[9] Therefore, I bring to the study of humanitarianism insights from the study of sentimental sympathy as a mediating factor in gender, race, and class relations, a field of study thriving especially in the feminist Americanist tradition.[10] The (Anglo-)Americanist scholarship on sentimentality is particularly precise when it comes not only to the Romantic period and its literatures of sensibility but also to relating the legacies of this period to present-day sentimental politics.[11] By forging a conversation between the study of humanitarianism and the study of sentimentalism, and by elaborating on the current predicament, as seen from a Nordic vantage point, of sentimental cultures of feeling, I hope to be contributing to both of these fields. I argue that privilege sensibility—as a felt, encountered, and countered imperative to consider the causes and effects of real and imagined global privilege—is rendering the sentimental humanitarian culture of feeling if not obsolete, then increasingly untrustworthy to Scandinavian constituencies. In the Nordic societies, humanitarian culture is, as we shall see in the following chapters, of a distinctly darker hue than the sentimental humanitarianism emanating from the research literature.

Sentimental Politics

In sentimental cultural texts, moral philosophers and reform-minded intellectuals have found a source for the moral improvement of peoples and the political change of societies owing to the sympathy and compassion that these texts produce in a reading public. Since the 1990s, however, scholars of sentimentalism have, in agreement with the literature on humanitarianism, focused on the asymmetrical power relations that sentimental politics simultaneously presupposes and renders acceptable. According to these bodies of work, the principal relation of sentimentalism is asymmetrical. This relation, existing between "sympathizers" and "sufferers," is mediated by sentimental cultural texts, and it is, more precisely, characterized by sympathizers identifying sympathetically with the sufferers in question.[12] Sentimental identification, however, also permits the consolidation of differences, as the literary historian Lynn Festa's history of the eighteenth-century origins of humanitarian sensibility teaches us. In *Sentimental Figures of Empire in Eighteenth-Century Britain and France*, Festa demonstrates how, in the colonial encounter, the trope of sentimental identification allowed metropolitan readers "to carve out communal identities based on the distinction between the community of feeling subjects and shared, but excluded, sentimental objects: the poor, the wretched, the old, and the enslaved, who furnished a seemingly infinite supply of emotional fodder for the mode" (Festa 2006, 11). Also writing on the eighteenth-century literature of sensibility, Ellison similarly suggests that "the feeling of identifying or sympathizing with someone else, as a number of scholars have pointed out, depends not so much on similarity but on difference. Sensibility is not just a 'feeling toward' others but also, as a rule, a 'feeling down' by those in positions of relative privilege toward those of lower social standing who are in need or in pain" (Ellison 2012, 41).

Lauren Berlant's work on sentimental publics is particularly relevant for my conceptualization of the politics of skeptimentality. In a significant essay on the role played by trauma and suffering in American identity politics in the 1980s and 1990s, Berlant diagnoses an age of sentimental politics in which issues of social disparity and conflict are transposed from a register of power to a register of sincere emotion (Berlant 1999). In this age, Berlant argues, public discussion and policy are structured in line with a "politics of true feeling," according to which the most reliable evidence of societal injustice is produced when someone *feels* bad, while conversely, justice is most recognizable as *feeling* good (Berlant 1999, 58). In *The Female Complaint*, Berlant (2008) explores further the politics of sentimentality in an American national culture held together by the capacity of citizens, chiefly the classically privileged, to hold moral feelings for subordinate social groups and the sufferings endured by these populations.[13] This national culture is sentimental to the extent that it considers good, authentic feeling to be the core of a just society. In the archives of sentimental national culture, Berlant argues, sympathy and compassion for subaltern characters function as "great equalizers," which produce *a sense of* equality and universality, even though such an equality is in reality materially nonexistent. This argument that a distinct sentimental feeling culture confirms the unity of society in the face of its structural disparities, while also authenticating the morality and goodness of those benefiting from the disparities in question, is a core argument against the feeling culture of contemporary humanitarianism as well.

In common with other scholars in this tradition, Berlant considers Harriet Beecher Stowe's abolitionist novel *Uncle Tom's Cabin* (1852) an urtext of American sentimentalism. In Berlant's pinning-down of national modes of sentimentality, Stowe's novel constitutes a form of original text to which the American public habitually returns when wanting to comment on the political and aesthetic optimism for which the novel stands: the belief that unjust social institutions can indeed be overturned if the privileged would just identify strongly enough with the underprivileged and the belief that art and literature can facilitate exactly that kind of sympathetic identification. In studying American culture's many literary and cinematic versions of Stowe-style sentimentality, Berlant finds that such renderings—in ways similar to the urtext itself—make it possible for characters, readers, and viewers alike to identify *contrary to* their own privileged position—that is, downward in the social hierarchies (Berlant 2008, 43). Sentimental tropes give form to socially marginalized suffering, and the sympathetic identification with this suffering imperceptibly dissolves, through the power of warming tears, the feeling subject's own privileged position. In the land of sentimental emotions, everyone can be equal.

For Berlant, sentimentality is thus a form of intimacy: Sentimental rhetoric and the sentimental aesthetic generate affinities and identifications where, mostly, it would seem material differences pertain. In sentimental publics, an emotional universalism prevails in which the individual's subjectivity feels general, and in which people have a feeling-generated sense of community. Indeed, sentimental national culture *has* had a transformative and inclusive impact throughout the history of the nation, Berlant confirms. Yet, while sentimental politics have been vital to the experience of belonging to, or at least of being, in time, able to belong to, a national middle class, the humanizing strategies of sentimentality have simultaneously protected the privileged classes, for whom the sentimental claim has primarily been to *feel* right (Berlant 2008, 35). In this sense, a sentimentalist is someone who focuses on the emotional, rather than the economic, costs of injustice.

In *The Biopolitics of Feeling*, Kyla Schuller (2018) develops a deeper analysis of the link between sentimentality and race distinction already implied in Berlant's work (see also Wexler 2000). According to Schuller, emotional responses awakened by sentimental literature and visual art in nineteenth-century North America contributed to the molding of a white middle-class sensibility, given that the projection of an ennobling virtue onto subaltern characters played a role in the construction of a shared affective register for identification and compassion in an emergent middle-class public. The crucial point, as identified by Schuller, is that white sensibility was generated in the light of an idea of black people's lack of that sensibility (see also Ngai 2005, chapter 2; Freeman 2019). In this sense, sentimentalism is a multibranched biopolitical discourse on emotional flexibility and sensory suppleness and, in more concrete terms, on the emotional mobility of some sections of the population and the emotional inertia of other communities. Sentimentalism thus contributed, according to Schuller and other scholars, to the nineteenth-century concept of racial difference.

The next two chapters further develop the notion of skeptimentality through readings of the Swedish director Ruben Östlund's award-winning feature film *The Square* (2017), the Swedish filmmaker Roy Andersson's cinema, and the recurring Danish televised fundraising show *Danmarks indsamling* (Denmark collects, 2007–). In various ways, these cultural texts are concerned with skeptimental publics and thus register the diffuse distrust of humanitarian feelings distinguishing these publics. Who needs help and sympathy, really? What does an act of helping actually mean? Who can in truth provide help? Can "we" be helpers and not merely exploiters? Rather than as simple moral imperatives, these cultural texts cast sympathy, benevolence, aid, and moral goodness as cultural *problems*. By so doing, they point up that what may seem to be privately uglified moral sentiments are, in fact, matters of mass public culture. In particular, *The Square* and *Danmarks indsamling*, unlike as they are, both make use of the privilege genre I call privilege montage for their open-ended posing and tentative answering of the fundamental question of Scandinavian privilege sensibility: Is this okay? I shall think through the range of hesitant responses to humanitarian imperatives presented in these bodies of work in order to arrive at a fuller picture of the ongoing, incoherent, activity in contemporary Scandinavia of bargaining with the issues of global economic inequality, responsibility, and solidarity.

2.

Skeptimental Publics

WE DO NOT yet have a genealogy of Scandinavian sentimentality in line with the one Americanists have mapped out for the nineteenth- and twentieth-century United States. To what extent, we could ask, has sentimental rhetoric contributed to the political and cultural discourses in which Nordic welfare states have historically found legitimation, if at all? Which tropes are recurrent and perhaps specific to Nordic sentimentality? Which urtexts would we identify? What, for instance, is the relationship between "worker sentimentality" and the strong foothold of social democracy in the region? And to what extent is the Nordic colonial aesthetic a sentimental one? Undoubtedly, social sympathy has been important both to the foundation of the Nordic welfare states and to their later self-image as humanitarian superpowers: to feel sympathy for the homeless, the single mother, the unemployed, vulnerable children, and impoverished populations elsewhere in the world. Conversely, the history, policies, and discourses of the Nordic welfare state and its egalitarian ways have also worked to throw suspicion on any politics of sentimentality and its feeling-based distribution of public goodwill. Today, in my hypothesis, Scandinavian publics generally have limited confidence in the sentimental politics of moral sentiments and the aesthetic of sympathy accompanying it.

I am suggesting we regard contemporary Scandinavian publics as operating according to a skeptimental rather than sentimental politics. A skeptimental public is a public that suspects that inequality is a prerequisite for the sentimental *sense of* equality. In skeptimental publics, expressions of moral feeling are most often perceived as elements in asymmetrical power relations, and such expressions therefore appear as elements alien to an egalitarian imagination preoccupied with the moral evaluation of privilege. As my archive demonstrates, our historical moment is one in which the Nordic middle classes have gained a sense of, and a problem with, living at the expense of others. This does not mean that all Scandinavians are, or see themselves as being, weighed down with privileges but, rather, that the predicament of privilege is a structuring element of Scandinavian public culture. An individual or collective subject typically says something to the effect of "check your privilege" (in the politically highly variable Nordic versions of this phrase) when a morally "good" emotion assumes shape and public articulation; in general, a skeptimental public responds to a moral expression of feeling with variations on a negative response, fundamentally saying, How very morally embarrassing that you should present yourself as morally good.

What I identify as the sensibility of privilege is one explanation as to why moral sentiments do not function culturally as "great equalizers" in Nordic societies. The professed Nordic "true desire for equality" and its intimate association with independence and freedom in what Berggren and Trägårdh call a "theory of love" is another and related explanation (Berggren and Trägårdh [2006] 2022). However, skeptimentality, like the sentimental itself, has widely varying historical and political inlets, including topical antihumanitarian currents. Public criticism of what Sylvi Listhaug, then a minister for the Norwegian far-right Progress Party, called the "goodness tyranny" of self-righteousness, and of those seen by critics as mobilizing their sense of guilt to at least *feel* politically relevant, is fairly mainstream (for more on the alleged Norwegian "goodness regime" and its tyranny, see chapters 5 and 9).[1] I want to emphasize that in *the skeptimental* we should also hear *the scandalous*: There is sometimes the smack of something socially impermissible, in other words, in the skeptimental resistance to the sentimental. For instance, the Danish pastor Søren Krarup's criticism of a sentimental "benevolence industry," to which I shall return in the next chapter, was once scandalous. It is, however, now closer to being straightforwardly skeptimental, by which I mean that it has slipped into the general sensibility of privilege as one among several components of the skeptical collective metaresponse to morally good feelings that I call skeptimentality.[2]

A Cry for Help

On a public square in Stockholm, a chugger—someone who approaches people on the street asking for donations or subscriptions to a specific cause—is asking the busy crowds if they would want to save a human life. Although engaged in a typically face-to-face fundraising confrontation, this chugger does not look anyone in the eye; no one is paying her, or her appeal, any attention. This urbane Swedish public is not, we gather, a sentimental humanitarian public. The crowd does not respond to the humanitarian imperative *par excellence*: save lives, relieve suffering, help. This is one of the first scenes in the film *The Square* (2017), in which the Swedish director Ruben Östlund—"possibly the foremost chronicler of social unease and moral precarity in Scandinavian cinema" (Grønstad 2020, 20)—is particularly concerned with the issue of help, inequality, and the sensibility of privilege in the Scandinavian welfare state.

In 2014, Fredrik Reinfeldt, the then–prime minister of Sweden representing the Moderata Samlingsparti (the Moderate Party), described Sweden as a "humanitarian superpower."[3] The chugger in *The Square* is, however, confronted with something quite different: a Swedish public that raises not so much as an eyebrow at the prospect of being able to help or save a human life.[4] No humanitarian interpellation occurs; no one turns around in recognition that he or she is a humanitarian subject: This is not a public convinced that their conscience and morality could in fact change the world. When a desperate cry for help resounds across the public square, this same public again turns a deaf ear. Except, that is, for the central character in the film, Christian (played by Claes Bang), who turns toward the desperately shouting woman and tries to help her. But he should not have done so. The cry for help is a scam; Christian is robbed of his cell phone and has to see himself transformed into one of those people who ask for help: Excuse me, may I borrow your phone? The film then rolls out the sequence of events triggered by Christian's arrogantly high-spirited vigilantism, ending up with him losing his job as chief curator of a contemporary art museum in a fictitiously postmonarchical Swedish capital.

In an interview, Ruben Östlund spoke of the effect of witnessing inequality: "I think that we, as a species, are very upset when we see an imbalance. When we see inequality; when we see poverty. We really get provoked by that. So I still think that we are definitely caring about each other, but it's also not how we're building cities. The main idea with cities today is, 'go to this place; consume'" (Östlund in Utichi 2017). Taken as an introductory statement to *The Square*, this is an equally obvious and surprising observation. Obvious because with this film, as in films such as *Play* (2011) and *Triangle of Sadness* (2022), Östlund himself makes a considerable visual investment in questions of inequality; surprising because the characters in the film are not remotely provoked by witnessing inequality. The Swedish urban life depicted in *The Square* is full of inequality, poverty, and imbalance that seems not to excite any concern among the city dwellers. Beggars, homeless people, and people making unanswered requests for help are fixtures of this Stockholm cityscape. Östlund's camera lingers on them, as if they were urban ornament, but otherwise they garner little attention. The film makes it its business to present a Scandinavian public in which you leave well enough alone, mind your own business, whether it be from convenience, habit, discomfort, or fear. On a formal level, the film's approach to these "imbalances" is to display them as privilege montages, in which images of the haves are juxtaposed with images of the have-nots. Why are we refraining from helping people in need? Why do we remain bystanders? Rarely are these questions posed with such insistence as they are in Östlund's film.[5]

The Square itself would seem to be divided. In a scene late in the film, Christian is tormented by a ghostly voice crying for help. Who precisely is asking for help? Can Christian help, and will he? Has he even got the right to believe that he can help, and if so, does it help anything or anyone? Are the cries for help ringing purely inside the heads of the privileged? The film does not know. On one hand, *The Square* seems to long for a public that acts upon the moral feelings of sympathy and compassion; on the other, we quickly sense that the sentimental public and its cultural forms are not presented as the solution to the inequalities emphasized by the film. Thus, the film has no language for the moral-political framework it is seeking out. Christian cannot by way of sympathy save the variously vulnerable characters with whom he is confronted: homeless people, beggars, an ill-treated child. Nor does the film allow its audience to feel warm-heartedness and benevolence for these characters; on the contrary, it satirizes such ways of producing a mere *sense* of equality. This schism rending the film is the skeptimental schism.

My description of *The Square* as a film in the skeptimental mode is based, firstly, on its depiction of a society in which benevolent, moral feelings have no resonance chamber, unlike in sentimental publics. Secondly, the film takes a critically detached stance vis-à-vis central elements of the sentimental aesthetic of sympathy, including its depiction of socially marginalized and racially marginalized characters. As an example of the former, the film's portrait of a skeptimental public, I shall highlight two sequences. Each of them reflects on the basic structure of skeptimentality: that something which seems morally good, touching, and proper turns into or is revealed as something morally improper rather than having its moral and affective value sentimentally doubled.

The first sequence is the aforementioned good deed undertaken by the central character, Christian, when he hears a cry for help and the subsequent corruption of this good deed into an "immoral" threat of revenge, which is directed at all the residents of a housing project, a "ghetto."[6] Unless they return Christian's cell phone and wallet, the residents will be hunted down, as he and his co-conspirator colleague tell the residents in a threatening letter. He does not simply react with annoyance over the incident and report it to the police: One key point of *The Square* is, exactly, the reversal of a "moral good" into something "immoral." First, Christian's impulse to offer help is occasioned by deception—the cry for help was a confidence trick—and then the impulse altogether degenerates into an immoral readiness to deal out collective punishment to an underprivileged social group in the shape of the residents of a housing project. If the name *Christian* suggests a Christian morality of benevolent acts, the crux of the film is a demonstration of the crumbling of this morality: Christian cannot save himself by saving others; on the contrary, he becomes an avenger. My point here is not, however, that Christian's emotions are represented as skeptimental but, rather, that the skeptimental structure of feeling operates as a matrix for the film's central storylines.

The other sequence I shall highlight as exemplifying the film's portrait of a skeptimental public revolves around the art piece of the film's title, *The Square*, the thinking behind and fate of which can be interpreted as an allegory of the political concept of *folkhemmet*, "the people's home," introduced in 1928 by the Swedish Social Democratic Party, and of the Nordic welfare model more generally.[7] A statue of a historical military commander in front of the fictitious X-Royal art museum in Stockholm is dismantled to make space for a square-shaped installation of light and cobblestone, this being *The Square*, an art piece with an accompanying plaque promising that the luminescent square will performatively constitute an equality-generating and benign social form: "The Square is a sanctuary of trust and caring. Within it we all share equal rights and obligations."[8] Unlike the statue and so much public art, the luminescent square will not pay tribute to violence and social hierarchy. Rather, it promises to be a good, solicitous, social-aesthetic form to the benefit of all. But the skeptimental sensibility taken up by the film cannot simply accept this as a matter of course. To have moral and commercial relevance—the two criteria here prove to be identical—this sympathetic art form has to mutate.

In his role as curator at the museum of contemporary art, Christian has hired an advertising agency to promote *The Square*, the artwork. The advertising agency decides that the sympathetic values the piece professes are all well and good but far too vague to support a marketing campaign. Hence, in a skeptimentalizing gesture, they change the moral signature of the work, from the morally virtuous to the morally dubious: For the accompanying video campaign, they decide to pull a visual trigger on the promises offered in the art piece by including footage of a very young, presumably homeless, child entering the square—and being blown up in there.

With this storyline, to my mind, the film is suggesting two important points about skeptimental sensibility. Firstly, that the skeptimental mutation of the sentimental, here in the shape of skeptimental scandal, does not necessarily register an aversion to the commercial, to consumption, to spectacle. In the age of the universal advertisement already diagnosed by Theodor Adorno and Max Horkheimer ([1947] 2002), the skeptimental mode is of course no less consumer-friendly than the mode of sentimentality. The advertising agency's campaign might indeed trigger a media storm, but bad press is, as the adage goes, better than no press.[9] As Elizabeth Ezra points out in her reading of the function of this campaign in the film: "Thinking outside the box results in a bigger box within which formerly unacceptable thoughts become acceptable" (Ezra 2020, 107). Secondly, we can understand the fate of this morally good art piece as one of the film's many comments on the idea of art as transformative event and terrain for affective, moral, and political reform, which is so key to the sentimental tradition that we could designate, along with Berlant, the *Uncle Tom* tradition. If the art piece *The Square* is sentimental by inviting the art participant to experience a good and charitable world, which does not yet exist, then the film *The Square* is, by contrast, preoccupied with the skeptimental public in whose hands this sentimental potential detonates.

White Skeptimentality

In a famous essay on the sentimental American protest novel, James Baldwin ([1949] 1963) describes the "self-righteous, virtuous sentimentality" in *Uncle Tom's Cabin*—"a very bad novel"—as a result of Stowe's consistency in purifying her black characters of all the evil and sin that they nonetheless represented according to the "medieval morality" of Stowe and her world (Baldwin 1963, 486–87). Uncle Tom is humble and "phenomenally forbearing," Baldwin writes; "he has to be; he is black; only through this forbearance can he survive or triumph" (1963, 487). The god-fearing will to embrace the gentle, pure, and unadulterated in the black characters—to "robe them in white"—was, according to Baldwin, Stowe's means to deliver the salvation of the sentimental reader and author alike.

The Square, by contrast, works hard so as not to air the repertoire of sentimental tropes and the clichés of suffering, innocent, humble, and forbearing brown or black characters from which this repertoire and its feeling-based racial hierarchies continue to draw sustenance. Yet, while the nonwhite characters in Östlund's film are not your typical objects of sentimental sympathy, they remain, nonetheless, objects, around which the transactions of a white affective economy play out: Östlund's interest is primarily the privileged white emotional life and its qualms at being just that. Skeptimentality in *The Square* is, therefore, no less a white aesthetic and structure of feeling than the sentimental, when we consider the latter's position in the history of sympathy and sentimental culture.

Let us take a brief look at two examples of the film's skeptimental depiction of socially subordinate characters, who are racialized as nonwhite: a woman and a boy. On several occasions, Christian meets a presumably homeless woman (played by Sofica Ciuraru) who sits near a 7-Eleven asking people for money. The woman is possibly Romani. The first time they meet, Christian either will not or cannot give the woman money, but he will gladly give her a ciabatta sandwich from the shop. I regard this scene as a skeptimental modification of a household sentimental trope, especially because the woman's expected expression of gratitude—expected, that is, from the vantage point of the repertoire of sentimental tropes and tonalities—fails to materialize. Not only is she not grateful, she is utterly unimpressed by Christian's gesture of sympathy and, moreover, displeased that there are onions in her ciabatta sandwich. The woman is presented as an object not of the viewers' sympathy but, rather, perhaps, of our (and Christian's) puzzlement.[10]

The plotline that renders *The Square* a skeptimental tragedy follows from Christian's confrontation with a boy (played by Elijandro Edouard) who lives in the housing project targeted by Christian's letter accusing tenants of being thieves and threatening reprisals. Although the boy, possibly from a North

African background, is not the thief, Christian's threatening note leads his parents to suspect that he is, and so they ban him from playing on his PlayStation. The boy now writes a note to Christian in which he threatens to bring chaos to *his* life unless he apologizes to him and his parents.

On the one hand, we have here a familiar sentimental trope: an innocent, nonwhite, and socially marginalized child treated unjustly by a white man. On the other hand, Östlund has rid the boy not of all sin but of all sentimentality. The boy might well be innocent in the eyes of the law, but that does not make him a typical object of sentimental sympathy: He is not humble or patient, he does not hold back in demanding his rights, and his innocence is not a sign of pure-hearted primitivity—the boy is not innocent in the sense of being unaffected by the corrupting influences of late capitalism. If he is affronted, it is mostly because he wants his PlayStation back. He does not want sympathy, but he does demand an apology.[11]

Danish writer Theis Ørntoft criticizes *The Square* for presenting a politically, and planetarily, irrelevant sensorium, namely the existential problems of the forty-five-year-old privileged Nordic welfare-state citizen. In a sense, Ørntoft's criticism is a privilege-sensitive criticism of a privilege-sensitive film. He says:

> What makes the film so terrible is that for the 117th time it records the same satirical portrait of the privileged and elitist Generation X and their *oh-so-empty-and-artificial-luxury lives*. We don't want to look at them anymore. . . . The beggars who surround the main character try in vain to call out to the privileged world, but they are never really brought into the space of action. *The Square* pretends—like so many Generation X writers—to be morally indignant. But in reality it is hypernarcissistic in its focus on what it means to be a postmodernist, postironic forty-five-year-old person. (Ravn 2018)[12]

As I argue in chapter 11, in staying within the interpretative framework of evaluating an object or a subject to be hypocritical, to be, that is, only *pretending* to be virtuously inclined, we risk merely reiterating rather than subjecting to analysis the skeptimental logic of the moral sentiments and its aesthetic mode.[13] As I see it, *The Square* wears its hypocrisy on its sleeve, so to speak, and purports to be itself an analysis of it. Therefore, I would like to alter Ørntoft's hypothesis slightly and suggest that *The Square* examines those publics, including the public generated by the film itself, in which the morally and emotionally right thing—to Ørntoft this would perhaps be a more genuine kind of indignation—comes across as sentimental and hence morally unsustainable. For instance, bringing "the others" into a space of action, as Ørntoft recommends, is a fairly common privilege-sensitive cultural strategy for responding to the paradoxes of the predicament of privilege; how to do it without being either sentimental or paternalistic is one of the questions raised by the skeptimental objects mediating skeptimental publics.

It is surely a question raised by *The Square*. One of Östlund's earlier films, *Play* (2011), was criticized for its stereotypical depiction of nonwhite Swedish teenage boys as unlikable, emotionally impervious, criminal types: "immigrant youths" (Khemeri 2011; Jonsson 2011; Stubberud and Ringrose 2014; Karlsson 2014; for a more positive interpretation of Östlund's work on racial stereotypes, see Lübecker 2015). This stereotype is the flipside of the innocent brown child; the two images are like the heads and tails of sentimentality. In my understanding of *The Square*, the film attempts to wrench itself away from the visual conventions of sentimentality, including this specific image-couple's evocation of, respectively, fear-contempt and sympathy-compassion. However, as the film itself contemplates with, for instance, the art piece *The Square*, the rhetoric of skeptimentality has a tendency to risk immoral stereotypes rather than morally "good" and venerable ones.[14]

Bystanders

Kyla Schuller has pointed out that the sentimental repertoire of feeling is today upheld, in particular, by cinematic clichés, which reestablish a preexisting relationship between a familiar trope and the viewer's repository of emotional response: "Sentimental visual tropes such as a dying child, a pretty girl in love, or an affluent woman dedicating herself *to helping the less fortunate* train the affective and corporeal dimensions of the body for particular repertoires of feeling" (Schuller 2013, 181; emphasis added). The skeptimental repertoire of feeling is trained culturally too. Skeptimental tropes will typically appear as mutations of sentimental motifs, themes, and tonalities, generating a range of tropes inviting our affective response to images of "the less fortunate," while simultaneously sabotaging the moral and affective uplift of the response en route—thus contributing instead to the sedimentation of a skeptimental culture of feeling. Let me give another example, one in many ways close to Ruben Östlund's work, of the skeptimental mistrust of the moral sentiments and their aesthetics of sympathy.

Admittedly, the Swedish filmmaker Roy Andersson is not someone whose work you would immediately associate with the predicament of privilege as I describe it—that is, a heightened collective awareness of one's own relatively privileged position in an unequal world and a nagging sense, or accusation, of somehow living at the expense of global "others." The predicament of privilege hinges on a shared capacity for moral evaluation. But with few exceptions, the characters in the social situations staged as *tableaux vivants* in Andersson's cinema do not pass moral judgment in favor of "the less fortunate." Moreover, in acclaimed films such as *Sånger från andra våningen* (Songs from the second floor, 2000) and *En duva satt på en gren och funderade på tillvaron* (A pigeon sat on a branch reflecting on existence, 2014), people simply have too many problems of their own to worry also about global hierarchies and unjust privileges. Nonetheless, Andersson's films ask questions very similar to those raised by *The Square*, *Play*, and other films by Östlund: How do we respond to inequality? What to do with our sense of injustice? Why do we remain bystanders? Do we care? But Andersson's cinema poses these questions mostly by showing people *not* caring.

Since Roland Huntford's 1971 book *The New Totalitarians*, at least, the "Swedish model" has been portrayed by observers in and outside of Scandinavia as flirting with totalitarianism in the guise of a superstrong state fully supported by its trusting citizenry. With its spectacular reference to Nazism's machinery of death, and the "banality of evil" on which it relied, as the shadowy side of a thoroughly rationalized, bureaucratized, and gray-on-gray Swedish society devoid of human warmth and responsibility, Andersson's short film *Härlig är jorden* (World of glory) from 1991 played into this discussion of a heartless, alienated society in which man has sold his soul to the system. The opening tableau of *World of Glory* displays a group of white, middle-aged people in gray office clothes with their backs to the camera. They silently look on while a group of white, naked people, including a screaming young girl, is led into a truck. The doors to the truck are closed, and a hose is connected from the exhaust to a hole in the car. We assume that the people inside are gassed. Screams sound low, the truck drives off, and a woman among the onlookers helps herself to a jacket from the pile of clothes left behind. As spectators, we are thus invited to consider a fundamental violence, and complicity with this violence, in Swedish welfare life. In the wake of *World of Glory* this cinematic environment should become an emblem of Andersson's work: a sepia-tinted and strangely timeless, yet somehow dated, urban Swedish society, in which care and joy appear scarce or exist only in estranged forms. As the film scholar Daniel Brodén notes, "Few, if any, film-makers have scrutinized the development [of the Swedish welfare state] with the same depth, consistency, and zeal as Andersson" (2014, 99).

Yet the pronounced critique of the welfare state in Andersson's cinema is not your average neoliberal critique of "too much state." What seems to be under attack, rather, is a more fundamental and absurd condition characterized by atomic individualism, loneliness, meaninglessness, alienation, and the reification of human relations, all of which are portrayed in the context of a bleak *folkhemmet*, "the people's home." This critique of modern welfare society draws its energy and style from the European critical tradition of the postwar period, including influences from German critical theory, the French critiques of everyday life, the philosophy of existentialism, and, above all, the theater of the absurd.

Andersson's first feature film, *En kärlekhistoria* (A Swedish love story, 1970), already demonstrated his penchant for imaginatively depicting "the emptiness and materialism in contemporary Sweden" (Brodén 2014, 105). With its focus on youth, love, and movement and its recognizable postwar setting, *A Swedish Love Story* is difficult to reconcile with Andersson's later cinema in a number of ways. But his distinct attention to the ways in which objects and commodities mediate the relations between people in the boom-ing welfare society is already in place. This legacy of Jacques Tati in Nordic cinema is palpable in all of Andersson's films (which do not, however, fea-ture a place like the old Paris in which Tati's Monsieur Hulot could regain a sense of being human). For instance, *A Pigeon Sat on a Branch Reflecting on Existence* opens with scenes suggesting that even confronted by death, people stay tragicomically attached to objects. After a man has dropped dead on the floor of a ferry cafeteria, the question of what to do with his already-paid-for beer and sandwich baffles the cashier. And when an old woman on her deathbed refuses to let go of her bag, her son almost picks a fight with her, trying to wriggle the bag out of her hands. "What makes Andersson's tragicomedy work," the film scholar Ursula Lindqvist notes, "is the ironic juxtapositions he builds into each shot" (Lindqvist 2016, 555).

In this manner, dark sides of the welfare society are at the forefront of Andersson's cinema. In general, however, this darker side is different from that conveyed by the other cultural texts in my study. With Andersson, the shady side of Nordic welfare society is not primarily about global asymmetries, hierarchies of wealth, and their continuation of imperial projects. It is, rather, about alienation, quotidian violence, greed, egoism, a deficit of mutual human care, and the reification of social relations in the modern welfare society. If these Swedish publics are at all aware of owing a moral debt, it is to the human in themselves rather than to a global underclass akin, for instance, to the one we saw represented in Östlund's *Triangle of Sadness*, in which the fierce reversal of a brutal yet naturalized and institutionalized hierarchy between North and South, the haves and the have-nots, provides much of the action.

Andersson's work, Lindqvist argues, shares with the "next generation of Nordic filmmakers," including the cinema of Ruben Östlund, an aesthetic of "sparse or banal dialogue; dramatic irony and oppositions; fixed camera positions resulting in detached, objective perspectives; and long, drawn-out scenes that emerge slowly in the cinematic environment" (Lindqvist 2016, 549). What distinguishes this Nordic strand of cinema in particular, Lindqvist points out, is its manifest humor, which ranges "from the absurd to the darkly satirical, and . . . usually serves as an instrument of social critique" (Lindqvist 2016, 560). We *could* argue that the films by both Östlund and Andersson belong to the genre the literary and film scholar Nikolaj Lübecker calls the "feel-bad film," to which he assigns Östlund's *Play*. *Play* is, in Lübecker's reading, a feel-bad film in the aesthetic mode of "unease," a feel-bad mode slightly less visceral and confrontational than the mode of "assault." Placing its spectator in a position of intense discomfort, the feel-bad film rests on a distinct "feel-bad experience." Thus, this genre "produces a spectatorial desire," Lübecker submits, "but then blocks its satisfaction; *it creates, and then deadlocks, our desire for catharsis*" (2015, 2; emphasis in original).

While this definition works well as a common descriptor of Östlund's cinema, it sits uneasily with that of Andersson. Certainly, Andersson's *is* a cinema of unease. Yet this unease is, importantly, repeatedly produced by the remarkable *lack of spectatorial desire* elicited by his films. Similarly, whereas Östlund's films often exemplify what I call skeptimentality and its aesthetic of complicity, as was the case with *The Square*, I hesitate to call Andersson's cinema in general skeptimental. Skeptimental tropes play out as modifications, sometimes radically so, of sentimental tropes; the skeptimental aesthetic of complicity invites our affective response to images of "the less fortunate" but then blocks any moral and affective uplift pertaining to the response. In Andersson's films, however, images of "the less fortunate" do not, in general, invite affective response from either characters or spectators. Indeed, the heavy-handed distancing effects of this cinema, such as the white face paint used on actors and the radical emotional restraint brought about by the tableau aesthetic, places Andersson's work on the far side of any sentimental aesthetics of sympathy.[15]

A Colonial Imaginary

The film that, to me, *does* mark a new interest for Andersson in what I call the predicament of privilege, and the collective skeptimental structure of feeling at its center, is *A Pigeon Sat on a Branch Reflecting on Existence. A Pigeon* is introduced by an intertitle stating that it is the final installment in a trilogy on being human; it thus concludes Andersson's "Living Trilogy," which also includes *Songs from the Second Floor* and *Du levande* (You, the living, 2007). The film presents a series of tableaux loosely tied together by recurring lines, notably "How nice to hear that you are doing fine," and by the presence of two recurring characters, Jonathan and Sam, whose attempts to sell novelties and party tricks in a drab urban environment consistently fail. Jonathan's joyless (and futile) display of vampire teeth and horror masks contributes to the absurd mood of several tableaux, each of which is marked by highly awkward affective contrasts: fun and displeasure, desire and discomposure, pain and indifference, sensitivity and pragmatism, and most generally, tragedy and comedy. These strikingly dissonant tonalities are emphasized by the contrast between the lightheartedness of the film's nondiegetic polka music and the weightiness of the human encounters portrayed.

Employing its aesthetic of complicity, one sequence in particular registers the collective skeptimental structure of feeling I am mapping in this part. The central elements in this "organ sequence" include a massive brass cylinder with trumpet-like openings, white male soldiers in uniforms, the soldiers' barking dogs, and black enslaved male and female characters, including a baby, in shackles and minimal loincloth-like clothing. The setting suggests savannah. To the sound of barking dogs, whipping, and commands, the soldiers order the enslaved characters into the cylinder. One soldier closes the door, and a fire is lit under the cylinder, which then starts to slowly rotate. We assume that the people trapped in the cylinder are tortured to death. Then a strange music emanates from the cylinder's trumpet-horns, and we understand that the machine, for which the enslaved characters serve as human fodder, produces not only death but also pleasure. We notice that the word *Boliden* is embossed into the rotating brass cylinder.

This tableau is immediately followed by one in which a group of old white people in evening gowns enjoys the music the cylinder produces. First, we see only a white building with a set of glass doors in which the preceding tableau is reflected. Two men, one of them appearing to be Jonathan, pull the curtains from the doors; now the cylinder is reflected even more clearly. Thus, in a sense, the cylinder tableau overlays the people looking out through the doors. Then the doors are opened, and the partygoers silently step out onto the terrace in front of the building, taking in the strange beauty of the rotating cylinder and its music, their glasses being filled by the two men attending to the company. The group of black and enslaved subjects is invisible to the white people sipping champagne.

In chapter 4, I argue that glimpsing pain, historical injustice, extraction, and exploitation in the everyday objects and environments surrounding you is a common way of seeing for the subject of skeptimental publics. The skeptimental gaze is characterized by a kind of double vision in which the privilege-sensitive subject perceives, often subliminally so, a certain historical injustice in all sorts of situations, settings, and consumer items encountered by the privilege-sensitive sensorium. With this tableau-image, the brass cylinder superimposed on the image of the group of white people, *A Pigeon* provides us with a distinct concretization of this skeptimental way of seeing—a structure of seeing always balancing delicately on not-seeing. For now, however, I suggest we view this sequence as a reflection on the skeptimental structure of feeling organizing skeptimental publics.

In several ways, the organ sequence is in conversation with the opening scene of *World of Glory*; twenty-three years after that film's antitotalitarian critique, Andersson thus expands the critical scope of his cinema to include an anti-imperialist critique, too. With its superimposition of a spectacularly envisioned historical violence onto a group of white, well-off people, the tableau demonstrates the ways in which what Julianne Q. M. Yang (2017) calls the "anachronistic aesthetic" of *A Pigeon* is also an aesthetics of complicity. Overall, the anachronistic aesthetic is a way for *A Pigeon* to make the past visible as unfinished business—more precisely, to voice a critique, Yang suggests, of Sweden's imperial past. By slipping into the diegetic present imagery referring to historical matters, two sequences in particular invoke imperial legacies. In the first sequence, the Swedish monarch Charles XII (1682–1718) and his entourage visit a roughly present-day bar. In Swedish history, King Charles XII is known as the king of war, *krigarkungen* (Liljegren 2018). He was the last king in Sweden's "Great Power Era," an epoch of colonial enterprises and a Swedish empire around the Baltic Sea, including contemporary Finland and parts of Russia, Lithuania, Estonia, Poland, Germany, and Norway. In *A Pigeon*, the king's soldiers ruthlessly expel all women from the bar before the king himself enters on his horse.

The second sequence marked by anachronism is the organ sequence. Suggesting that we view the group of white people in the latter part of the sequence as Swedish, Yang notes that "an interpretation of the bystanders as Swedish is encouraged by Jonathan's presence as a waiter" and contends that the fact that "the bystanders look both old and privileged can also evoke associations to Swedish aristocracy" (Yang 2017, 590). But how about the hyperbolic colonial imagery of the cylinder and the enslaved characters? How might that tableau refer to a distinct Scandinavian history?

By adding the name *Boliden* to the brass machine, which refers most explicitly to colonial imaginaries, *A Pigeon* discreetly conjoins this colonial imagery with references to the contemporary extractive capitalism of Nordic welfare society. According to its web page, the Swedish mining company Boliden is a "world-class metals company."[16] However, according to the local government of Andalusia, Southern Spain, the Swedish multinational owes 89 million euros in compensation for the 1998 industrial-ecological disaster at its mine in the city of Aznalcollar, a spill that contaminated rivers and wetlands with heavy metals including arsenic, cadmium, and mercury.[17] And according to the two prizewinning Swedish documentaries *Blybarnen* (Toxic playground, 2010) and *Arica* (2020) by Lars Edman and William Johansson Kalén, in 1983 Boliden engaged in a kind of "toxic colonialism" by dumping twenty thousand tons of toxic waste in the city of Arica in northern Chile. This specific kind of neocolonial North-South relationship is summed up by a headline at the homepage of the Environmental Defender Law Center (EDLC) about the lawsuit against Boliden in the Arica case: "Mining Waste from Sweden Poisons Chileans."[18]In this light, I propose we follow Yang's suggestion that the cylinder is "a metaphor for colonialism in the past and global capitalism in the present" (Yang 2017, 591). Toxic colonialism is what haunts this sequence and the public to which it alludes.

In *The Square*, Christian was haunted by a ghostly voice crying for help. In *World of Glory*, the main character (a salesman like Jonathan and Sam) is haunted at night by screams, the reality of which he has difficulty determining. His alienated way of being present in his life is put into perspective by the mass murder in the beginning of the film, to which the man was a witness in the crowd. At night, the man's wife rebukes his inappropriate sorrow. He really ought to get some sleep, she says, because tomorrow is yet another hard day. In *A Pigeon*, the tableau with the old people slips into a scene where Jonathan sits despairingly in his room and tries to grasp whether the unnerving thing he has witnessed was in fact a nightmare. The music from the organ sequence still sounds even though we are now in the diegetic present. Jonathan has the sense of having participated in something absolutely horrible for which "no one has asked for forgiveness. Not even me," he tells Sam. "Is it okay to use other people solely for one's own pleasure?" he asks repeatedly. As in *World of Glory*, however, Jonathan's moral despair is corrected. The building guard comes down the hall to Jonathan's room to see, like Sam, what's wrong. Sam and the guard remind him of the unseemliness of his anguish: "Is it appropriate to talk about such things at this time of day? People have to go to work tomorrow."

This national culture, as portrayed by Andersson, does not, as in the sentimental national culture depicted by Berlant, consider compassionate, authentic feeling to be the core of a good society. With the grief of Jonathan and the salesman in *World of Glory*, Andersson provides rare examples of a form of sentimental identification—albeit an "identification" with a ghostly presence of sorts. As we have seen, the principal relation of sentimentalism is asymmetrical; this relation, existing between "sympathizers" and "sufferers," is characterized by sympathizers identifying sympathetically with the sufferers in question (Hendler 2001). Jonathan is deeply affected by the depraved injustice he seems to have witnessed. In a sentimental public, Jonathan's haunting sense of being a bystander to phenomenal injustice would possibly have given rise to scenes of collective sympathetic response; his dismay could have been contagious and spurred expressions of compassionate engagement. But the community to which both Jonathan and the salesman in *World of Glory* belong has no patience with such extravagant sympathy; here, sympathetic response to an injustice vaguely perceived by the sympathizers is met by disapproval. This collective will not pass moral judgment on the events that inexplicably haunt these oversensitive sympathizers; it will only pass negative judgment on the presence in private and public settings of their unsuitable moral emotions.

This is the skeptical collective response to morally "good" feelings that I call skeptimentality. There is absolutely no moral or affective uplift involved in these moments of overwhelming sympathetic emotion. Rather, such moral sentiments are shown to be, at best, irrelevant to the community. In the archives of sentimental culture, sympathy and compassion for subaltern characters function as "great equalizers," producing a sense of equality and universality. For Andersson's Swedish public, however, they are inconvenient, embarrassing, even condemnable. Similar to the public futilely addressed by the humanitarian chugger in *The Square*, the public in Andersson's cinema does not respond well to humanitarian imperatives to help, to relieve suffering, or to come together as a compassionate community. Moral sentiments remain pathetic, not ennobling. And tomorrow is yet another day.

With Jonathan's grief and sense of complicity, *A Pigeon*, like the organ sequence in its entirety, thus registers the predicament of privilege: Jonathan's despairing question to himself and his environment is, in a nutshell, Is this okay? In contrast to Christian in Östlund's *The Square*, however, Jonathan is not framed as a classically privileged subject, albeit white and male. Jonathan is not a representative of what Ørntoft described as "the privileged and elitist Generation X and their *oh-so-empty-and-artificial-luxury lives*." Compared to the enslaved subjects in his vision, Jonathan is of course "privileged" in the sense of being a spectator, if less so when compared to the old white people, for whom he is a waiter, or to the Swedish public, to whom he and Sam try in vain to sell their wares. In this manner, it is perhaps not too speculative to suggest that according to the cinema of this self-professed working-class filmmaker, unjust privilege is a predicament not exclusive to the elites of the Nordic welfare society. At any rate, staging privilege as a relative condition is a feature of all of Andersson's films, as it is in Östlund's work.

In *The Swedish Theory of Love*, the historians Henrik Berggren and Lars Trägårdh suggest that the Swedish social contract—that is, the negotiation between "community" and "individual autonomy"—can be described as "statist individualism." When the Swedes embrace a strong state, according to Berggren and Trägårdh, it is not because of a particularly complacent national character but because this is the best way to achieve the high degree of individual autonomy they want, without undermining social cohesion. The Swedish strong-state model—which is, however, "not so much a model as a historical product"—offers to its citizens the promise of emancipation from "the traditional bonds of community without jeopardizing the moral order of society" (Berggren and Trägårdh [2006] 2022).

Underlying this Swedish social contract, Berggren and Trägårdh suggest, is a strong desire for social equality. Because only with a high degree of equality—equality before the law, but especially social equality in the form of the citizens' unmediated relationship with the state—have individuals historically been able to become truly independent of family, church, local community, and charitable organizations. In contrast to, for example, the American model, the promise of the good life in Swedish political culture does not lie in social institutions like these. They have, by contrast, been associated with negative forms of sociality such as "privileges, inequality, hierarchical and patriarchal power structures, and even personal degradation and humiliation" (Berggren and Trägårdh 2022, 25). Rather than from a strong notion of community (what the sociologist Ferdinand Tönnies called "Gemeinschaft"), the Swedish model has historically derived its legitimacy from "its citizens' desire for social equality and individual autonomy" (Berggren and Trägårdh 2022, 29). The driving force behind the development of a strong state has thus been, Berggren and Trägårdh argue, the desire to abolish privileges.

Thus, at the heart of this social contract, as they describe it, lies, we could say, a certain anthropology. It suggests that human beings can be *free* only if they are *independent* of each other, and they can only be truly independent if they are *equal*. Berggren and Trägårdh call this equation "a theory of love." In Sweden, they argue, popular support for the social contract provided by statist individualism is premised on "a widespread belief in the importance of being independent of other people, of being autonomous and not subordinate or made indebted—whether that debt be economic, emotional, or social. At the heart of this conviction is the idea that true love and friendship—indeed, any authentic relationship—is built not on mutual dependence but on equality, freedom of choice, and autonomy. We call this *the Swedish theory of love*" (xi; emphasis in original). This particular configuration of individualism, independence, equality, and welfare-statism is, I would contend, not a gospel unique to Sweden but shared across Scandinavia, which is both hinted by the authors and supported by numerous works on the equality-desiring Scandinavians.

In my view, the cinemas of Ruben Östlund and Roy Andersson affirm Berggren and Trägårdh's hypothesis of a Nordic theory of love. Above all, the mark with which it is affirmed is the pronounced idealism impelling and structuring their films, obsessed as they are with unequal relationships, power asymmetries, and everyday violence. But, and this is what matters to my study, the films touched upon in this chapter also question the Swedish theory of love. Or, more precisely, they recontextualize it historically and geopolitically. While the theory of love, like the statist individualism that for Berggren and Trägårdh is its result rather than its cause, does not in itself have much to say on *transnational* equality, solidarity, and independence, these films seem to suggest that the Swedish model is based not merely on a strong urge for social equality. Rather, it is based, also, on imperialism, toxic capitalism, and the racialized hierarchies organizing these phenomena. According to this Nordic cinema, the equal relations promised by the Nordic social contract rely, to some extent, on transnational unequal relations. Apparent symmetry in one country rests on asymmetries elsewhere.

In a sense, this awareness is a scandal to the Scandinavian theory of love—a scandal that in the view of these films almost renders the theory sentimental. This scandal is, of course, what gives rise to what I call the predicament of privilege. How does statist individualism à la Norden respond to a historical conjuncture of increasing national inequality? If this social contract safeguards a formal kind of equality among its constituents, then how can one address the actual inequalities still organizing, according to the filmmakers, these publics? And given that humanitarian reason and its moral sentiments seem inappropriate to the privilege-sensitive Scandinavian publics, then how, in a historical context of global capital, will these publics address the issues of global inequality, hierarchy, and exploitation, which continue to haunt them? These are some of the questions raised by this strand of Nordic cinema.

Hence, films like *The Square* and *A Pigeon* look again at the Swedish theory of love and ask about its continued relevance in an unequal world of late capitalism. While this cinema affirms the egalitarian ambitions of the Nordic welfare states, it most importantly lingers on and dramatizes the unmet promises and unfulfilled dreams of this particular configuration of a national social contract. In *The Square*, we see Christian insist on the reciprocity of equal relationality: If a beggar can ask Christian for help, he, too, can ask the beggar for help in turn. According to Christian and the "theory of love" he embodies, men are equal, and therefore their relationships are reciprocal. But *The Square* is a film that immerses itself in the fact that men are not equal in contemporary welfare society. And in Andersson's Swedish public, if the "autonomous individual" is surely *lonely*, he is in no way *independent* from abusive bonds. By contrast, there is always some midlevel manager, some brutal layoff, some miserable market, some petty competition abusive to the individual and her world. In this manner, while I find in the cinema of Östlund and Andersson a commitment to "the Nordic model," it is a commitment to its unfinished business with equality and solidarity.

Importantly, *The Square* and *A Pigeon* also affirm the Swedish theory of love by not suggesting, as a way of responding to the "social and existential ills of Swedish society," that the privileged simply ought to be more compassionate toward the disadvantaged (Brodén 2014, 102). This could perhaps have posed an attractive and credible solution in a sentimental public culture, had these films had any faith in the aesthetics of sympathy. Yet there exists, I believe, a longing in this Nordic cinema not only for a recommitment to formal equality and solidarity but also for a convincing moral-political and aesthetic language in which to address social injustices. As I see them, these films suggest that the deep-seated Scandinavian suspicion of compassion and sympathy as socially mediating emotions, what I call skeptimentality, has effected a vacuum in which national and transnational solidarity now call for a credible moral and affective grammar.

A Pigeon sides with the despairing Jonathan. It sides with the sense of guilty complicity, albeit not in any optimistic or sentimental way. Both filmmakers epitomize the unmet pledges of the welfare state through the recurring character of the bystander, who observes instances of violence and harassment without intervening. The bystanders do not seem to have any legitimate ground from where to intervene. The eponymous artwork *The Square* could not provide such ground. In skeptimental publics, the bystander's sympathy is blocked, inoperative, and it is chronically rendered morally suspicious, irrelevant, and awkward. To those considering the Nordic welfare societies to be the apex of social equality this may seem like a paradox, but to me, *The Square* and *A Pigeon* portray a Scandinavian welfare society lacking a morally, affectively, and politically compelling language in which to talk about, and respond to, socioeconomic inequalities and injustices.

3.

Privilege Montage

AS WE SAW in the preceding chapter, Ruben Östlund's *The Square* is inter-ested in the issue of reciprocity and, especially, reciprocal vulnerability. It is not only "the others" who have to ask for help, the film submits; so does the privileged white man (in general, white masculinity is under some de- and reconstruction in Östlund's films). However, as a privilege-sensitive film in the skeptimental mode, *The Square* must necessarily have an ironic take on reciprocity and vulnerability as social facts. There is, again, the skeptimental schism: on the one hand, subscribing to an emotional universalism—we all suffer, we all need help and care—and, on the other, a sense of something sham and unreasonable in this universalism and its semblance of equality and shared humanity.

As mentioned, this split operates as a formal matrix for a number of scenes in *The Square*. Consider, for instance, the scene in which Christian starts out sitting on a bench in a large department store, his purchases in expensive branded bags at his side. A poor-looking Muslim man (played by Copos Pardaliam), whom we have just witnessed praying, asks him for money; Christian shakes his head (fig. 1). Christian then needs to find his daughters in the large store. He now has to ask the man for help: Will he keep an eye on Christian's shopping while he looks for his daughters? The man is indeed willing to do so, and thus the film pictures for us the way in which the sentimental notion of the "universally human" is simultaneously true (Christian and the man both need help) and false—but mostly false and exploitative, or so the scandalous-skeptimental shot of the man now guard-ing the expensive shopping bags would seem to suggest.

These images are examples of what I call privilege montage. I wish to emphasize immediately that by *montage*, I am referring to a general cultural technique for bringing together widely disparate images, rather than, say, to

FIGURES 1 AND 2. Christian with his shopping bags, and poor man with Christian's shopping bags. Film stills from *The Square*. Copyright © photographer Fredrik Wenzel and Plattform Produktion, 2017.

a specific film editing technique or to a specific media such as photomontage. Privilege montage is a basic aesthetic technique for juxtaposing and integrating images signifying poverty, vulnerability, violence, war, and disaster with images signifying Nordic welfare ordinariness. It is a visual and discursive genre for articulating some sort of knowledge about the radically different and yet mutually linked conditions of life in the "safe world" and the "unsafe world." Even if, in the technical sense, it is not a collage, the scene from *The Square* is a typical privilege montage—albeit global inequality is here figured in a domestic form in the shape of an immigrant beggar. In Scandinavian public culture, privilege montage is the most straightforward and most frequently employed way for a cultural artifact to open up the dossier of global economic inequality and its attendant skeptimental structure of feeling. A form for holding together the contrasts between the domestic and the global that organize the sensibility of privilege, privilege montage is now a staple in Scandinavian culture, and the form is thus central also to the cultural texts whose interpretation of the predicament of privilege I analyze in this book.

In the essay "The Misadventures of Critical Thought," Jacques Rancière tracks the development of collage, an artistic form that is "particularly representative of the critical tradition in art" (2011c, 26). Rancière is interested in collage not in the technical sense of the term but as a more general technique for instigating a "clash on the same surface of heterogeneous, if not conflicting, elements" (2011c, 26). In surrealism, Rancière notes, collage was mobilized in order to make visible the dreams and desires running like undercurrents through bourgeois reality, while to Marxism collage served to express the violent heterogeneity between class domination and quotidian "peace." Collage also proved to be a highly successful form to the politically committed art of the 1960s and 1970s: One of the main examples Rancière offers is Martha Rosler's *House Beautiful: Bringing the War Home* photomontage series (ca. 1967–72). By mounting images from the Vietnam War onto images of luxurious American domestic interiors, Rosler made palpable the shocked sensation of witnessing the first "living room war." Splicing together magazine images of American soldiers and American kitchens, of Vietnamese female captives and American commercial femininity, of spacious modernist homes and dying bodies, Rosler's montages gave form to a shattered sense of national self. Part awareness-raising, part accusatory, Rosler's photomontages sought to "bolster activist energies hostile to the war," Rancière argues, by accentuating "the heterogeneity of the elements" (2011c, 28).

Commenting on Rosler's *Balloons* montage from the series, Rancière points to the conflicted message of this artwork. In *Balloons*, the image of a Vietnamese man carrying a wounded or dead infant is inserted into an image of a bright and sophisticated domestic space. The conflictedness pointed out by Rancière has to do with the impetus of the work to reveal a truth to the spectator and simultaneously to reveal the spectator's disavowal of that truth. I quote the passage in full:

> The connection between the two images [Vietnamese man with infant and sophisticated living room] was supposed to produce a dual effect: awareness of the system of domination that connected American domestic happiness to the violence of imperialist war, but also a feeling of guilty complicity in this system. On the one hand, the image said: here is the hidden reality that you do not know how to see; you must become acquainted with it and act in accordance with that knowledge. But it is not obviously the case that knowledge of a situation entails a desire to change it. That is why the image said something else. It said: here is the obvious reality that you do not want to see, because you know that you are responsible for it. The critical procedure thus aimed to have a dual effect: an awareness of the hidden reality and a feeling of guilt about the denied reality. (Rancière 2011c, 27)

This conflicted message of politically committed collage is both repeated and reversed, Rancière suggests, in a later work by the German artist Josephine Meckseper, whose 2003 photograph *Untitled* documented a protest march held in Washington, DC, against the US invasion of Iraq. In the foreground of *Untitled*, we see an overflowing garbage bin; in the background, a crowd waving banners in front of what seems to be a government building. Again, the convergence of the two elements of "distant war and domestic consumption" is meant to say something about a national self and its conflicted desire to act against a war fought in its name. But instead of supporting the activism depicted in the photograph, *Untitled* deprecates it, Rancière finds, because it underscores the "basic homogeneity" between, on the one hand, "the empire of consumption" waging an imperialist war and, on the other hand, the protests against it; in Rancière's reading, the litter presumably left by the protesters seems to suggest that protest is yet another form of consumption (2011c, 28–29). Thus, the heterogeneous elements whose collision encouraged antiwar activism in Rosler's *Balloons* were in *Untitled* "reduced to one and the same process governed by the commodity law of equivalence."

Yet, and this is where the reader realizes that Rancière's discussion of collage as critical form is not exactly a tribute to the art of the politically committed artist of the 1960s and '70s, to him, *Balloons* and *Untitled* are both examples of the same critical paradigm. The essay's title serves to testify to the misadventures of this paradigm. To each image, it is "a question of showing the spectator what she does not know how to see, and making her feel ashamed of what she does not want to see" (Rancière 2011c, 29). To Rancière, the success of the collage form is thus indicative of the development of a critical paradigm that has turned into a melancholic kind of leftism by repeatedly pointing to the participation of critique itself in the system it naively labored to bring down.

The participation of critique itself in the system it criticizes is the topic of part 4 of this study. For now, I suggest that we recognize the importance of the collage form to the skeptimental sensibility of privilege. Rosler and Meckseper might have had different strategies, but both of them, in their respective historical situations, gave the problem of global privilege, hierarchy, and asymmetrical power relations a recognizable visual form. As an idea and an aesthetic form, this kind of collage, what I call privilege montage, goes straight to the heart of the predicament of privilege as an affective predicament—as also implied by Rancière's pinpointing of the feelings of guilt, shame, and complicity invited by this tradition of political collage. As a means for responding to the predicament of privilege, privilege montage is remarkable for its ordinariness: Privilege montages are everywhere in contemporary Scandinavian culture, surfacing in sentimental and skeptimental modes alike. The fact that privilege montage is operative in humanitarian genres, too, attests to the elasticity of the form and also indicates that, in order to make itself relevant in skeptimental publics, humanitarian culture must now run the risk of highlighting global economic injustice. Yet to humanitarian culture, privilege montage is a hazardous form, because it always risks implicating the viewer deeper and deeper in the entanglements of the predicament of privilege to which humanitarian donation is intended to be a suitable response.

The key difference between privilege montage in the critical paradigm discussed by Rancière and privilege montage in conventional humanitarian communication is that, according to the latter, the system connecting "distant war and domestic consumption" is not a system of domination but one of care. Consider once again the Médecins Sans Frontières Denmark "Donor Without Borders" video campaign, with which we became acquainted in the introduction. This two-minute sequence shows, as in Rosler's work, colliding scenes of distant war and sunlit domestic everyday life. A white dad is unpacking groceries, his kids playing in the garden, while a white female MSF doctor saves a young black child from a warlike scenario. The doctor then runs with the child in her arms, covering the distance from there to the Nordic here in a split second, arriving at the safe and bright domestic space, where dad and kids quickly convert their dining room into an emergency room. It is, the appeal implies, because of the care of these people that the child from the generically war-torn country ends up receiving the help needed.[1]

In this particular humanitarian privilege montage, the "basic homogeneity" between the two settings consists in Nordic care unfolding both "there" and "here" in the shape of the caring humanitarian doctor and the caring father, respectively. The father being a stand-in for the caring donor, this association of caring characters suggests to the potential donor that her act of donating is indeed as useful and "active" an action as that of the doctor, as also indicated by the campaign title. The Scandinavian man is presented as a domestic caretaker benefiting from the roomy living conditions made possible by the Nordic welfare state, while the woman is the global caretaker representing the region as a moral and humanitarian power. The visual rehearsal of the sentimental master trope of white people saving brown people from brown people is presented in a framework that looks much like that of commercial Nordicity: well-designed and gender-equalized domestic and global caring. While *Balloons* and *Untitled* ask critically about the capacity of the spectator to respond to the capitalist war machine, the humanitarian privilege montage instead makes the spectator aware of the simple form of response and agency lying before her: donating to a humanitarian organization. In humanitarian communication, privilege montage is thus meant to be a form for *generating* agency in scenarios where no agency seems to be immediately found. Whether or not this form of agency is in fact experienced *as* a form of agency is part of what is currently at stake in everyday humanitarian culture.

By tracking instantiations of privilege montage in the largest humanitarian benefit event in Denmark, *Danmarks indsamling* (Denmark collects), the remainder of this chapter makes some forays into the life of privilege montage in contemporary humanitarian popular culture. It is my contention that in privilege-sensitive publics it is becoming increasingly difficult for the globally privileged to trust their own impulse to provide humanitarian care to the globally underprivileged. That is why humanitarian products often try to make allowance for the hesitation of skeptimental publics vis-à-vis the humanitarian ethos and its sentiments.

As we saw in the introduction, this also applies to the "Donor Without Borders" appeal, in which a paratextual address to the humanitarian constituency takes into account that this constituency may in fact feel uneasy about the contrasts of living conditions conveyed so forcefully by the video itself: "With this campaign, we also wish to tell Danes that it is okay to enjoy a good and safe life in this country, with a clear conscience. As long as one also looks up from time to time and does not shut the door on those who live in a world that is neither safe nor good."[2] In this manner, the campaign has integrated a conceivably reassuring response to the fundamental skeptimental question undoubtedly raised by the humanitarian campaign: Is this okay? Is it okay to be moved by this humanitarian appeal? In contrast to the general contention that humanitarian interpellation comes with the benefit of moral and affective uplift, the use of privilege montage in humanitarian settings, I argue, attests to a perceived need for managing the predicament of privilege.

Donation Hesitation

Danmarks indsamling is a humanitarian event full of glitter, communal joy, and excited applause. Every winter, Danish television viewers are invited by the main national broadcasting station and a selection of humanitarian organizations to participate in this nationwide fundraiser. Mobilizing families, schools, workplaces, and the general public in the weeks preceding the broadcast, *Danmarks indsamling* includes elements consistent with its aid telethon genre: entertainment by Danish celebrities, publicity for companies contributing to the fundraiser, a lottery, various forms of compassionate consumption, and somber vignettes about suffering and development on, predominantly, the African continent. And, of course, the jolly donation race itself: How many millions will the Danes collect this particular year? In 2017, *Danmarks indsamling* could celebrate ten years of the campaign and "millions of human lives saved." This five-hour anniversary show opened with a discursive version of privilege montage, which is in effect the organizing matrix of *Danmarks indsamling*. One female host said to the other, "We're fortunate in Denmark, but that's by no means the case everywhere in the world. There's hunger, there's illness, there's war, there are children dying, there are displaced people." The other female host responded, "Yes, and they need our help" (*Danmarks indsamling* 2017).[3] Imagining the Danish nation as one of happiness, prosperity, unity, and generosity is the framework through which the diverse elements of these annual events come together. Most recently, the 2023, 2024, and 2025 shows featured the headline "Small Country, Big Heart."[4]

Yet, for all its glitter, *Danmarks indsamling* is a humanitarian event that also demonstrates the impasse of humanitarian reason in skeptimental publics. The political scientist Lene Bull Christiansen suggests that initiatives such as *Danmarks indsamling* have had a cultural and political role to play in the wake of the 2005–6 Prophet Muhammad cartoons crisis as elements in "a new articulation of Denmark's global role—a re-articulation of global caring via development aid" (Christiansen 2015, 3). In this vein, we could read the campaign as a response to a sense of crisis in Danish self-understanding as a benevolent humanitarian world actor in the face of undertakings such as the Danish participation in the war in Iraq, the cartoon controversy, the mainstreaming of anti-immigrant nationalism, and the emerging public assessment of colonial pasts and presents. These historically specific blows to Denmark's self-image as a pioneering country when it comes to human rights, development, and peaceful diplomacy do not, however, register in *Danmarks indsamling* as concrete historical references; on the contrary, such historical events are never alluded to. They register instead, I suggest, in the show's skeptimentalizing of, and crab-walk distantiation from, the sentimental humanitarian feeling culture to which the show nonetheless itself belongs.

According to *Danmarks indsamling*, the Nordic humanitarian subject is perfectly okay, despite this subject's possibly mixed intentions and ambivalent moral impulses. This general conviction comes most clearly to the fore in statements such as "We don't care if you donate your money to *Danmarks indsamling* because you would like to win these prizes or because you do it with all your heart" (DI 2018).[5] With acknowledgments of this kind, the program devalues, so to speak, the emotional and moral investment required of a humanitarian subject, so that this investment comes across as less suspicious to a skeptimental public. Other sequences reflect, without irony, the experience that being globally privileged is in reality a morally and emotionally tough job. In a short animation film from the 2017 show, a family comprising father, mother, and child represents the Danish people, responding to the humanitarian call to help as a matter of course. "Because they were well aware," says the film's empathetic voice-over, "that it's tough to be the happiest country in the world while the rest of the globe is bleeding." "It wasn't that they were perfect," the voice-over concludes, "but they were really okay" (DI 2017).[6] Rather than articulating substantial ethical and affective claims on viewers, *Danmarks indsamling* affirms that the humanitarian constituency is absolutely okay in all its colors.

In a similar vein, *Danmarks indsamling* signals that it is okay to collect and donate money to the humanitarian event in ways that are not necessarily seen as morally appropriate. Consider, for instance, a video sketch by the comedy duo Rytteriet (The cavalry) included in the 2019 show, which shows us an elderly white man who collects for the fundraiser in, and literally *in*, his underpants. Over the years, a number of weirdly inapt, sexually explicit sketches have been featured in *Danmarks indsamling*, but this sketch simply lets the man tell his story via a first-person voice-over while we watch a gentle picture sequence of him standing by the sea. The man tells us that, one month before the fundraiser airs, he puts on his collection underpants, and then every day during that month he drops twenty kroner into these underpants. He also asks his occasional guests to contribute coins or notes to this very private fundraising campaign. In contrast to the serene, meditative visuals, the conclusion of the sketch is a striking expression of piqued pride: "Some people think it's an unsavory way to make a collection. But I don't give a shit. . . . I'll do my collecting how I like" (DI 2019).[7]

While the viewer may find himself scoffing at the idea of collection underpants, the message of the sketch nevertheless remains clear enough: Any humanitarian donor is a good-enough donor, and don't you let them make you think otherwise. In the midst of this self-celebratory humanitarian format thus appears a sketch featuring a feeling subject who perceives a need to defend himself against negative evaluation of his manner of engaging in the humanitarian project.[8] In this little man's self-defense echoes, perhaps, the big public-service channel's riposte to the criticism aimed every year, from widely differing political persuasions, at *Danmarks indsamling* and its participating humanitarian organizations: Yes, the sketch seems to be saying, we do shoulder morally and affectively "unsavory" ways of collecting donations too. The sketch is thus telling us something significant, I believe, about the navigation strategy of late-humanitarian culture vis-à-vis a collective sensibility that regards humanitarian and morally gratifying sentiments with a measure of circumspection: Better to hold on to *some* sense of humanitarian purpose by admitting to possibly being morally inappropriate, the campaign seems to reason, than risk bringing down the entire humanitarian enterprise by claiming to be in fact morally appropriate. In this manner, in *Danmarks indsamling* the task of the morally unsuitable is to rescue the idea of the morally suitable.

To be sure, sentimental forms from the history of humanitarian visual culture *do* abound in *Danmarks indsamling*. The show presents itself as an "entertainment program with touching stories."[9] This is a precise characterization insofar as sentimental visual tropes are mounted as the said "touching stories" in what is in essence a family entertainment program. Pitiful program items include short videos depicting scenes of harsh everyday life in villages or urban slums in the global South. These scenarios are usually mediated by a deeply moved Danish focalizer informing the viewer about, say, the dreams for the future of a surrounding group of smiling black people.[10] The "touching stories" may also take the form of short videos with a dramatizing voice-over and possibly background music. It might be footage of a teenage girl in Madagascar, her girlfriends tending her baby while she has sex with a client; it might be pictures of people in a Nairobi slum or a story about the prison experiences of a boy in Southeast Asia.[11] These items give free rein to the repertoire of neocolonial, sentimental features of humanitarian aesthetic and feeling culture, and we are reminded of Elizabeth Freeman's description in *Beside You in Time* of the affective economy of sentimentality. Here Freeman suggests that sentimentality involves a racialized emotional grammar, whereby white people's "fragility, interiority, receptivity, porosity, and expressivity are produced and maintained in relation to other subjects and populations cast as overly susceptible to their sensations or as impervious to feeling" (Freeman 2019, 9).

Mounting these sentimental humanitarian items in the family entertainment format severely compromises their sentimental pull on us, however—if not their whiteness-maintaining effects. At the end of such touching stories we are returned to the studio show, the audience clapping while a smiling host says something cheery like "Oh, it breaks your heart" or "Right, now we could do with a spot of good music." Or, the show simply goes on, straight into the next entertainment item. But the tangible emotional, ethical, and aesthetic awkwardness of this abrupt juxtaposition of sentimental humanitarian program items and the liveness of a Saturday evening family broadcast is not a real problem for the show. Rather, this type of insensitivity is exactly what *saves* the sentimental humanitarian elements from being simply too suspect. Admittedly, the skeptimental experience of responding ambivalently to a heartbreaking program item may be amplified by the family entertainment context. Yet this context also works to neutralize and render harmless the discomfort of not knowing how to respond to the humanitarian elements, since a "negative" emotional metaresponse potentially evoked by these elements will be deflected or given a new object by the next wacky program item. Undoubtedly, some viewers find campaigns such as *Danmarks indsamling* ethically fraudulent and affectively cheap due to the jolly entertainment atmosphere of it all. But, as we shall see, this experience of ethical "cheapness" may pose less of a problem to the skeptimental sensibility than would an aesthetic of sympathy proper.

The Benevolence Industries

Ever since its first show in 2007, *Danmarks indsamling* has been publicly criticized for taking part in the "benevolence industry," a term usually associated with a *Tidehverv*-ian criticism of humanitarian reason for demanding salvation by works and for a sentimental understanding of charity. *Tidehverv* is a theological collective and periodical that has existed in Denmark since 1926, fashioning itself as an ecclesiastical and cultural confrontation with "idealistic sentimentality" in church and cultural life alike.[12] From the 1980s until his death in 2023, Søren Krarup—a leading member of the Tidehverv movement, pastor, and former member of Parliament for Dansk Folkeparti (Danish People's Party)—cautioned against prioritizing human rights and humanitarianism on the assumption that these phenomena distort Christian charity by cultivating a programmed global benevolence at the expense of the *local* neighbor, who exists within the parameters of the nation.[13] Today, the term *benevolence industry* is, however, no longer tied as intimately to Tidehverv, but rather serves as a kind of conceptual meeting place for various types of skepticism about humanitarian phenomena, including the basic caveat that humanitarian organizations "live off" the suffering of others.

I would suggest that *Danmarks indsamling* responds to this kind of criticism by assuming, paradoxically, the mantle of "benevolence industry" as a shield against the distrust incited by sentimental humanitarianism, an approach indexed not least by the clashing "on the same surface" of commercial and humanitarian forms of address in the show. This clash appears,

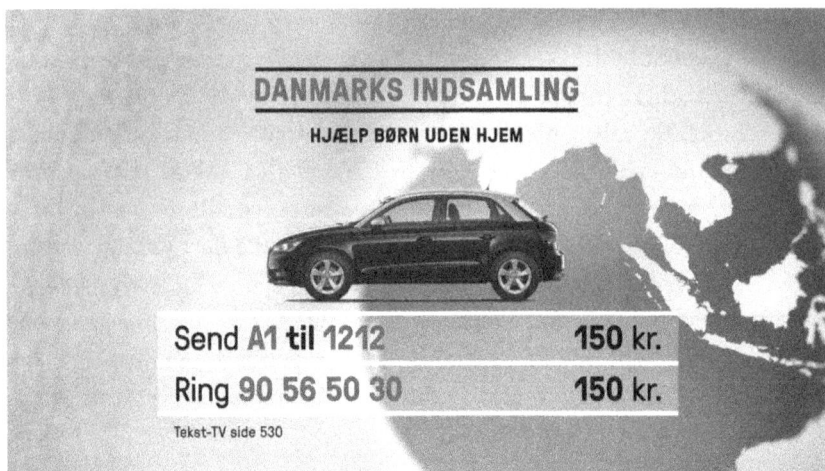

FIGURE 3. The Audi. *Danmarks indsamling* 2018. Copyright © DR Archive.

however, not so much *as* a clash but rather as an exposé of the general intimacy between advertisement and humanitarian form. In part 3 of this book, we shall dwell awhile on philanthrocapitalist discourse, but for now, I would like to introduce here the idea not of humanitarian reason saving capitalism but of commodification salvaging humanitarian reason.

In the 2018 *Danmarks indsamling*, one recurring image on the television screen was a collage showing a dark Audi mounted on a faint image of the globe, headlined by the imperative to "help children without a home."[14] Every year, car advertisements and a car lottery figure largely in the show.[15] Thus, touching humanitarian program items are often followed by a representative from the car industry highlighting the features of the new model being advertised. Insofar as it juxtaposes the class of children without a home with a world of affluence represented by the Audi, the Audi image is a humanitarian privilege montage.

An Audi, however, is not an obvious image of global care. Indeed, it might even seem surprising that the broadcasting station and the humanitarian organizations behind *Danmarks indsamling* do not find the presence of all these cars in the humanitarian campaign too morally disturbing regardless of the income generated. I would venture two reasons why, in a skeptimentalized humanitarianism, car advertising sits well enough with the humanitarian format. Firstly, car advertising deflects the distrust that would otherwise take the humanitarian sentiments as its object, suggesting, perhaps, that "well, this is just advertising, at least we're clued up about this kind of affective manipulation." Consequently, in this advert-mutation of the humanitarian privilege montage, manifest commodification is a way of giving visual form to the discomfort about the very humanitarian interpellation that is the professed business of the image: Commodification comes to provide a formal framework for the humanitarian deed, so that the noble moral emotions are carefully screened out in the act of promoting them. In fact, to this particular humanitarian privilege montage, moral sentiments are not really of importance, it would seem. Rather, the montage presents the *disappearance* of such feelings. This disappearance is figured by the black Audi taking up the spot in the appeal that would conventionally feature a brown or black child presumably "without a home." The sentimental object is left out of the picture. Hence, the wonder of the Audi montage is that it is an image of the commodification not exactly of humanitarian sentiments but of the withdrawal of such sentiments. With montages like this one, *Danmarks indsamling* permits us to see that today humanitarian reason must capitalize not only on our altruistic feelings but also on our hesitation and anxiety about them.

Secondly, the Audi montage corroborates and performs, as do a number of other program elements, two important discourses of late-humanitarian communication: win-winism and the notion that the ends justify the means. The inappropriateness of the cars is okay, so the reasoning seems to be, because the humanitarian ends justify the commercial means: If more Danes donate to the fundraising campaign because they have the chance to win a car, then the presence of the cars is morally justified. The ideological function that this humanitarian "ends justify means" discourse aims at is, perhaps, maintaining the belief that even in this day and age there still *is* a causal link between means and humanitarian ends. The Audi montage has the additional function of rendering win-winism tangible: It shows that as a humanitarian benefactor you may be a beneficiary too. An Audi A1 costs upward of 240,000 Danish kroner. The donor winning the car may have donated 150 kroner. That is to say, the Audi montage represents a scenario in which the two positions in the humanitarian relation coincide, and in which a humanitarian benefactor gets more out of this relationship than the beneficiary. Potentially, this convergence of humanitarian benefactor and beneficiary in one and the same person is hazardous for a humanitarian campaign, because it might look like an admission that humanitarian reason primarily benefits the humanitarian benefactors. The ideological function of this discourse of win-winism is, perhaps, to make the audience hold on to the assumption that the others nevertheless also win a little something.

Like other skeptimentalized humanitarian artifacts, *Danmarks indsamling* speaks to a desire for rendering humanitarian emotionality harmless, while still holding on to the ability to respond to what does not seem right in the world. The becoming-advertisement of humanitarian privilege montage is a way of responding to, by taking on, the discontents of humanitarian reason and of making public what otherwise seems merely private about the uglifying metaresponses to the moral sentiments: The fact that in *Danmarks indsamling* humanitarian mobilization comes across as "business as usual in the benevolence industries" functions as a kind of cover, overlaying the mistrust of humanitarian reason with a more familiar, and in that sense reassuring, mistrust of, but also tolerance toward, the modus operandi of the language of advertisement. In this manner, the humanitarian format draws legitimacy from the advertising form, suggesting that to skeptimental publics it may be more acceptable to be affected by genres of advertisement than by genres of altruism.

The final privilege montage we shall examine in this chapter paved the way for the *Danmarks indsamling* 2019 show, under the headline "The Girl Shop." In that particular year, the campaign was raising funds for "Verdens piger" (the girls of the world), and "The Girl Shop" thus functioned as a theme-specifying campaign, a subcampaign running on YouTube in the weeks prior to the show itself. True to their genre, the "Girl Shop" montages highlight the contrast between commodities conceivably belonging to, on the one hand, the regular life of a young Scandinavian girl and, on the other hand, the far more brutal and oppressed lives of girls elsewhere in the world. This "clash on the same surface" of two essentially different ways of life is emphasized on a formal level by a clash of two genres: the special offer advert and the humanitarian appeal. In "The Girl Shop," the overt language and style of advertisement is meant to convey the scandal of girls in our world leading such diverse forms of life: be-helmeted, pink-clad child cyclists versus child soldiers. Nordic well-being is juxtaposed to the other world's vulnerability, children's play against children's brutish reality. Here, to an even greater extent than in the Audi montage, the humanitarian appeal is merely implicit in the advertising form, and thus on the face of it the humanitarian message is actually hard to spot.

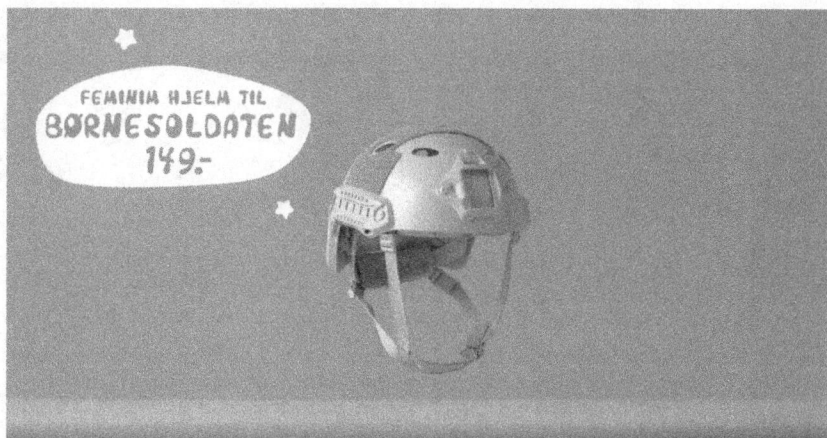

FIGURE 4. Feminine helmet for the child soldier. "The Girl Shop," campaign for *Danmarks indsamling* 2019. Copyright © DR Archive.

The "Girl Shop" campaign derives significance from the so-called world gifts, which we shall look at more closely in part 3. In world gifts, humanitarian donation assumes the form of a useful gift to be employed in an everyday life with illness and privation—for instance, UNICEF (United Nations Children's Fund) Denmark offers in their web shop a vaccination set for ten children or a school kit for an entire school class. In "The Girl Shop," however, this world gift format is mutated into a scandalous form, inasmuch as the commodities on display are conspicuously improper, many of them in a sexualized way. This impropriety is, of course, legitimized by the fact that the actual scandal is not the products or their backdrop but the scandalous reality of girl life to which the montages refer. Yet, the unseemliness of, for instance, "Wedding dress of the year for the child bride" or "CE marked cosmetic kit for the young prostitute" takes the latent scandalous pitch of the skeptimental mode to the next, and arguably final, level.[16]

In the "Girl Shop" montages, I submit, humanitarian form as advertising is brought to a provisional conclusion. Here, we are not invited to perceive ourselves as "donors without borders" or even as sympathizers, really. On the contrary, the donor's agency is utterly frustrated by the scandalizing tone, and the montages seem to virtually disparage the idea that the humanitarian subject can donate herself out of the collision of realities represented by the image. Any sense of humanitarian agency left is further complicated by the

FIGURE 5. Wedding dress of the year for the child bride. "The Girl Shop," campaign for *Danmarks indsamling* 2019. Copyright © DR Archive.

fact that "The Girl Shop" is actually false advertising: Unlike the vaccination kit from UNICEF Denmark, the products in "The Girl Shop" exist only as imagined commodities, not as real ones; there is nothing for the humanitarian subject to buy in this shop. "The Girl Shop" is, so to speak, humanitarian communication only to the extent that it is fraudulent advertising. In these montages, the sentimental mode so typical for humanitarian communication has received more than just a twist: The scandalous-skeptimental mode of the "Girl Shop" montages operates not by offering moral uplift but by screening out sympathetic emotions in the very act of promoting them.

As I see them, these skeptimental montages risk jeopardizing the very idea of well-intentioned agency through donation so essential to twenty-first-century humanitarian culture. The "Girl Shop" montages are hard-hitting and consumer-disparaging in tone, a legacy passed down by both Rosler and Meckseper. While the commercial exploitability of the privilege collage was evident already in the energetic magazine aesthetic of Rosler's *Bringing the War Home* series, in late-humanitarian culture the function of the commercial aesthetic of privilege montage is to take on and render harmless the suspicion that in skeptimental publics clings to doing good. As a device in humanitarian communication, this form is, however, most likely a precarious aesthetic strategy. For one thing, privilege montage always risks implicating its viewer in a way that she will find accusatory, as argued by Rancière, and the relationship between "them" and "us" drawn up by humanitarian privilege montage is notoriously difficult to stabilize as benign. For another, the advertising form is in itself a form of address that skeptimental publics will more often than not regard as being party, in some nebulous fashion, to the scandal of global economic inequality staged by privilege montage. Here, the system connecting "distant war and domestic consumption" is not a system of care but one of—yes well, what exactly? Not only is there nothing to buy in "The Girl Shop," there is nothing for the late-humanitarian subject to buy into, either. Whereas a sentimental humanitarian appeal is both emotionally and economically "appealing," in "The Girl Shop" the two are separated and equally stymied. There is no idea of agency left. In portending to be business as usual, these late-humanitarian privilege montages admit to having nothing to offer the skeptimental public.

Just as sentimental publics are mediated by cultural objects and commodities such as novels, magazines, songs, and cinema employing specific sentimental tropes, so too are skeptimental publics mediated by skeptimental cultural artifacts, examples of which I am exploring in this study. Whereas we associate sentimentality with an aesthetic of sympathy, skeptimentality is characterized by a critical mutation in the aesthetic of sympathy resulting in what I call an aesthetic of complicity. The "interplay of opposites" at the crux of privilege montage, the privilege genre examined in this chapter, may at times appear to belong to a repertoire of sentimental tropes asking the privileged subject to feel right, to cultivate sympathetic emotions for the less fortunate, and to dedicate himself to *helping* these less fortunate by, say, donating or consuming compassionately (Rancière 2011c, 27). Yet more often than not, privilege montage plays out in a skeptimental key, calling forth emotional ambivalence and an experience of complicity.

Privilege montage is, then, rarely a genre hailing us as straightforwardly virtuous humanitarian subjects, not even when the genre pops up in late-humanitarian communication. The kind of analysis that lingers implicitly in the "interplay of opposites" organizing the genre is an analysis that cannot help pointing to "a causal logic between the situation of the haves and the situation of the have-nots" (Robbins 2014, 262). Discussing the distinction between humanitarianism and the transnational egalitarian discourse he calls "the discourse of the beneficiary," Bruce Robbins suggests that "humanitarian discourse forbids the positing of a causal logic between the situation of the haves and the situation of the have-nots. . . . An analysis that makes this causal link is doing something more ambitious than humanitarianism" (2014, 262). This assumption is as important to my study as it is to Robbins's work, and we shall return to Robbins's formulation in chapter 11. For now, I want to emphasize, however, that this kind of causal analysis is not necessarily a reflection of analytical or political ambition (although it is certainly possible). In Scandinavian public culture now, this kind of "analysis" is an expression, rather, of a historical common sense that filters through and modifies humanitarian discourse and practice.

Part 2

On Seeing

4.

Humanitarian Spectatorship

THE WAY OF seeing lying at the center of this part of my study is captured in a scene from the novel *Telefon* (Telephone, 2018) by the Danish author Ida Jessen. In this scene, the fifty-one-year-old female protagonist Lisa and her partner Frederik are in their living room watching the news on television, in disbelief, as they see footage of refugees crossing the border into Denmark from Germany:

> They sat watching the late news, and saw the trains stop at Padborg Station, and the refugees run across the fields in a country they didn't know, a country that scared them, *their* safe country where no one should be scared. A young mother was running, a little boy in one hand and a wheeled suitcase in the other; she couldn't handle both, and let go of her son. A woman was hitting herself in the face, young children were screaming from the depths of darkness, and teenage boys were loping along like calves. Lisa and Frederik took each other by the hand. There they sat in their living room, looking not only at the television, but also at the living room, and at their entire home, at the rooms in which they lived. (Jessen 2018, 99)[1]

This scene speaks to the hybrid affective environment in the Nordic countries at the 2015 onset of what was quickly termed "the refugee crisis," a term little concerned with when, why, or to whom the intensified pattern of migration and fatalities among refugees in fact posed a crisis. In Scandinavia, widespread collective acts of everyday humanitarian solidarity, neighborly care, and mass volunteering sparked by moving media coverage of what was, in a Nordic context, an uncharacteristically disorderly arrival of thousands of refugees from the Middle East and North Africa co-existed with a wide spectrum of anti-immigrant political and public rhetoric. In Denmark, where Jessen's novel is set, these mixed public emotions were marked by a surprised disappointment that many of these refugees seemed to have no desire at all to live in Denmark but were resolutely heading for neighboring Sweden in order to seek asylum there. So how desperate were these people? Danes asked themselves. And how come so many immigrants were carrying smartphones? This was a vexed moment in the history of, and a continued Scandinavian investment in, the egalitarian imaginary.

The living room scene in *Telefon* marks a recurring theme in Jessen's body of work: altruistic middle-class individuals encountering the subaltern classes and the disorienting shock over what life near the social bottom looks like. There, at the bottom, things and behaviors are rarely as they ought to be, it occurs to the privileged protagonists; yet it remains frustratingly difficult for them to find fruitful ways in which to share their own good-life attitudes and privileged manners. In this particular scene, Lisa is attentive to the scrambled conduct of the foreigners. To her, they appear not only as strangers but also as "affect aliens," to borrow Sara Ahmed's phrasing, inasmuch as they behave like scared creatures in what Lisa wants to hold on to as being in fact a Nordic zone of safety and care (Ahmed 2010, 142). The scene is entwined in a cluster of Lisa's ruminations about the meaning of neighborly love in a changing world, where even foreign street beggars do not behave as Lisa and her generation of welfare-state citizens would expect them to. They beg too humbly, with tears and pleading voices rather than with the self-esteem and dignity Lisa wants them to feel now that they have arrived in the Nordic welfare state with which she has shared a trajectory of growth and decline.

For decades now, the issue known in visual culture scholarship as the predicament of looking at "the pain of others" has been organized according to a cluster of questions such as, Is it okay to represent violence, vulnerability, and pain in this or that particular way? Is it okay to look at this? Is it okay to feel like this when looking at that? Which looking practices and sentiments are the most "ethical" or "political" when faced with an "image of suffering?"[2] In this imagined scene of twenty-first-century Scandinavian domestic life, however, the question that the television footage provokes in Lisa would seem to be more implicatory, perhaps something along the lines of, Is this life that we have built in fact okay? How come we have all this? Or Whose pain is reflected in our belongings, in the way in which we live? In this and the next two chapters, then, my focus will be the sense of double or deep vision inherent in the final sentence of the passage quoted from *Telefon*. Lisa and Frederik look at the images on the television, and they look at their life, their home becoming an object of contemplation, the meaning of which changes in the light reflected by the images before them.

Susan Sontag famously argues that images of war and destitution cannot really convey to the spectator his or her complicit relation to power: "To set aside the sympathy we extend to others beset by war and murderous politics for a reflection on how our privileges are located on the same map as their suffering, and may—in ways we might prefer not to imagine—be linked to their suffering, as the wealth of some may imply the destitution of others, is a task for which the painful, stirring images supply only an initial spark" (Sontag 2003, 103).[3] The extensive research literature on images of "the pain of others"—crisis photography, atrocity photography, images of war, violence, conflict, destitution—is, at large, infused with a critical discourse on innocence, which in broad outline goes, When the Western privileged spectator is seized by sympathy and pity, she misunderstands her own relationship to the suffering of others, inasmuch as she believes herself to be politically and economically unrelated to—that is, innocent of—the suffering she is watching. Therefore, the spectator regarding the pain of others has no sense of being an accomplice to the suffering in question, albeit in reality she is.[4] Let us call this the hypothesis of the spectator's false sense of innocence. We recognize in this hypothesis the critique of sentimental politics and its aesthetic of sympathy, with which we have become acquainted.[5]

The hypothesis of the spectator's false sense of innocence is, I suspect, accurate insofar as "we," the structurally privileged viewers, would prefer not to imagine our lives, our privileges, linked to "their" suffering. However, this is nevertheless the link that "we" imagine every day, as evidenced by the culture of Nordic privilege sensibility. To be sure, the predicament of privilege also gives rise to all sorts of collective reinvestments in forms of (white) innocence and moral purity, and sometimes the anxious question, Is this okay? indeed manifests a yearning for okayness in the form of innocence and indisputable benevolence. Yet it is relevant to ask, Who looks at images of poverty, violence, suffering, vulnerability, and pain and feels, actually, innocent? In privilege-sensitive publics, the hypothesis of the spectator's sense of innocence does not describe humanitarian spectatorship particularly well. Rather, to the Nordic sensibility tracked and traced in my study, a sense of innocence most often constitutes an alluring but ultimately untenable mirage. For that reason, and based on this book's archive, I propose two alternatives to this hypothesis. Firstly, in skeptimental publics, spectators typically understand themselves precisely as accomplices. Secondly, these spectators very much understand themselves as accomplices *because* they are spectators. This latter, and specifically visual, experience of being implicated will be the pivotal point of the chapters in this part of the book.

These chapters examine humanitarian spectatorship in the skeptimental mode. By *humanitarian spectatorship*, I mean the practice of looking at images (still, moving, digital, or analogue) that invite the viewer to interpret them as representations of humanitarian crises—that is, as records of poverty, famine, disaster, epidemics, terror, or war.[6] In my usage, humanitarian spectatorship in the skeptimental key is a way of looking that configures what is seen according to the visual understanding that "our privileges *are* located on the same map as their suffering" (Sontag 2003, 103; emphasis added). As we saw in chapter 1, a skeptimental structure of feeling differs from a sentimental structure of feeling by being conspicuously ambivalent: The skeptimental structure of feeling predisposes the feeling subject, which may be a public, to a "negative" metaresponse when experiencing a "positive" feeling of care. A skeptimental gaze differs from a sentimental gaze by, in short, organizing what is seen into a privilege montage.

Yet skeptimental spectatorship is not necessarily the gaze of someone who *knows* herself to be an accomplice to the injury of which an image speaks. The sense of being implicated that I wish to identify is not primarily a question of subjectivity, although it cannot avoid being that too, but one of visuality. The privilege-collaging gaze with which Lisa looks around her living room is a result of a historically specific matrix for relating things seen and heard and halfway comprehended. This particular way of framing a field of vision does not, however, chart one specific interpretation of what the privilege-collaging gaze actually sees. In chapter 3, we saw how, in Rancière's interpretation, Martha Rosler worked with the form of collage as a visibility mechanism in order to present the spectator with his or her complicity, which the spectator would otherwise not be able or willing to see. The literary portrayal of an implicatory structure of seeing in Jessen's *Telefon* is more a depiction of the way in which the subject *already* sees. Lisa is no critical artist. Her visual integration of scared refugees with her own belonging and belongings is presented to us as obvious and ordinary, if also saddening and upsetting to her. The crucial point here being that the implicatory, skeptimental framework organizes someone's field of vision in such a historically distinct manner that when this someone is looking at her living room it appears to her like a privilege montage.

Glimpsing or detecting pain, historical injustice, extraction, and exploitation in the everyday objects and environments surrounding you is, I argue, a common way of seeing for the citizen-subject of skeptimental publics. Therefore, when calling for the privileged spectator's awareness of being implicated in what is seen, the scholarship on images of violence overlooks the ordinariness of the implicatory sensorium that privilege sensibility already entails. How are emerging looking practices modifying the forms of engagement shaped by the sentimental visual politics of humanitarianism? Unless we align the scholarly inquiry with the historically distinct sensorium, we will be in no position to respond to such questions. One way to align the literature with the historical sensorium is, I suggest, to pay closer attention to those objects of late-humanitarian visual culture that actually exhibit great ambivalence toward the sentimental politics and its aesthetic of sympathy. Then the issue of what visual agency might be under conditions of complicity could also be treated with greater care. An implicit ideal in much research on images of suffering is that these images provoke political action to remedy the specific suffering in question, and it is widely held that realizing that "our privileges are located on the same map as their suffering" is in itself mobilizing. Judging from my Nordic archive, this view is not necessarily accurate. What *is* a solidary act of looking under conditions of complicity? To the skeptimental spectator, this is everything but clear. His implication, however, most often is.

Returning to Ida Jessen's novel and the living room situation, we realize that the novel's narrator has found no reason for racially marking either Lisa or the arriving refugees appearing on her television screen. But humanitarian spectatorship is never a raceless experience. To the reader of Jessen's novel, it will seem obvious that in this literary scene of humanitarian spectatorship, as in most such scenes, real or imagined, white characters are regarding the pain of nonwhite characters. In a Scandinavian setting, humanitarian spectatorship is generally synonymous with looking and feeling across racial difference, meaning across the physical differences of skin color, which are interpreted as profound cultural differences. But it is not only in the Nordic context that the humanitarian imaginary is premised upon global dividing lines that are not merely geographical and economical but also racial. The visual culture of humanitarianism thus acts as a central element in the humanitarian biopolitics that keeps producing "benefactors" and "beneficiaries" according to geopolitical and racial wealth gaps and other fault lines.[7] Humanitarian visual culture, and the forms of spectatorship instigated by it, is one component in a more overarching symbolic and material maintenance of racial difference, albeit the global symbolic production of race cannot be reduced to the humanitarian visual politics alone: In large sections of Western public culture, blackness connotes guiltiness, whereas in the visual culture of humanitarianism, "beneficiaries" are usually raced black in accordance with the sentimental visual matrix and its focus on the childlike innocence, humility, and forbearance of people of color. This is the moral grammar we saw described by James Baldwin in chapter 2.

Seen in this light, humanitarian visual practices are a regulatory mechanism, which, in line with other such scopic regimes, contributes to the framing of black and other nonwhite bodies in a grid of, respectively, guilt-fear-disdain and innocence-sympathy-compassion. In this chapter I seek to make the point that the skeptimental gaze has a sense—specifically, a visual awareness—of participating in this kind of visual politics. To humanitarian spectatorship in the skeptimental mode, therefore, the overdetermined correlation of humanitarian identities (benefactors and beneficiaries) with racially marked identities is becoming a problem. Skeptimental spectatorship is marked by a wariness with regard to the repertoire of tropes and frames engaged by conventional humanitarian visual culture: Alongside the affect called forth by a particular image, there is a sense, a visual understanding, that humanitarian spectatorship is raced—an impression that by looking at "the pain of others" one is, in a sense, made white. Ida Jessen's description is thus also significant in what it does *not* tell us about humanitarian spectatorship as a racialized cultural practice. Or rather, Jessen's depiction shows us that humanitarian spectatorship habitually involves *performances of not-noticing race. Performances of not-noticing race* is the historian Robin Bernstein's pertinent term for sentimental racial innocence, on which I shall draw in chapter 5's account of humanitarian spectatorship in the skeptimental mode (Bernstein 2011, 6).

The visual productions I analyze in the following two chapters are explicitly about self-implicating forms of seeing as much as they are about "the pain of others." The two bodies of work I engage are, firstly, a selection of outputs from the awareness campaign and fictitious humanitarian organization Radi-Aid (2012–22) developed by the Norwegian Students' and Academics' International Assistance Fund (SAIH) and, secondly, the now classic art documentary *Episode III: Enjoy Poverty* made by Dutch visual and performance artist Renzo Martens (2008). Starting from the supposition that global relations of inequality have their own visual life, and that the visual culture of humanitarianism forms an intricate part of that life, both serve as satires on the visual regime of humanitarianism—one an apparently light satire, the other ruthless. In this manner, both are really *about* the visual politics of humanitarianism, aiming also for the disruption of this particular visual regime. Yet, as satirical cultural texts, Radi-Aid and *Enjoy Poverty* also record (and contribute to) looking practices that are now becoming habitual in skeptimental publics. My analysis centers especially on the way in which these visual productions make the conventional correlation of humanitarian subject positions with racialized identities stand out.

5.

The Race to Help

IN HIS BOOK *Det internasjonale gjennembruddet* (The international break-through), which caused a stir in the Norwegian public when it was published in 2017, the historian Terje Tvedt describes the development from the 1960s onward of Norway's "humanitarian-political complex." *The international breakthrough* is Tvedt's term for a double internationalization of Norway in this epoch. It refers, on one hand, to the establishment of Norway as a humanitarian superpower with one of the world's largest aid budgets, a world champion in peace and development and, on the other, to Norway's development "from homogeneous nation-state to multicultural country" (as one of the book's chapter titles describes it). It is the mutual influence and exchange of norms, resources, and personnel between these two policy fields that have created the humanitarian-political complex. This complex is, in turn, the moral vehicle of what Tvedt calls "the national goodness regime."[1]

In the latter half of the twentieth century, Norway met the world, Tvedt writes, and became an "aid country." This development was shaped by international processes and was thus "part of a general European historical process" (Tvedt 2018, 17). While Norway was not, therefore, alone in developing a large humanitarian sector, what is special about the country, Tvedt suggests, is that the humanitarian-political complex here gained a particularly strong position in relation to other policy fields "when it came to influencing the national culture and education and the power over national conversations about the world and the country's place in it" (Tvedt 2018, 269).[2] Accordingly, the "Norwegian Samaritan" became the nation's foremost identity marker, and a well-intentioned population supported this new form of state philanthropy in the global South, Tvedt writes.

But Norway did not just encounter the world; the world also came to Norway. When "Norway received thousands, and eventually tens of thousands and hundreds of thousands, of residents from countries outside the Western cultural hemisphere . . . the old nation-state ideology no longer functioned," Tvedt argues (Tvedt 2018, 136).[3] The state's political leadership now needed a new language, a new ideology, in order to navigate new "multicultural dilemmas" (136). Multiculturalism, in conjunction with the universalism of human rights discourse, became this new political strategy and ideology, Tvedt contends: "For several decades, the state itself and central political environments systematically promoted multiculturalism as a societal norm and societal ideal" (Tvedt 2018, 137).[4] In terms of culture and values, the state should now be neutral. As a state-building ideology, multiculturalism, Tvedt maintains, has therefore led (according to both the political leadership and the majority of the Norwegian population) to the annulment of Norwegian values or Norwegian culture: The dominant Norwegian value, in other words, is that there are no Norwegian values.

What Tvedt calls the humanitarian-political complex thus arose from the tangible influence of Norway's international work for development and peace on the "semantics and use of concepts in the area of immigration policy."[5] A cornerstone of Tvedt's national history is his account of the emergence of an entirely new elite whose raison d'être was not primarily personal gain but to represent the morality of the Norwegian state on the global arena. According to Tvedt, the Norwegian regime of goodness is thus led by "aid jet-setters" and "tyrants of goodness": "Many of the actors within this regime of goodness staged themselves as stewards of the 'good'" (Tvedt 2018, 264, 268, 270).[6] With its self-legitimating power of goodness, the humanitarian-political elite, including the journalist profession, has succeeded in shaping a national doxa, Tvedt suggests, and in organizing the public conversation about the world and Norway's role in it: The goodness regime operates "as a field of politics above politics and as a representative for the universal, and for the Good and for the Just" (278).[7] This doxa did not arise out of the blue; it came in to being, rather, only as a result of concrete political initiatives and billions of kroner invested in "producing world-images and self-images" (Tvedt 2018, 278).

While this is not the place for a review essay, to me, Tvedt's scholarship comes across, if polemical and controversial, as sound and generally engaged with relevant theoretical discourses and historical examples, notwithstanding that certain passages approach the aggravated outlook and tonalities of a more routine right-wing ridicule of humanitarian politics. Importantly, however, instead of arguing for or against the germaneness and applicability of *Det internasjonale gjennembruddet*, I take Tvedt's passionate argument about the existence of a Norwegian goodness regime to belong to the general ecology of skeptimentality. That is, I regard it as a historical object of contemporary Scandinavian public culture—and, more precisely, as a skeptimental object suspicious of humanitarian reason and its politics of sentimentality. For instance, in employing a vocabulary including phrases like *aid jet-setters* and *tyrants of goodness*, Tvedt demonstrates the broad appeal held by the mode of *scandalous* skeptimentality to those wishing to expose something as self-charitably sentimental. In this manner, scandalous skeptimentality is a historical mode, also, in the sense that it is employed to judge history.

Remarkably, Tvedt is not concerned with internal fractures in, or opposition to, Norway's "regime of goodness." Thus, the story of the far-right and anti-immigrant Progress Party (Fremskrittspartiet), which had already become Norway's second-largest party in the 2009 election with more than 22 percent of the vote, does not figure in Tvedt's contemporary history. In fact, the term *goodness tyranny*, which Tvedt uses actively in *Det internasjonale gjennembruddet*, was used in 2015 by Sylvi Listhaug, today the party's leader, to describe a Norwegian goodness regime not unlike the one Tvedt portrays.[8] Nevertheless, the considerable skepticism toward humanitarian publics and noble moral sentiments, which Listhaug and the Progress Party represent, does not play a role in Tvedt's contemporary history of Norway.

In Tvedt's historical narrative, humanitarian reason is extremely effective ideologically, both as doxa and in its capacity to structure feeling. In the vocabulary of my study, the Norwegian public is, according to Tvedt, a sentimental-humanitarian public, in which the moral feelings naturally follow the logic of sentimentality; here it actually feels good to do good, and neither the public nor the elite hesitate in front of this feeling culture and rhetoric of goodness. In the Norwegian public, so the argument goes, humanitarian tropes do their sentimental work without interruption: Rather than with skepticism and mistrust, humanitarian self-images are associated with moral and affective uplift. This also applies to a key sentimental trope that Tvedt acidly calls "a mighty Norwegian pietà" (268). This trope is one of piousness, "where the Virgin Mary, mourning her son Jesus, was replaced by a minister or a celebrity, preferably squatting, surrounded by African children; preferably many children, and obviously grateful children" (Tvedt 2018, 269).[9]

This sentimental trope of piousness appears, Tvedt shows, in the humanitarian organizations' campaigns and in "the nation's great rituals," such as the recurrent NRK telethon (*TV-aksjonen*) and Operation Day's Work (Operasjon Dagsverk). "As the humanitarian-political complex grew and the competition between the organizations over the aid market sharpened," writes Tvedt, "the temptation to exploit both one's own moral capital as a kind of modern Samaritan and people's desire to demonstrate their empathy with the African poor intensified" (Tvedt 2018, 55).[10] It is this deeply sentimental trope, the "mighty Norwegian pietà," that we shall see undergoing a joyful skeptimentalization in Radi-Aid.

Optimism

The spoof charity song "Radi-Aid: Africa for Norway" was released in the Christmas season of 2012, just a few months after the Kony 2012 campaign had turned humanitarian communication, its potentials and problems, into a matter of hectic public debate (in the United States at least). In the "Africa for Norway" video, we encounter a group of smiling young black people identifying as Africans who get together around the good cause of helping Norway.[11] They collect radiators from their fellow Africans in order to ship them to Norway, where people are freezing. A lot of Africans are unaware about what's going on in Norway right now, Breezy V, a young man in sunglasses and a Radi-Aid T-shirt, laments in front of the camera. What *is* going on in Norway—the freezing—is in fact just as bad as poverty, Breezy V suggests, and that's why he's gotten together the team now going from door to door collecting radiators. "Africa, we need to make a difference in Norway," his rallying cry echoes, "spread some warmth . . . spread some smiles" (SAIH 2012). Then begins the performance of the charity song, sung by a choir of fine-looking young black people accompanied on the piano by a piano player resembling Ray Charles. From this point, the video follows the genre conventions of the charity song. We see singers arriving in the studio, cheery and glowing with moral uplift, while the piano player strikes the first chords. In a mock privilege montage, the glossy performance of the song is crosscut with footage of distressed white people slipping on icy roads, protecting their faces from the intense winter cold, trucks buried in snow along the roadside. The lyrics of the song encourage fellow Africans to donate their radiators—"There's heat enough for Norway if Africans would share"—while also assuring them that while Norway has previously helped Africa with its problems of poverty, corruption, HIV, and crime, "now the tables have turned," and "now it's payback time" (SAIH 2012).

The "Africa for Norway" video ends with the campaign team waving off a truckload of radiators to be shipped over there, to Norway. This is followed by a piece of information that comes as a surprise, to some viewers undoubtedly a disappointing or alarming one.[12] We see the Radi-Aid logo and then the credits: The video has not been produced by, say, an African grassroots organization, but by the Norwegian Students' and Academics' International Assistance Fund (SAIH; Studentenes og Akademikernes Internasjonale Hjelpefond), and is thus supported by Norad, the Norwegian Agency for Development Cooperation.[13] Hence, while "Africa for Norway" takes the form of a satirical call from South to North, it is actually more of a visual manifestation of what Bruce Robbins calls "the discourse of the beneficiary" (Robbins 2017, 6), meaning an appeal from "beneficiaries" in the North (Westerners benefiting from global inequality) to fellow Western beneficiaries about the injustice of their shared privileges—in this instance, the unacceptability of a specific visual convention.

Akin to other Radi-Aid productions, "Africa for Norway" is an educational campaign aiming for a humanitarian solidarity built on greater awareness and fewer visual stereotypes.[14] The aesthetic aim of the video is to replace the Afro-pessimism so naturalized in humanitarian communication with a kind of realism by figuring smart, urban chic, young (South) African people, whose global middle-classness is indicated visually by means of hoodies, caps, smart-tech savviness, and beach culture recognizable to the Euro-American good-life imaginary.[15] Africans are not what you think they are, the video suggests; they are not poor, starving, crying, dying, half-naked, smiling gratefully, or whatever other images the humanitarian imaginary has made available to you. The Radi-Aid spoof messes around with the humanitarian genre of the charity song by "turning the tables," as the lyrics have it—by inverting, that is, the familiar humanitarian relationship between "them" and "us," including the racial and geographical implications of this relationship. It engages with and makes fun of the humanitarian imaginary by putting one Scandinavian nation on the same footing as an entire continent and by equating Norway with deadly frostbite and dangerous drifts of snow in the tradition of framing countries that receive humanitarian aid as places of disaster.

FIGURES 6 AND 7. "Africa for Norway." Radi-Aid campaign. Copyright © iKind/
SAIH.

The fact that humanitarian images are imbued with racial meaning and
that they imply racialized viewing habits is the principal visual knowledge documented by the Radi-Aid enterprise. The simple move of switching the racial-
regional identities of humanitarian beneficiaries and benefactors activates and
foregrounds the visual knowledge that humanitarian spectatorship usually
implies white people seeing white people helping people of color—this racial
logic of humanitarian spectatorship most often hiding, in Scandinavia at least,
in plain sight. While we do not yet have a critical vocabulary developed enough
for discussing the role played by humanitarian images in shaping a racial world
"order" and the everyday experiences of that order, visual productions such

as those of Radi-Aid remind the spectator that humanitarian imagery is one occasion for observing the reproduction of racial difference.

One of my theses in this book is that, in skeptimental publics, even conventional humanitarian productions will move toward skeptimentality by, in one way or another, integrating a skeptimental suspicion of the affects, tropes, and genres of sentimental humanitarianism. *Danmarks indsamling*, as we saw in chapter 3, is an example of this tendency. Rather than conventional humanitarian productions, Radi-Aid's productions are parodies, yet it is exactly their charming satire that tells us of the way they nonetheless seem to nurture an optimism about humanitarian reason. Therefore, Radi-Aid's productions are an occasion for closely studying a conflict, very common to skeptimentality, between the optimism of sentimental humanitarianism and the pessimism concerning humanitarian reason that skeptimental suspicion typically implies. How can one manage skeptimental suspicion in such a way that it is possible, still, to hold on to that promise of a better world through helping others that animates humanitarian reason? Radi-Aid provides us with an example of one such way.

For, on the one hand, Radi-Aid is a declared optimistic enterprise, saying that better humanitarian images result in less visual containment, less symbolic violence, and thereby a better humanitarianism, which in turn results, hopefully, in a better world. The good news brought to us by Radi-Aid and like-minded satires is that the symbolic containment—the sentimental and degrading framing of nonwhite bodies, that is—can be overturned by circulating other images. On the other hand, however, the Radi-Aid productions seem to be marked by a more fundamental mistrust of the humanitarian culture of feeling and its visual features. Intimating, as the "Africa for Norway" video does, that sending radiators to cold Norwegians somehow mirrors humanitarian aid is also an allusion to the risk that the humanitarian beneficiary is not so much benefiting from the aid as providing a good cause for performing benevolence. In a similar vein, another Radi-Aid production, the "Who Wants to Be a Volunteer?" video (SAIH 2014), mockingly takes on the phenomenon of voluntourism, while the "Radi-Aid App: Change a Life with Just One Swipe" video (SAIH 2016) deals a blow to the "apptimism" and "clicktivism" so central to the "technologization of action" in humanitarian fundraising (Chouliaraki 2010, 117). Indeed, while Radi-Aid's productions feel good, their chipping away at white humanitarian sentimentalism records a more fundamental mistrust of humanitarian culture.

Thus, Radi-Aid's productions seem pedagogically conflicted: an earnest humanitarian-reformist framework colliding with a discrete impetus to altogether unsettle the humanitarian ethos and culture of feeling. This conflict is the schism of skeptimentality; it is a symptom of the skeptimental modification of sentimental humanitarianism that I am tracing in this book. Yet in the Radi-Aid productions, skeptimental mistrust of humanitarian reason does not take the form of immoral scandal, examples of which we find in this book's skeptimental archive. Rather, here the mistrust thrives in the laughter—in the playful, tenderly cruel ridicule of white sentimentality and humanitarian benevolence. Take another Radi-Aid spoof, the "Let's Save Africa—Gone Wrong" video (SAIH 2013), in which we follow Michael, a "fundraising actor child" and his encounter with Western communicators who want him to perform the role of sad African child in their appeals. The video is damning in its charming satire of the racial aesthetic of humanitarian appeals. Like the "Africa for Norway" video, "Let's Save Africa—Gone Wrong" plays with stereotypes and with turning the tables by presenting silly and ridiculously sentimental white humanitarian celebrities as the ones in need of care and help. This creative ridicule haunts the Radi-Aid productions' determined will to optimism, because it exposes the basic elements in humanitarianism as racial ideology: white benevolence predicated upon childlike black innocence and the aesthetic conventions that give this ideology its shape and feel. Michael, the fundraising actor child, is not innocent in the sense of being untouched by the customs and vices of the white world. He is a fast-food-eating black boy who routinely performs African childhood innocence and deprivation for white humanitarian spectators.

The determination to, above everything, steer clear of cynical reason sometimes renders skeptimental cultural texts improbably optimistic. The concluding textual comments of the "Let's Save Africa—Gone Wrong" video cry out in bold capitals "STEREOTYPES HARM DIGNITY" and "CHALLENGE THE PERCEPTIONS." While these pedagogical exclamations are indeed significant and fitting, they also come across as being somehow overly edifying and "useful" summaries of a body of work that critically takes on basic elements of humanitarian imagery and of the humanitarian imaginary. Radi-Aid presents us with the fact that humanitarian images are racialized objects that confirm a certain racial order. At the same time, the humorous presentation of this fact is suggesting that with disarming humor and wit we can indeed move forward together into more progressive representations, leaving neocolonial tropes behind, toward a reeducated humanitarian reason. But this representational optimism is contested by the skeptimentalizing laughter it itself provokes.

Racial Innocence

Thus far, my suggestion has been that humanitarian spectatorship in the skeptimental key involves both an awareness of being implicated in what is seen and noticing racial difference as a basic ingredient of humanitarian visual objects. Furthermore, I have been arguing that the Norwegian Radi-Aid project shows that noticing race may have consequences for humanitarian visual culture: Radi-Aid makes visible the tacit skeptimental knowledge ("tacit," at least, for white spectators) that the visual politics of humanitarianism is a raced politics and that the humanitarian aesthetic thus contributes to the shaping and maintenance of global racial identities and hierarchies. Pedagogically conflicted, the Radi-Aid enterprise catalogs, and sediments, the hesitant reluctance to participate in "regarding the pain of others" that is at the heart of skeptimental spectatorship. In the following, I look at another element of the Radi-Aid work, the research element *Radi-Aid Research*, which raises questions about who gets to be a humanitarian spectator—questions at the center, also, of Martens's *Episode III: Enjoy Poverty*, to which we will turn in the next chapter.[16]

Examining humanitarian spectatorship in six African countries, the research project *Radi-Aid Research: A Study of Visual Communication in Six African Countries* (2018) is not, on the face of it, really about Scandinavian humanitarian spectatorship, which is the focus of this chapter. Nonetheless, as part of the Norwegian SAIH's Radi-Aid project it does indicate both a certain aesthetic embarrassment about conventional humanitarian iconography and, in a sense more fundamentally, a skeptimental moral and visual embarrassment about humanitarian communication. Conducted in 2017 and 2018, *Radi-Aid Research* examined the representational preferences among focus group participants in Ghana, Zambia, Malawi, Ethiopia, Uganda, and South Africa by asking participants which of the images used in a range of real and mock humanitarian campaigns they preferred over other images and why. The design and execution of this research endeavor once again speaks to the raison d'être of Radi-Aid: the energetic attempt to open up the white Western echo chambers of humanitarian communication, in this case by doing what may have appeared simple—asking those at "the receiving end," as the research report frames it, what types of humanitarian images they preferred (SAIH and Girling 2018, 6). In other words, they are asked to signal their preferences in a visual field that contributes to shaping a global racial order.

If SAIH had assumed that *Radi-Aid Research* would bring results seamlessly aligned with the organization's own advocacy work, they were, on the face of it, wrong. The two key results highlighted in the research report are not exactly in line with SAIH's main hypothesis that visual representations of "African problems" are often stereotyped and negative misrepresentations of an entire continent. Summing up the conclusions of the study, the authors of the report remark that "most respondents said they would use negative images in their fundraising ads, and they felt that the pictures they were shown were an accurate depiction of reality" (SAIH and Girling 2018, 32). One part of the study asked respondents to indicate their preference from three different images of a "local 7-year old girl, Katrina Nassali," shown in close-up on an indistinct background (SAIH and Girling 2018, 7). The three images show the girl as, the report explains, happy, neutral, and sad, respectively, but are otherwise alike. A majority of respondents chose the "sad image" (13). The questionnaire also asked, "To fundraise, is it better to show an image of the problem, the outcome, the root cause or a neutral image?" (29). Respondents leaned toward showing the problem. This preference among respondents for "negative imagery" (32) is perhaps surprising. Does it suggest that respondents identify with stereotypes of "sad Africans" living on a "disaster continent"?

To further assess *Radi-Aid Research* and its implications for thinking skeptimental humanitarian spectatorship, I will draw some comparisons with the famous study known as the "doll tests," carried out in North America in the late 1930s and the 1940s by the psychologists Kenneth and Mamie Clark.[17] With the doll study, Clark and Clark wanted to examine how African American children experienced racial difference. Asking hundreds of African American children from ages three to seven to choose the doll, brown-black or pinkish-white, they liked the best, Clark and Clark discovered that a majority of test subjects identified a white doll as the "nice" one and chose a black doll as the one that "looks bad" (Clark and Clark 1947, 175). Subsequently, when asked to pick the one that "looks like you," approximately two-thirds of the children chose a brown doll, while a third claimed a white doll as looking more like themselves. Over the years, the Clarks repeated the experiment with some variations, but the conclusion they drew remained: Even very young children were familiar not only with racial difference but also, and traumatically so, with the cultural evaluations of that difference.[18] What the Clarks proved, according to popular reception of the findings, was that a damaged American culture was responsible for a damaged psyche of black American children.

While the Radi-Aid study and the Clarks' study differ widely in object, scope, and political importance, the doll tests provide us, I suggest, with an interpretative framework for pinning down the wider relevance of *Radi-Aid Research*. Like the doll tests, the Radi-Aid research project confronts its respondents with racialized objects, in this case humanitarian images, that invite specific patterns of performance. Both research projects ask their respondents, children and adults respectively, to process a certain cultural configuration of racialized identities. In terms of identifying with negative stereotypes, could the case of African respondents preferring "negative" humanitarian images of black African "beneficiaries" be likened to African American children in the Clarks' study identifying with the doll that they have just pointed out as the "bad" doll? And if so, in choosing "negative" images over "positive" ones, are the respondents in the Radi-Aid study then professing symptoms of internalized stereotypes?[19] And, if not, how else are we to assess the cultural significance of *Radi-Aid Research*?

In a both critical and affirmative reading of the Clarks' experiments, historian Robin Bernstein (2011) assesses their conclusions, arguing that a black child choosing to play with and cuddle a white-pinkish doll over a black-brown one was not necessarily proof of anything other than that the child was an expert on a historically specific culture of play in which black dolls scripted servitude and violence. Understanding dolls as "scriptive things"— material objects that in use invite some historically located practices and discourage other such practices, thereby scripting one set of performances rather than another—Bernstein argues that the black dolls in the experiment did not, and could not, manifest *only* the idea of race. The dolls always also contained the idea of black *doll*, and black dolls most often "prompted play scenarios in which black dolls served white ones" (Bernstein 2011, 203). Thus, rejection of the brown-black doll could be read instead as resoluteness on behalf of the test subjects to reject degradation and servitude too. In this manner, Bernstein's interpretation of the Clarks' study takes seriously the history and materiality of the object in question, the black doll as racialized thing, allowing for an understanding of the child respondents as experts on a particular culture of play.

To Bernstein, the deepest cultural and political significance of the doll experiment thus lies not within the terrain of internalized racism but in the image the study provided of an innocent black childhood. From the mid-nineteenth century through the early twentieth century, Bernstein argues, "two qualities defined childhood innocence: whiteness and obliviousness." But in the 1940s, what Mamie and Kenneth Clark and their respondents collaborated to prove was that African American children were no less innocent and impressionable than white ones (241). The dramatic structure built into the Clarks' experiment, in which the final question constituted a climax often resulting in children sobbing or running out the door after having had to identify themselves with either a "nice" white doll or a "bad" brown one, was in itself a performative denunciation of the cultural assumption that black youth was indifferent to pain and suffering. Bernstein therefore concludes that the Clarks "wrought a spectacular performance of black childhood innocence" and that this spectacular performance contributed to "culturally desegregating childhood innocence itself" (241).

The concept of "racial innocence," also the title of Bernstein's study, is particularly relevant for my discussion of humanitarian spectatorship as raced practice. In the mid-nineteenth century, Bernstein points out, the white child's inherent innocence was in some cases transferrable to, for example, adult African Americans. One of Bernstein's illustrations of this dynamic is Harriet Beecher Stowe's *Uncle Tom's Cabin*, in which little Eva's pure-white virtuousness rubs off on Tom, whom Eva hugs and idolizes, thus sharing her childlike innocence with him.

The special mark of this childhood innocence, which had decisive political impact, was that it was not an innocence, in the sense of absence of knowledge, vis-à-vis anything and everything, but, on the contrary, an innocence specifically of social categories such as gender, class, and, not least, race. Little Eva does not notice Tom's status, his gender, or the color of his skin; her innocence consists precisely in transcending these "adult-world" categories. However, Bernstein reminds us, white children and black adults were no more unraced, ungendered, or unclassed in the sentimental culture of nineteenth-century North America than they are today: "Innocence was not a literal state of being unraced but was, rather, the *performance of not-noticing*, a performed claim of slipping beyond social categories" (Bernstein

2011, 6; emphasis added). Illustrations of Eva with her hand on Tom's shoulder, or on his thigh, visualize this innocence precisely as "performances of not-noticing" along with the transferability of innocence. Here we see Eva depicted "in the act of not-thinking about race, gender, age, or sexual desire" (Bernstein 2011, 7). This innocence, this active not-noticing, was decisive for the century's production of whiteness and racial difference, writes Bernstein: "What childhood innocence helped Americans to assert by forgetting, to think about by performing obliviousness, was not only whiteness but also racial difference constructed against whiteness" (2011, 8). The white, childlike innocence and its transference would have, Bernstein argues, a role to play in such diverse political projects as abolitionism and post-Reconstruction romanticization of slavery, respectively (2011, 6).

Dolls, according to Bernstein, "provide especially effective safe houses for racial ideology" (Bernstein 2011, 19). As do, I suggest, humanitarian visual objects. Humanitarian images are, like the illustrations of Eva and Tom, visual artifacts that invite the spectator to contemplate racial difference in a racially innocent way, this imagery thus being an occasion for sentimental publics to play racially innocent. Bernstein's analysis of the Clarks' study shows that the recognition of black childhood innocence in the United States of the mid-twentieth century was decisive both judicially and culturally for racial desegregation. Today, it is conversely clear that the cultural assumption of a childlike innocence of people of color, an assumption pivotal to humanitarian visual culture, contributes, on a global scale, to maintaining racial ideology—the flip side of the harmful exclusion of black youth from the category of childhood being, exactly, "the well-known libel of the 'childlike Negro'" (Bernstein 2011, 19). In the genealogy Bernstein is tracing, childhood innocence is raced white, whereas contemporary humanitarianism thrives on a childlike innocence raced nonwhite. Yet this latter nonwhite innocence has an equivalent capacity for transferability across racial difference, and thereby also for political application. In the extensive sentimental tradition characterizing US popular culture and conventional humanitarian visual culture alike, visualizations of black childlike innocence, suffering, and pain are scripts for the compassion of the privileged classes and thereby for the emotional experience of justice, which is a key attraction of sentimental cultures.

Returning to the Radi-Aid study, the absence of white people from any of the campaign images shown to the respondents is remarkable. While the doll tests involved choosing between pinkish and brown dolls, respondents in the Radi-Aid study are not given the opportunity to choose an image figuring a white beneficiary or a white benefactor. Yet the study suggests that respondents do in fact notice racial difference, even when it is not explicitly presented to them. The handful of responses conveying irritation toward the uniformly racialized character of the aid iconography is a case in point. One male respondent from Ethiopia asks, "Why don't we see posters with white children that are in need? . . . We are good for begging just because we are black? Do we make for good poster children because of the colour of our skin?" (SAIH and Girling 2018, 20). A female respondent from Malawi says, "I feel that outside there in the Western world, there are also some people that are poor. But we have never seen them here in pictures" (SAIH and Girling 2018, 24). By thus noticing racial difference as paramount to humanitarian visual culture, respondents perform what we could perhaps call racial *noninnocence*, whereby they simultaneously question the script of humanitarian images as racialized objects. Hence, from being vehicles of the visual reproduction of racial difference and hierarchy, in the hands of respondents these humanitarian images instead become occasions for probing the valences of that exact racial order.

Adapting Bernstein's methodological framework, we could say that, as a scriptive thing, a humanitarian image depicting a black African person cannot manifest *only* the idea of "Africanness" or any other racial-regional identity; it necessarily also refers to ideas of "humanitarianism," including distinct ideas of a humanitarian relationship between benefactors and beneficiaries and the scenarios scripted by that relationship. The Radi-Aid study does indicate that respondents do not really perceive the humanitarian images to be vehicles for identification or self-representation. Take, for instance, the entry in the Radi-Aid questionnaire that shows a young black girl as, respectively, happy, neutral, and sad and then asks respondents, "Which advert do you like and why?" (SAIH and Girling 2018, 9). As we saw, a majority preferred the sad image. From the responses, however, we realize that respondents do not at all identify with this preferred disposition. An Ethiopian male respondent explained his choice: "As long as we are trying to fundraise to solve the problem, the sad picture is the one that drives the message home" (SAIH and Girling 2018, 12). When asked, "To fundraise, is it better to show an image of the problem, the outcome, the root cause or a neutral image?" respondents leaned, again, toward showing the problem (SAIH and

Girling 2018, 29). But they did so from the vantage point of humanitarian communicators and benefactors rather than speculating on the kind of image they would like to see as a visual representation of their own situation; one female respondent from South Africa, for example, responded, "You need to ask why you are asking for money. What is it for? How are you going to use it? Who will benefit from that? I would highlight the problem" (SAIH and Girling 2018, 29). In terms of humanitarian communication, these responses would seem commonsensical and pragmatic, and they suggest that respondents react to the image as a material object rather than as a reflection of self. Or, more precisely, that respondents treat the images as scriptive things, objects designed for a historically specific purpose, namely to elicit donations from spectators living elsewhere.[20]

According to Bernstein's analysis, the most significant cultural impact of the doll tests was the *spectacular* performance of black childhood innocence. For our understanding of skeptimental late-humanitarian spectatorship, the most significant impact of *Radi-Aid Research* is, I suggest, that it is a *nonspectacular* performance of black African *noninnocence*. The powerful performance of an innocent and vulnerable African American childhood in the Clarks' study depended upon the affectively convincing response of the children. In contrast to these children, whose responses were interpreted as a collective response and thus culturally disruptive, the responses of African test subjects in the Radi-Aid study are not convincing in the sense of indicating a shared sense of self. Respondents are not performing collectively as either the happy, the neutral, or the sad African; they do not form a generically unambiguous character. The Radi-Aid study does appear convincing, however, in that it conveys responses that are conventional, ambivalent, and pointing in a number of directions. The respondents in the study perform as humanitarian spectators, fundraisers, communication advisers, and benefactors, respectively—in other words, as noninnocent discussants of and experts on humanitarian visual culture. To some extent, at least, this nonspectacular interruption of the coherence of respondents as a class of victims carries with it the interruption of "us" as a class of saviors.[21]

In her book *Picturing Pity* (2007), the anthropologist Marianne Gullestad provides one possible framework for further contextualizing the *Radi-Aid Research* project and for relating it once again to what Gullestad, Tvedt, and other scholars describe as a Norwegian "goodness regime."[22] *Picturing Pity* examines the imaging of "the others" facilitated by a Norwegian Protestant mission in northern Cameroon from the beginning of the mission in the 1920s until today (Norway has a rich tradition of evangelical missions and has sent out more missionaries per capita than any other European country). Particularly relevant to my analysis of *Radi-Aid Research* is Gullestad's discussion of an effort by the Norwegian Missionary Society (NMS) to "repatriate" missionary photographs by returning a collection of these photographs to publics in Cameroon. "Pictures that were originally taken to elicit interest about Cameroon in Norway," she explains, "were in the year 2000, seventy-five years after the Norwegians started working in northern Cameroon, returned to become a new cultural resource in the region" (Gullestad 2007, 250). This event—an act of "belated reciprocity"—demonstrates, Gullestad suggests, an emerging communicative modality in the history of missionary photography, a modality she calls "partnership" (248–50). Partnership is one of three communicative modes identified by Gullestad in the archive of Norwegian missionary images. This archive documents, she suggests, a historical movement from an "evangelizing" mode to a mode of "development" and then, with late twentieth-century initiatives such as the returning of missionary images to publics in northern Cameroon, to the communicative mode of partnership (14).[23]

I suggest we recognize in *Radi-Aid Research* an ethos similar to the NMS's returning of Norwegian missionary images to Cameroon, a project that was, like Radi-Aid, funded by Norad. To be sure, *Radi-Aid Research* does not aim to constitute a cultural resource in the six African countries, as the research seems to be addressed primarily to humanitarian donors and organizations in Northern Europe. Yet the communicative mode of partnership is one way of understanding the impetus of *Radi-Aid Research* to "return," so to speak, a collection of humanitarian images to an African audience, asking this audience to assist in disrupting the discourse within which the subject-object of humanitarian care has been constructed. Whereas the spoof Radi-Aid campaigns illustrated a skeptimental aesthetics of complicity by shifting and satirizing a sentimental visual grammar, *Radi-Aid Research* instead exemplifies this aesthetic by shifting the audience of humanitarian communication. As an event in the history of humanitarian imagery, *Radi-Aid Research* thus mirrors the history of Norwegian missionary photography, which is, Gullestad argues, "also a history about how the missions have gradually become aware of local people's reactions to the way they have been represented in Europe, and how they now want to remedy the resentment that this has created" (249).

I opened this chapter with Terje Tvedt's description of a Norwegian humanitarian-political complex because the supposed existence of this complex raises questions about how we should best understand Radi-Aid: as the reorientation of humanitarian reason or as a critique of that very reason? On one hand, Radi-Aid can be said to have the Norwegian "regime of goodness" as its context and its origin, but on the other hand, this body of work performs a critique of this regime's self-understanding and, above all, of the forms of humanitarian spectatorship on which it depends.

From a point of view like Tvedt's, Radi-Aid's charming, yet damning, satire on the "mighty Norwegian pietà" could perhaps be explained away as humanitarianism's corrective self-criticism—that is, as an update of the goodness regime's techniques and thus an optimization of the power of goodness. In Tvedt's account of the humanitarian-political regime, Norad, the Norwegian Agency for Development Cooperation, which finances SAIH and the Radi-Aid campaign, plays a central role alongside the large humanitarian organizations. These actors developed into a system, Tvedt maintains, "organized around influencing opinion or educational activities, largely on behalf of the government through the Ministry of Foreign Affairs—and intended for the Norwegian population" (Tvedt 2018, 277).[24] Tvedt's interest here is thus also the educational role of the welfare state (and an alleged absence in the population of aversion to this role); he uses terms such as *state-funded pedagogues, pedagogical contractors of the parent state*, and *social engineering*, in particular about the "aid industry," the journalistic profession, and school curricula (277–80).[25] In this way, we could understand Radi-Aid's intervention as stemming from the "tyranny of goodness" itself. Optimizing "self-images" and "world images" by ridding them of racist stereotypes would then appear to be a way for "state-funded pedagogues" to galvanize their moral superiority.

In this reading, a Norwegian regime of humanitarian benevolence holds absolute power. Its "power of goodness" is incontestable. By contrast, I am interested in the cultural means by which people *do* incessantly process and modify the humanitarian grammar of goodness, whether such modifications come from "inside" or "outside" the humanitarian "system." Instead of settling doubts about the radicality of a project like Radi-Aid, I therefore suggest we pay attention to the work such doubts do in the cultural texts under study. Perceptual dissatisfaction with sentimental-humanitarian tropes is most often related, tacitly or not, to moral and social dissatisfaction, too, and questions about complicity and critical relevance are always at the heart of the sensibility of privilege and the cultural artifacts responding to it. Therefore, rather than trying to decide on them, I aim at charting their cultural productivity. In this manner, what is relevant to my study is the ways in which cultural texts such as the Radi-Aid enterprise play out a skeptimental conflict between optimism and pessimism vis-à-vis the notion of Scandinavia's "helping role toward the world's poor" (Tvedt 2018, 273). This is the cultural work that skeptimentality does for us: As a cultural mode it responds to, and sometimes seems to solve, the problem people have with the sentimental kernel of humanitarian reason.

6.

Visual Economies

IN HER BOOK *White Innocence: Paradoxes of Colonialism and Race* (2016), the cultural studies scholar Gloria Wekker makes an important observation about racism and egalitarianism in contemporary Dutch public culture. In a society founded on a sense of self based on notions of (white) innocence and social equality, such as that of the Netherlands, she argues, the problem of describing an object, an action, or an expression as racist is twofold. The problem is not just that one points out that the originator of the statement or action believes herself to be superior to others and thus practices an unequal relationality; rather, the problem is also that by identifying something as racist, you would seem to establish an unequal relationship between yourself and the originator of what appears racist, insofar as you apparently see yourself as morally superior to them. Thus, Wekker concludes that "an accusation of racism runs deeply counter to the strand of egalitarianism that is also [in addition to innocence] such a strong ingredient of the Dutch sense of self" (Wekker 2016, 79).

This observation goes straight to the heart of the often-awkward response by skeptimental culture to racial inequality. In sentimental publics, sympathy and compassion may soften (by rendering heartbreaking) the violence of racial hierarchy. Skeptimental publics, however, have misgivings about that merely emotional sense of equality, where the privileged relate sentimentally to the underprivileged. Thus, a skeptimental public finds itself confronted time and again with the problem of how to respond to the social fact of racial inequality in a way that will appear egalitarian. To be sure, one well-rehearsed response is to simply deny the existence of racial hierarchy. The cultural mode of scandalous skeptimentality, with which we shall become more acquainted in this chapter as well as in chapter 9, is another.

In this chapter, I analyze the Dutch artist Renzo Martens's 2008 art documentary *Episode III: Enjoy Poverty*, which I consider to be an art film in the skeptimental mode. While my focus in this book is primarily contemporary Scandinavian societies, I have also wished to emphasize that the predicament of privilege is not exclusively a Scandinavian problematic. What makes the Scandinavian case special is that, here, privilege sensibility takes on a remarkably urgent character due to the historically sedimented welfare statist preoccupation with equality on the one hand and the notion of benevolent internationalism on the other. Yet in itself, the condition of privilege sensibility already testifies to the global context of its emergence, and so cultural texts of various (but not any) origin can indeed be in the skeptimental mode. Thus, Martens's (in)famous art documentary is the arch-example of how a cultural object takes up the mode of skeptimentality to reflect on the utter inadequacy, in an unequal world, of humanitarianism and its racializing visual politics. Incidentally, *Enjoy Poverty* has enjoyed a large audience in Scandinavian artistic environments and has been screened repeatedly at Nordic art and documentary venues since its release in 2008. While Martens's work thus belongs to a cosmopolitan scene of acclaimed, politically engaged visual art, it also speaks in profound ways to the highly ordinary discomfort with, and mistrust of, humanitarian spectatorship that I take to be crucial to skeptimental sensibilities.

In his book *The Embarrassment of Riches: An Interpretation of Dutch Culture in the Golden Age* (1987), the historian Simon Schama describes the central paradox of being Dutch as "the moral ambiguity of good fortune" (Schama 1988, 7). While Holland in the sixteenth and seventeenth century became a world leader in trade, art, and consumption, humanist and Calvinist orthodoxy had from the very beginning of the Dutch republic guaranteed "the continuous pricking of conscience on complacency," which according to Schama "produced the self-consciousness that we think of as embarrassed" (1988, 8). Hence, prosperity posed a moral problem to the collective personality of the Dutch, who developed an ambivalent moral sensibility in response. "The same collective personality that heard diatribes against Queen Money and Dame World from the pulpit," Schama suggests, "rejoiced in flaunting its power on their streets and in its homes. And that peculiar ambivalence was as true for the sixteenth century as for the eighteenth" (1988, 295). Thus, Schama identifies a "disparity between principles and practice" as key to being Dutch in the Golden Age and beyond.

This "embarrassment of riches," this moral pulling and pushing, is not exactly the problem I describe as the predicament of privilege. The cultural and religious pedagogy described by Schama—the Protestant imperative that riches had better embarrass—is more about not letting the human soul be corrupted, about not letting avarice and cupidity "turn free souls into fawning slaves," than about the experience of living well at the expense of others (Schama 1988, 334). In her eminent essay "Hegel and Haiti" (2000), the political philosopher Susan Buck-Morss suggests that in fact "the others" and the price they paid for Dutch affluence are conspicuously absent from Schama's historiography of the Dutch Golden Age. In this essay, Buck-Morss deals with the paradox that "slavery" in the eighteenth century's Western political philosophy had become a key metaphor for all the worst that could happen to man at roughly the same time as the "capitalist enslavement of non-Europeans as a labor force in the colonies" was intensifying (Buck-Morss 2000, 821). Buck-Morss pursues this "glaring discrepancy between thought and practice" in the European philosophers of freedom, thinkers such as Hobbes, Locke, and Rousseau, in order eventually to hone in on the extent to which Hegel's famous concept of the master-slave dialectic was in fact informed by the Haitian revolution and abolitionism—an obvious connection, albeit one not made by Hegel scholarship. Before turning to Hegel, however, Buck-Morss pays attention to the Dutch case, pointing out that, by reading Schama's *The Embarrassment of Riches*, one would "have no idea that Dutch hegemony in the slave trade . . . contributed substantially to the enormous 'overload' of wealth that he describes as becoming so socially and morally problematic" to the Dutch (Buck-Morss 2000, 823).

In a similar vein, Gloria Wekker also relates her analysis of the Dutch sense of innocence to Schama's historical framework. In the final pages of *White Innocence*, she suggests that the Dutch need new histories and moral pedagogies of "Dutchness"—ones that recognize the significance of colonialism, slavery, and race to the Dutch sense of self. "In an environment in which the seventeenth century, the Golden Century, has always been looked upon with pride in the Netherlands, and where we have been taught to see trade and prosperity as something neutral, we need," Wekker argues, "another 'embarrassment of riches'" (Wekker 2016, 173).

White innocence is Wekker's term for the way in which the Dutch in general understand themselves and their nation: as a small, but ethically correct country, color-blind and thereby without racism, and furthermore a pioneering country in regard to global justice. The principal thesis of *White Innocence* is that "an unacknowledged reservoir of knowledge and affects based on four hundred years of Dutch imperial rule" has given shape to dominant white Dutch self-representation (Wekker 2016, 2). Thus, this deep-rooted Dutch self is a racialized self, Wekker argues, to which claims of innocence form a central but paradoxical component, insofar as the white Dutch claim of innocence is typically upheld by an aggressive disavowal of the issue of race and racism being at all relevant in a Dutch context: "There is a fundamental unwillingness," Wekker points out, "to critically consider the applicability of a racialized grammar of difference to the Netherlands" (Wekker 2016, 23). Yet race *is* firmly present, in material culture, public feelings, and in language, Wekker demonstrates, referring, for instance, to the Dutch conceptual pairing that marks someone as either "native" or "foreign" regardless of how many generations back the "foreigners" migrated to the Netherlands.

White Innocence is, in a sense, a North European counterpart to Robin Bernstein's analysis of racial innocence in North American popular culture, which informed my analysis in the previous chapter of the Norwegian Radi-Aid enterprise.[1] And Wekker's account of the ways in which "an innocent, fragile, emancipated white self is constructed versus a guilty, uncivilized, barbaric other" (2016, 15) is an apt description of strong and loud forces in current Nordic nationalisms too. However, descriptions of white innocence such as Wekker's are not particularly well suited to encapsulate the sensibility in which I am interested: the collective subject regarding itself and its privileges as global problems. I suggest we think, rather, of the predicament of privilege as a mutation in the cultural complex of white innocence. At times, this privilege-sensitive mutation reinforces the attachment to white innocence. Most often, however, it carries out a different kind of cultural work, centering instead on forms of complicity.

I am exploring how visual artifacts register the guilty sense of complicity that, because it relates intimately to the privileged position of the spectator, is raced white. Conventional humanitarian visual culture is, I argue, configured around the flip side of the moral grammar of racial innocence described by Wekker: In humanitarian culture, the maintenance of whiteness and its association with benevolence and moral superiority is instead predicated upon the childlike innocence and suffering of people of color. In this manner, my interpretation of Martens's *Enjoy Poverty* as a film in the skeptimental mode views it as indexing white complicity and guilt rather than innocence.[2] I want again to emphasize immediately, however, that by *guilt* I mean an affective *structure*: an emotional interpretation of a perceived guilty relationship not necessarily entailing feelings of guilt. For as demonstrated by the archive of my study, a collective conscience preoccupied by guilty relationships, including racialized ones, may trigger a range of affective moods and attitudes.

Resources

The moral and visual pedagogy of Martens's *Enjoy Poverty* is, I believe, a late-humanitarian "embarrassment of riches" deeply concerned with the predicament of spectatorship. *Enjoy Poverty* is a fable about white hegemony and on the visual politics that underpin this hegemony; the film exhibits Western businesses' underpayment, exploitation, and resource extraction in the Democratic Republic of Congo, but it also serves as documentation of an artistic-educational project conceived and realized by the artist himself. Over a period of two years, Martens traveled in the Democratic Republic of Congo with the aim of examining poverty as a resource that ought to be claimed by the Congolese themselves. With his video recorder often turned on himself, Martens films at an art show in Kinshasa, at a press meeting arranged by the World Bank, in refugee camps, in plantations, in clinics, in villages. In all these places, he talks to high and low about working conditions, child malnutrition, poverty as a resource, and the visual practices that render exploitation in the country, respectively, visible and invisible. Martens is met with bewilderment or objections by the Western aid workers and photojournalists he meets, whereas the Congolese mostly seem to perceive his project as testifying to the situation in post–civil war Congo with a hopeful expectation that the film will generate funds and political change. The film speaks to the powerlessness experienced by the First World spectator. But it does so only by placing this sense of powerlessness in close and discomforting conjunction with the power of humanitarian visual governance to which it also attests.

Enjoy Poverty evolves around two central, and gradually converging, narratives. The first narrative considers poverty as a resource similar to other natural resources in the Democratic Republic of Congo. Poverty, the film suggests, is a resource that attracts a number of Western players, including photographers, development workers, journalists, and artists, all of whom see it as freely accessible and as a source of earnings. At a press conference in Kinshasa, where a representative of the World Bank pledges $1.8 billion to DR Congo, Martens asks if this type of grant might not mean that poverty is one of the Congo's most important raw materials. The spokesman does not wish to go along with the idea of poverty being a natural resource, although he confirms that: "It is true that development aid brings in more money to the Congo than copper or coltan or diamonds. Even if combined" (Martens 2008). The film then declares the probability that, as is the case with these other natural resources, it is not the Congolese people who benefit from the revenue derived from the nation's poverty.

The second narrative investigates the significance of photography and image making and explores the relationships between visibility and invisibility: Which Western activities in central Africa are made visible, which activities are made invisible, and why is that so? When Doctors Without Borders (MSF) withdraws from the hardest hit and most inaccessible parts of the country, is it partly because there is no one around to document the good work? Why is it apparently impossible for refugees in a UN-run camp to get a tarpaulin without a UN logo on it? Why do aid workers from FIDA, the Finnish development program, take pictures of all the people to whom they smilingly hand out aid? And why is there no visual documentation of the UN aiding, with armed protection, Western companies exporting gold and other raw materials from the Congo? From Martens's seemingly haphazard questions and awkward camera movements, we understand that it is not only the massive production of images but the effort to render invisible, too, that together serve to organize the management of aid measures in Congo.

When it is possible to earn money from poverty, it must be relevant, *Enjoy Poverty* suggests, to ask who actually owns this resource. On this point, the two narratives in the film—poverty as resource and image economies—converge. Martens spends time with a group of white European photojournalists, including an Italian photographer from Agence France Presse, who explains that he covers the Congo, that there is a market for crisis photography, and that he typically receives in the region of fifty dollars for a picture in addition to his travel and insurance expenses. Martens asks the photographer, "Who is the owner of these pictures, whose property is the picture?" The photographer replies, "I am the owner," and confirms, furthermore, that he is within his rights to make an exhibition or a book of the photographs should he so choose. "And the people that are in the pictures, the people that you have photographed—are they the owners too or not?" asks Martens. No, the photographer replies, "because I took the pictures." Martens objects that the people in the images have "organized everything" and that the photographer merely turned up and took a picture: "The situation that you made a picture of, they made the situation." There are thousands of situations here, the AFP photographer responds, and he confirms that the images are indeed his because he has picked out the situations that will make for good pictures. Thus, the film is letting us understand that not only do the images mediate "the brutal nature of North-South relations of inequality" but the economy of images in itself amounts to just such a "relation of inequality" (Demos 2013, 98).

It is in this manner that visual economies come to play a decisive role in *Enjoy Poverty*'s vigilant investigation of poverty as a raw material. Performing as white educator-missionary-entrepreneur, Martens takes it upon himself to reeducate a small group of Congolese photographers who had been taking colorful pictures at weddings and other festive occasions and then selling them at a small street stall. Crisis photography is, Martens suggests to them, the better means by which they may finally capitalize on the poverty that is rightfully theirs.

On one hand, *Enjoy Poverty* follows the generic conventions of concerned documentary art cinema, its intention being a critical exposé of a deplorable order. The film thus repeats the elements and positions described by the media scholar W. J. T. Mitchell as characterizing the traditional photo-essay: "The 'taking' of human subjects by a photographer . . . is a concrete social encounter, often between a damaged, victimized, and powerless individual and a relatively *privileged observer*, often acting as the 'eye of power', the agent of some social, political, or journalistic institution" (Mitchell 1994, 288; emphasis added). What makes *Enjoy Poverty* atypical is, on the other hand, that the reprehensible order the film so critically displays is not an order external to the production of images; it is, rather, the production of concerned documentary images itself. More precisely, the main subject of the film is the very asymmetrical relation between privileged observer and the observed described by Mitchell.[3]

Thus, my categorization of *Enjoy Poverty* as an artwork in the skeptimental key is based on the film's apprehension of itself as a global problem. It presumes that "our privileges are located on the same map as their suffering," as Sontag expresses it, but it also explores, more specifically, how our image production and image consumption themselves are located on that very same map. The film continuously reimplicates its spectator. While watching *Enjoy Poverty*, we are in fact participating in a form of resource extraction, we realize, in that the film's conditions of production largely correspond to the conditions of other forms of resource extraction: The artist Renzo Martens arrives in the Democratic Republic of Congo, mercilessly wreaks some havoc, and then goes home again—in order to market his film in Europe, to us, the Western spectators.[4] At the same time, as spectators we are an *implicit character* in the film: Martens continuously explains to the Congolese photographers which motifs the Western viewer will be most moved by, which aesthetic style the photographers should try for in order to move the viewer and sell their pictures to media outlets. To bear witness by seeing is a humanitarian imperative—and a photojournalistic one. But *Enjoy Poverty* shows us that testimony is profitable, that the testimony has financial value, and that the critical value of bearing witness ought, therefore, to be evaluated in proportion to this financial value.

For long stretches of the film, Martens impersonates a *colonial-style* explorer whose Congolese porters go barefoot over land and water balancing his heavy iron boxes on their heads. *Enjoy Poverty* thus not only displays white culpability, it also identifies with it—stylistically too. As the art historian T. J. Demos writes, this neocolonial character cannot "avoid conjuring the long history of the visual iconography of colonial exploration and plunder," because the activity that the character documents and takes part in "turns out to be rather continuous with the colonial past in using the language of modernization and development, while in reality wages decrease, poverty grows, and average life expectancy shortens" (Demos 2013, 103). In chapter 9, I discuss the privilege genre I call the artful guilt trip, an aesthetic and social genre with which *Enjoy Poverty* shares a certain affinity. In this genre, the character who "trips" on guilt is typically a revived colonial master. As artfully created character, the white colonial master is a way, I suggest, to give the convergence of disparate affective attitudes central to this privilege genre—guilt *and* agency—a historically relevant and recognizable form: The figure of the white colonial master embodies historically unresolved questions of guilt while assuming the artistic freedom to actualize such questions.

Division of Labor

Enjoy Poverty exhibits a great interest in the division of labor between those who do the seeing and those who are seen. The film's attention is primarily directed to the materialism of this division: Those who do the seeing are connected to powerful image machines, which, like those for mining gold, are built for the purpose of extraction, while those who are seen do not get a share of the profits. In *Enjoy Poverty*, this fundamental division of labor between viewer and viewed is, moreover, configured as a moral and racialized division of labor: Those who look through powerful camera lenses are white European subjects who, like the film's viewers, are framed as accomplices to the exploitation. By contrast, those who are looked at are black Congolese subjects innocent of the exploitation from which they suffer. From the very first scenes, and throughout the film, we see white photographers snapping away in the image economy that the film lays bare for us as extraction; Congolese subjects, meanwhile, are "sitting for the white man's camera," including the *Enjoy Poverty* team's cameras (Wexler 2000, 65). We thus recognize the film's framing of a heavily equipped white force of looking in the Congo as a privilege montage—and, more precisely, as an exhibition of white, Western scopic advantage over black, African disadvantage.

The film professes to have the aim of intervening in this division of labor while documenting its own disappointed attempts at doing so. Martens wanted to retrain the Congolese wedding photographers to be crisis photographers: Rather than being the objects of humanitarian images, they ought to step into the role as image producers. Given that party photography brings in approximately a dollar a month, it is financially rational, Martens argues, to replace weddings with pain, since crisis photography has, as we have seen, a completely different market value. Just like a good humanitarian entrepreneur, Martens teaches the photographers about the economy and aesthetics of humanitarian visual culture. During a lesson in a camp among displaced people, teacher Martens stresses that the photographers must get closer to the vulnerable, that pictures of children are to be preferred, and that they must seek out the best humanitarian motifs—meaning the worst cases. This image intervention will be put to the test at a local MSF hospital, where the photographers from Kanyabayonga, with Martens as their spokesman, ask permission to take photographs. Having seen the photographers' portfolios, a doctor in charge, "Mr. Fred," refuses to give the photographers access to patients in the hospital. His initial reason is that, as a doctor, he will not allow the exhibition of his patients' suffering so that the Congolese photographers can earn money. Martens objects that photojournalists from, for instance, *The New York Times* and *Le Monde*, who also earn money from the suffering in question, are allowed into the hospital. Mr. Fred retorts that you would have to differentiate between making news and making money. Moreover, he says, the images in the photographers' portfolios do not live up to the aesthetic standard for humanitarian images.

The division of visual labor with which *Enjoy Poverty* is concerned is thus also a labor of division. The division is patrolled, and the Congolese bodies are designated their proper place according to the conventional division of labor. The MSF doctor finds it absurd to regard the Congolese photographers as humanitarian photographers. Similarly, the Italian photojournalist thought it absurd that he should not be the rightful owner of his photographs. Without a press pass, the photographers from Kanyabayonga cannot access the market for images, and, as their teacher notes, there are altogether too many obstacles for the image intervention to be a success. The small group of thwarted humanitarian entrepreneurs faces the fact that while poverty may truly be a valuable raw material, trading it in the form of pictures is still the exclusive domain of Western players. The material inequality, which is the driving force behind the film, the racial-imperial-regional wealth gap and its perpetuation, is thus certified by a specific "distribution of the sensible" in the form of a specific distribution of roles, the patrolling of which the film investigates (Rancière 2011a, 12).[5] In this manner, the film indicates that the division of labor structuring humanitarian visual culture plays a role in shaping the symbolic and material maintenance of racial difference globally.[6]

The Fall

In terms of both narrative and production, the film's intervention in the division of labor crucial to humanitarian visual culture thus fails. Yet the film succeeds, I believe, in intervening in a related distribution of the sensible: the assumption that seeing is contrary to doing. The literature on "regarding the pain of others" is steeped in this assumption.[7] Thus, the hypothesis of the spectator's false sense of innocence often entails an implicit or explicit claim on their being animated, engaged, and riled into action but also a lament that this does not seem to happen—due to either the particular iconography, the overwhelming quantity of images available, or the moral-affective disposition of the spectator. In contrast to this familiar assumption, *Enjoy Poverty* examines, as we have seen, the spectator's *participation in* rather than their *distantiation from* "the action." When we watch, the film suggests, we are actually taking action, in that we are participating in an effective image economy and image ecology. As mentioned, Martens's approach in *Enjoy Poverty* is to continuously reimplicate the film's spectator. This approach does not invite the discussions about the absence of agency that characterize scholarship in this field, but, rather, it invites discussions about the many ways in which the spectator already acts in the world.

The distinction between viewing and doing is famously addressed, and deconstructed, by Jacques Rancière in "The Emancipated Spectator," an essay in which he does for the act of spectating what Jacques Derrida did for the act of writing in *Limited Inc* ([1977] 1997). "What makes it possible," Rancière asks, "to pronounce the spectator seated in her place inactive, if not the previously posited radical opposition between the active and the passive?" (2011b, 12). Why do we identify gaze with passivity, and why do we suspect the spectator to suffer from the condition that "the more he contemplates, the less he lives"? (6). Rancière suggests an alternative view: Being a spectator is, in fact, not a passive state that we must seek to transform into activity; on the contrary, it is the normal state of the human animal. Accordingly, the dream of turning spectators into a community of active "doers" is an impossible dream of reducing the irreducible distance between an individual and the forest of signs to which the individual always relates *actively* as interpreter. The emancipation of the spectator, Rancière's concern in the essay, thus presupposes that we acknowledge and recognize the kind of activity particular to the spectator, namely a form of interpretive activity. By so doing, Rancière argues, we also confirm a fundamental "equality of intelligence" between various types of activity and positionality (2011b, 10).

There is a particular scene in *Enjoy Poverty* that, to my mind, greatly contributes to the blurring of the opposition between "the image and living reality," which is Martens's approach in a nutshell (Rancière 2011b, 7). Of the many grueling scenes in the film, this hospital scene is perhaps the hardest to watch (fig. 8). The small group of photographers has entered the modest clinic in a refugee camp. Small children are fighting for their lives. Martens once again matter-of-factly explains that as photographers working in the humanitarian field they will have to aim for the worst cases. Those are the pictures you can sell, he assures them. To the film's viewers, it is in itself disturbing to see the Congolese doctors disregard their medical activities in order to let a group of photographers approach children who are in a state of intense distress and malnutrition, because the doctors seem to have faith in the work of humanitarian images: a faith, that is, in the film's spectators,

FIGURE 8. The hospital scene. Film still from *Enjoy Poverty*. Copyright © Renzo Martens, 2008.

which we may have difficulty sharing. In the hospital scene, we witness the final transformation of the photographers from objects of the humanitarian gaze to its manufacturers, exactly the transformation for which their teacher was hoping. Taking up the humanitarian means of production, they are becoming humanitarian "doers" by being humanitarian spectators. The photographers are visibly ill at ease, awkward and unsure of their assignment and their new status as "privileged" spectators of the pain of others.

Why is the response to this scene more visceral, more somatically intense, than scenes involving the heavily equipped, white, Western photographers who also take pictures of pain, suffering, and death? Because, I believe, it contests the opposition between "the image and living reality" by breaching an important convention of humanitarian production: that there is an insurmountable distance between crisis photographer and those struck by crisis (Rancière 2011b, 7). "In order to point the camera at people in this situation, an imagined curtain has to separate those behind the camera and those in front of it," Ariella Azoulay suggests in her discussion of *Enjoy Poverty* (Azoulay 2019a, 294). According to Azoulay, the physical closeness that is a precondition of the humanitarian image is "actually the manifestation of an *unbridgeable distance* expected from cosmopolitan photojournalists" (294; emphasis added). This form of "distant proximity" is, Azoulay writes, a prerequisite for Western photographers who, as "middlepersons," mediate between those who consume crisis images and those who appear in the images (294). However, the genre convention of distant proximity not only organizes the photojournalistic practice, I would suggest; it also organizes the spectator's expectation of the humanitarian image and of the world in which it circulates. As spectators, we assume that the photographer behind a given humanitarian image belongs to the same community of Western spectators as we do.[8] The convention of "distant proximity" in crisis photography is one facet of the opposition between image and living reality, which the film disturbs by breaking this very convention. In this scenario, the Congolese photographers manifest more of a "proximate proximity," thus confronting us with the expectations we harbor of the visual practice of "regarding the pain of others."

The assumption of a radical opposition between image and living reality and between the passive and the active gives rise, Rancière suggests, to a "rather intricate dramaturgy of sin and redemption" (2011b, 7). Rancière is referring here to the sense of guilt habitually accompanying "passive spectatorship" and to the redemption conversely associated with the "activating" of the spectator in "living reality." Seen in that light, the hospital scene is organized as a scene of the Fall. Before our very eyes, the innocent are given a share in the guilt we assume reserved for the act of "regarding the pain of others." Before this Fall, the Congolese photographers were representatives of "living reality," of unmediated presence, of activity, and of black African innocence. The precondition for them appearing as such was, we now understand, that "we," the Western spectators, should perceive the Congolese photographers to be nonspectators. In order to be representatives of living reality, they had to be active as viewed but passive as viewers. Their teacher wanted to turn them into agents in the humanitarian visual culture. That is not possible, however, because according to a vital assumption of this visual culture, the photographers can be active only by being passive. As the film's viewers, we expect these Congolese subjects to be innocent and active in their own living reality, and thereby not "passive spectators" to suffering like ourselves. Their transformation from passive active to active passive is an aporia, difficult to come to terms with for the MSF doctor and the Italian photojournalist alike but also, I believe, for *Enjoy Poverty*'s viewers. In this scene, the photographers appear as poor not primarily because they *are* poor but because they have become spectators and thus poor in terms of vitality and "living reality."

By regarding the pain of others, they become, we sense, like us, corrupted by viewing without doing.

The hospital scene is unbearable, therefore, not only because of the scandalous suffering on display but because we watch the Congolese photographers witnessing it. In a way, the scene is what Rancière calls a "scene of equality": one in which prior assumptions, division of roles, and spectatorship's "dramaturgy of sin and redemption" are subject to a shock. For we realize that the photographers from Kanyabayonga were *never not* spectators of their world and the pain within it. If the scene is shocking, it is because it confronts the spectator with his enduring attachment to, and investments in, black African innocence, presence, and living reality. Perhaps it is harder for the film's viewers to abandon this fundamentally sentimental attachment than it is to recognize their implication? In the assumption of African innocence, integrity, and virtue—which according to the "dramaturgy of sin and redemption" of humanitarian spectatorship I am mapping is presumably contrary to being a spectator—perhaps lies a remainder of sentimental innocence for the skeptimental spectator too? What this scene rips from our eyes in blurring the radical opposition between image and living reality is the "imagined curtains" separating those behind the camera from those in front of it, separating spectators in the Congo from spectators in Northern Europe. But if we wish to read this scene as a "scene of equality" in the Rancièrian sense, as I am doing here, we need to take into account that it is also a scene that—like the film overall—questions the value of this form of equality in a radically unequal world.

It is a skeptimental visual knowledge, I have been arguing, that the spectator of humanitarian images is himself somehow implicated in what those images show. If in no other way, the skeptimental spectator will have a sense of being implicated in what is seen by the very *act of viewing* it and thereby participating in a common cultural practice, the benign impact of which will most likely be a matter of doubt to the spectator. The double or deep vision we saw exemplified in chapter 4 in the scene from Jessen's *Telefon,* with Lisa and Frederik looking both at images of refugees and at their own belongings in the living room, suggests that when skeptimental spectators "regard the pain of others," they see their own life reflected therein. From a humanitarian image is thus created, in the mind's eye, a privilege montage.

Envisioning, skeptically, what lies behind humanitarian imagery is a common skeptimental visual attitude. I have placed special focus on skeptimental reservations about the way in which humanitarian visual culture contributes to the cultural reproduction of racial difference. One reason skeptimental spectators mistrust the visual culture of humanitarianism is, precisely, that this culture invites the spectator to play racially innocent—while presumably *not-thinking about race*, that is, to contemplate racial difference in the particular humanitarian guise of white benevolence and moral superiority constructed against the childlike innocence of people of color. In an age of privilege sensibility, playing racially innocent is, however, rarely a robust strategy. The works discussed in this part of my study respond to the misgivings about humanitarian visual culture by staying with the distrust, so to speak, giving it visual form and cultural significance, the serious satire of both Radi-Aid and *Enjoy Poverty* pillorying sentimental spectatorship and its emotional economies. If regarding the pain of others indicates a "rather intricate dramaturgy of sin and redemption," in their own particular ways Radi-Aid and *Enjoy Poverty* examine the racial grammar of this dramaturgy. The pending cultural work identified by these works is, we could say, the desegregation of globalized structures of seeing and the assumptions about knowledge, innocence, and guilt upon which they rely.

Part 3

On (Ac)Counting

7.

Debtors

FOR HER ARTWORK *My African Letters* (2011), the Danish artist Ditte Ejler-skov grappled with the so-called "Nigerian email" as a genre of exchange between North and South. According to documents included in the work, Ejlerskov had received an email from a lawyer in the Republic of Benin named Amadi Omorose Azagba, telling her that one of his clients, a man called Gabriel Ejlerskov, had tragically died in a car accident, leaving an exorbitantly large fortune. Rather than deleting the email, Ejlerskov entered into the fictitious narrative through a lengthy correspondence with Azagba about these newfound riches, about the alluring delights of Africa, about the dreams of a different life, and, finally, about the advance fee of $5,000 that would give her access to the legacy, but which she refused to pay. Feigning a guileless indignation about the demand for an advance fee, Ejlerskov asks the lawyer why he cannot pay the relatively modest sum himself, given that he will be receiving a share of the multi-million-dollar estate. Their correspondence then comes to a halt with Azagba calling Ejlerskov a dreamer, whereupon they seemingly reconcile in the avowal that "dreams can come true" (Ejlerskov 2012, 55–65). Besides the correspondence and an artist statement entitled "Emails, Paintings, Loops," Ejlerskov's art project comprises a number of colorful paintings with motifs such as tropical plants, toucans, a lion, a pool—motifs for which Ejlerskov ostensibly found impetus in her correspondence with Azagba and the "white man's expectations of Africa" (Ejlerskov 2012, 19) that it activated.

My African Letters can be said to be a devious endeavor to artfully appropriate what is in itself a devious genre of appropriation, "the Nigerian email," a variant of the advance fee scam genre. Ejlerskov introduces the accompanying book by describing the project as "a presentation of exchanged imaginings . . . between European dreamer Ditte Ejlerskov and African dreamer

Amadi Omorose Azagba" (Ejlerskov 2012, title page 2). However, from her artist statement, placed before the correspondence, we glean that Ejlerskov's artist-I actually doubts whether the work really is simply such a straightforward exchange between dreamers on separate continents. In light of the artist's sudden sense of guilt, the relation described initially as *exchange*—of correspondence, dreams, and imaginings—also materializes as *exploitation*: "After the last email is sent, in the final stages of the painting project, the great burden of colonial guilt happens in me. That is how it felt; I got caught in my own game. I had exploited Azagba for the sake of art" (Ejlerskov 2012, 20). Ejlerskov's artist statement then expresses the artist-subject's stratagem to "find an alibi and a moral solution to the fact that I have exploited my pen pal" (2012, 20).

Having an alibi means you cannot be guilty. Yet the artwork presents as fact that the artist has exploited her interlocutor, thereby incurring both moral and financial guilt, and therefore, seeking a "moral solution," she speculates as to how she can compensate him. Should she pay Azagba the disputed advance fee as some sort of wage for contributing to the art project? Should she, rather, share with him any profit she makes from exhibiting the art project? Should she invite him to make a joint project with her? Or do these deliberations actually demonstrate her narcissistic preoccupation with appearing morally superior to "the lawyer"? Ejlerskov notes, "First I exploit him and then I want to save him? I am acting like a colonial businessman from the 19th century!" (Ejlerskov 2012, 20). In her own impulse to "save" another human being—the humanitarian impulse *par excellence*—the artist-I finds not only financial-moral charity but also financial-moral exploitation—a hybrid form she associates with colonial business methods. The skeptimental sensibility, which is busy detecting something morally ugly in the morally beatifying, is here presenting itself as a sensibility preoccupied with principles of calculation.

My African Letters is a Scandinavian art project that anxiously questions its own okayness by questioning its own way of bartering and accounting. The contemplative labor documented in Ejlerskov's artist statement is relevant, then, because it exposes the way in which the predicament of privilege also manifests itself as a predicament of counting and of accounting. When do we enter into an exchange, and when is it more a case of exploitation? When is something a gift, and when is it more of an installment in the repayment of an imperial debt?

I view *My African Letters* as a run-through of the questions of doubt posed by the predicament of privilege vis-à-vis the conventions of counting and, in extension thereof, also of *recounting*. On the one hand, *My African Letters* displays the primary convention of the advance fee scam genre: Confidence tricksters from the global South try to exploit people from the global North. On the other hand, the work asks privilege-sensitively if it is indeed possible to speak of exploitation by the South of the North at all. The artwork thus intimates that the Scandinavian sensibility of privilege also entails a degree of suspicion, or at least ambivalence, about any idea of simple reciprocity in exchange and trade. In the wider cultural archive, this suspicion sometimes manifests itself as a critique of capitalism; it might also be evinced as a drive for guiltlessness. However, this market irresolution generally appears as a diffuse uncertainty about the circumstances, if any, under which global exchange relationships are okay. When, it asks, is exchange actually not exploitation?

On the face of it, humanitarian accountancy rests on principles of equality and equivalence. Every human life counts, and counts equally in the humanitarian accounts of lives saved. It is this equality that humanitarian organizations corroborate by dint of their work domestically and internationally, particularly when working in hazardous conflict zones where the lives of their own personnel are put on the line. Yet contrary to this ideal commensurability of the value of human lives, Fassin has pointed to the "hierarchies of humanity," which he sees as structuring not only military bookkeeping but also the humanitarian "politics of life" (Fassin 2007, 516). On the one hand, Fassin concedes, humanitarian politics of life *are* a rejection of the "politics of lives that do not count" intrinsic to military valuation of, respectively, lives lost and so-called "collateral damage" (2007, 513). On the other hand, the humanitarian politics of life are afflicted by an inequality of lives similar to that of military bookkeeping. Fassin gives two examples of this humanitarian politics of life based on hierarchies of humanity: firstly, the implicit difference in life value, which causes humanitarian organizations to pull out of conflict zones when Western personnel are abducted; secondly, internal distinctions made by humanitarian organizations between "nationals" and "expatriates," which are decisive not just for wages and rights but also for safety measures.[1] With the concept of a humanitarian politics of life, Fassin is thus addressing "the contradictions that exist in contemporary moral economies . . . in what characterizes the political disorder of the world: the inequality of lives" (2007, 520).

The wars in Ukraine and Gaza have once again confronted Scandinavian publics with the inequalities inherent in humanitarian principles of accountancy.[2] These manifest value differences in the global (life) accounts are some of the problems of counting and accounting indicated by the predicament of privilege, and which manifest themselves as a skeptimental wariness of humanitarian moral economies. The impression of somehow forming part of global accounts, and of being accountable, are watermarks in the sensibility of privilege. The privilege-sensitive subject is thus typically both preoccupied with counting and bound by various financial rationalities that confuse the impulse to count: *How* do we count, and *who* is of account? In *My African Letters*, the artist-I eventually comes to this conclusion: "Well, I am only guilty if Azagba in fact is less privileged than I am myself" (Ejlerskov 2012, 20). She then asks, "Is the victim always the less privileged? And how do I measure that when I know nothing about him?" (Ejlerskov 2012, 21). This bargaining with guilt and debt in the light of the various ways in which the books may be kept is a central component in scenes of Scandinavian privilege sensibility.

The predicament of privilege, then, is also a predicament of accountancy. As I explained in the introduction, I use the term *privilege genres* for the cultural forms that mediate the sensibility of privilege. In this part of the book, I shall be looking specifically at economic privilege genres such as humanitarian gifts and microloans, both of which belong to the (moral) economies of humanitarianism.[3] I am particularly interested in the commingling of diverse economic and moral rationales to which humanitarian reason subscribes in an era of privilege sensibility and debt economy, including the amalgamation of gift and debt logics.

In chapter 8, I look at the humanitarian gift as a particular privilege genre. I delve into the implications of "sentimental economy" and ask how humanitarian economies respond to issues of debt and guilt called forth by the predicament of privilege. In recent years, a good deal has been written about neoliberal debt economy and guilt subjectivity; my take on debtor subjectivity harnesses it to the sensibility of privilege on the assumption that neoliberal debt economies have not completely supplanted other forms of power or rationalities of exchange: The latter part of the chapter focuses on the striking contemporary coexistence of humanitarian subjectivity and debt subjectivity, of humanitarian economy and debt economy. The difficulty of humanitarian accounting in the Nordic publics cannot be understood in isolation from the amalgamation of humanitarian economies outside Scandinavia; the chapter therefore takes detours to countries with a heavy debt burden, such as Haiti and Greece. In chapter 9, we return to the humanitarian gift, here in a scandalized version created by the Danish artist Kristian von Hornsleth in his art and development project, *Hornsleth Village Project Uganda* (2006), which I relate to the Swedish artist Lars Cuzner and the Norwegian-Sudanese artist Mohamed Ali Fadlabi's art project, *European Attraction Limited*. Both art projects embody the idea that scandal is a relevant riposte to national self-images that appear sentimental.

8.

Sentimental Economy

WE MAY BEGIN the investigation of late-humanitarian exchange genres by looking closer at the relations between capitalism and humanitarianism, which have an extensive historiography. Historians generally seem to agree that the major eighteenth- and nineteenth-century humanitarian reforms in Europe and North America were intimately linked to the contemporaneous development of capitalism. There is, however, a range of explanations as to *how* these two phenomena and their historical emergence are connected and, by extension, what this connection means for our evaluation of the new humanitarian initiatives begun during the period concerning the treatment of animals, criminals, the poor, insane, children, and the enslaved. The Anglo-American mapping of the relationship between humanitarianism and capitalism naturally places the historical problem of abolitionism at its center. How, historians ask, could antislavery become an intellectual and popular humanitarian reform movement at a time when a new style of economic sense dictated a disciplined work ethic, mass production of raw materials for sale on distant markets, and, above all, self-interest (Bender 1992)? Why did early capitalism produce antislavery sentiments in some white populations? Was this advance in morality and sense of responsibility in fact in the pecuniary interests of the new middle classes, or was it prompted by a more technical and, thereby, in terms of interests, a more neutral relationship between capitalism and the development of abolitionism (Haskell 1992)?

The historian John Ashworth has pointed to the role of sentimentalism as an ideology mediating capitalism, abolitionism, and the wider humanitarian sensibility of which the latter formed part. On the assumption that a society "based on the pursuit of self-interest" is a society in disintegration, Ashworth argues that capitalist societies need "certain institutions, certain practices that must remain outside the area in which self-interest can operate" (Ashworth 1992, 192). In newly capitalist societies, he suggests, it was the sentimental-humanitarian concepts of human dignity that came to act as a kind of defense against commercial interests penetrating every part of the body politic: While rapid developments in wage labor eroded traditional social institutions and, consequently, social stability, social institutions such as the family, the home, and the individual conscience came to act as a bulwark against these developments. As a historical source for this contrast between a cold, economic domain and a (feminized) domain warmed by human virtue and sympathy, Ashworth turns to the work of Harriet Beecher Stowe and her depiction of how, to the sentimental sensibility with its concerned focus on family and home, slavery made a shocking spectacle. Ashworth quotes Stowe for her opinion, voiced in *A Key to Uncle Tom's Cabin* (1853), that "the worst abuse of the system of slavery is its outrage upon the family" (Ashworth 1992, 197).

According to interpretations such as Ashworth's, humanitarianism was thus from the outset intimately linked with capitalism as its perceived *contrast* on account of a sentimental ideology and ethics whose function was to highlight home, family, and conscience as barriers against self-interest: "Abolitionists deliberately juxtaposed references to humanity's higher qualities with the language of trade and commerce in order to emphasize their *utter incommensurability*" (Ashworth 1992, 193; emphasis added). Now, turning instead to research on the current relationship between humanitarianism and capitalism, one overarching endeavor stands out: to describe the full integration of the two phenomena, meaning their utter *commensurability*. It is one thing that the huge increase in numbers of humanitarian organizations since the 1980s has created a genuine humanitarian sector, in which organizations compete for resources and therefore increasingly behave as businesses, corporate communication and branding strategies included (Chouliaraki 2013, 5). The many new philanthro-capitalist formats aimed at making capital benevolent and humanitarianism pro-business are quite another thing. Just think of corporate social responsibility (csr), microfinance, brand aid, and consumer philanthropy, about which we may use the concepts in this study and describe them accordingly as economic privilege genres, inasmuch as they all address, in various ways, the experience of global privilege (Roy 2010, 2012; Schwittay 2015; DeChaine 2022; Richey and Ponte 2011).

"Sentimental economy" is, I will suggest, a useful way of conceptualizing this commensurability, both historical and current, between capitalism and humanitarianism. A sentimental economy is an economy in which commodities circulate as emblems of benevolent feelings. More specifically, the cultural studies scholar Cheryl Lousley suggests that, in a sentimental economy, commodities charged with caring serve as "the basis of a re-imagined economy" (Lousley 2013, 10). In the history of sentimental economies, the commodity form, including the technologies of capital for mass production and circulation of commodities, has been crucial to the dissemination of sentimental fantasies of a better world, Lousley argues, "because they [commodities] can circulate among dispersed participants, giving the fantasy a tangible place in social practice" (2013, 13).

One example is the "commodity market of souvenir dolls, games and theatre productions" (Lousley 2013, 13), which accompanied Stowe's abolitionist novel. In this market, the sentimental commodities, including the novel itself, seemed to lose their commodity status and move into the realm of charity objects. This sentimental vision of an economy that does not base itself on detached self-interest can also be identified, Lousley demonstrates, in the popular culture associated with emergency relief, including the Band Aid and Live Aid initiatives of the 1980s, which also hinged on social fantasies about being able to establish, via benevolence and care, an alternative economic order and to change the world. For instance, the Band Aid record appeared to purchasers and purveyors alike as "a sacrosanct object of benevolence" rather than as a commodity (Lousley 2013, 13). Yet it is exactly *because* sentimental exchange perceives itself as distinct from cool commodity exchange that the former functions as a perfect "alibi" for capitalism, as Lousley puts it, by "making use of commodity chains to travel while displacing an object's commodity status in the act of possession and donation" (Lousley 2013, 13). Hence, sentimental economies have been equally crucial to humanitarian reform movements and commodity capitalism.[1]

Against a backdrop of the suffering of others, the humanitarian gift, much like the sentimental novel, facilitates feeling, imagining, and investing in caring communities across social and financial hierarchies. By joining Lousley in describing humanitarian objects of benevolence as commodities circulating in sentimental economies, we recognize that the humanitarian gift is essentially a commodity, that there is a market for these commodities, and that the genre conventions of the humanitarian gift entail *presenting* it as a contrast to the techniques of capitalism. The following section investigates

"world gifts" as a particular form of the humanitarian gift—that is, a particular form of this privilege genre.[2]

World gifts belong to the category of "third-party gift donations," what
could be called triangular gift giving: A humanitarian benefactor in the
North buys a gift; this gift is distributed in the South by a humanitarian
organization; the benefactor gives a voucher for this gift to a third party
in the North—family, friends, or acquaintances—as proof of the humanitarian gift. In 2006, Folkekirkens Nødhjælp (DanChurchAid, DCA, the aid
agency of the national Church of Denmark) launched "Give-a-Goat" (Giv
en ged) as a new humanitarian product in Denmark; fourteen years later, in
2020, 150,000 Danes had supported the campaign.[3] On its website, Dan-
ChurchAid writes that Give-a-Goat is a success and that Danes continue
to think it fun and meaningful to give a goat. The goat is probably the most
popular world gift given by Scandinavian publics from a catalog that also
lists poultry, rabbits, emergency kits, mosquito nets, tents, polio vaccine, and
school desk and benches.

Like other humanitarian gifts, the goat is a commodity on the shelves
of a sentimental economy, meaning an economy that seems far warmer and
more charitable than the cold commodity capitalism dealing in profit and
self-interest. The goat does not look like a commodity. In financial terms, the
goat is a nonvalorized signifier, which underscores the benefactor's caring
humanitarian investment in the actual betterment of lives of impoverished
others. Yet as humanitarian gift, the goat circulates via the very market whose
rationality it to some extent disavows in favor of a more caring economy, one
dependent on affective investment rather than monetary exchange-value. As
such the goat symbolizes that a certain form of globalized care is valorized
above the financial donation itself; indeed, the goat camouflages the category
of money and commodity upon which, as humanitarian gift, it is nonetheless
dependent.

One advantage of Lousley's way of connecting various moments in
the history of sentimental economies, which is also the history of reform
movements, is the emphasis it places on the humanitarian subject's continued desire to be an agent of social change. This is, Lousley proposes, the
supreme sentimental fantasy: to replace exploitative economic reason with
a caring economy. The fact that Give-a-Goat is yet another manifestation
of this sentimental fantasy does not seem to explain, however, why the gift

structure—the economic form of this fantasy—has been reconfigured and made more complicated by the inclusion of a third Give-a-Goat party. Why is this triangulation relevant to the late-humanitarian moral economy of today? Is it because, as the geographer Peter Jackson puts it, the goat "simply allows us to parade our generosity to our family and friends in a paternalistic gesture of guilt-free giving" (Jackson 2006, 202)?[4] This explanation would presuppose that humanitarian sentiments and deeds are indeed associated with uplift, esteem, and acclaim, as would be the case in a sentimental public. But, as I argue, this is rarely the case in Scandinavian publics. Promoting humanitarian benevolence may have a significant effect for businesses that donate publicly in skeptimental family shows such as *Danmarks indsamling*, where humanitarian reason is, as we saw in chapter 3, well mixed in with family entertainment and commercial formats that neutralize its moral claim on viewers. In general, however, skeptimental publics are characterized by mistrust of humanitarian sentiments, which will therefore typically be experienced and represented as morally embarrassing feelings. Promoting humanitarian affectivity and generosity, particularly in a gift relationship, is therefore a strategy involving some risk. In skeptimental publics, it is thus more relevant, I suggest, to ask why on earth the gift-giver would risk being met with disapproval, ingratitude, and criticism of the gift-goat for being paternalistic and self-righteous.

Conversely, it would seem obvious to associate, as Jackson does, Give-a-Goat with the issue of guilt. Rather than a "paternalistic gesture of guilt-free giving," however, I suggest we view these third-party gifts as a humanitarian-formatted response to the collective experience of somehow being a debtor in the global accounts. The third-party gift is an n+1 mutation in the conventional (humanitarian) gift relationship, a mutation turning the third party in the relation into gift-recipient and gift-giver simultaneously. I thus consider the element of renouncement, which is the central feature of the third-party gift, to be more essential for an understanding of the goat's popularity than the impetus to "parade our generosity." In a way, the goat is a gift-commodity signaling a break with its own gift-commodity chain. With my third-party gift, I set the scene for a temporary break from contributing more to the "everything" structuring "our" lives: Perhaps I decide to give one of these unconventional gifts to my sister because she already "has everything" and therefore has no need of anything else and because I too "have everything" so nor do I need more, not even the return gift that a conventional gift would have landed me at some point. It is in this sense that Give-a-Goat seems to be a gift serving also as a renouncement in a fashion extending beyond the more straightforward humanitarian gift relationship.

I consider Give-a-Goat and other humanitarian third-party gifts to be skeptimental mutations in a sentimental economy because the third-party gift responds to a cultural impulse to count, calculate, and give in new ways. If humanitarian counting and giving has previously seemed simple and sooth-ing of the deep anxieties of our times about how we choose to count under conditions of inequality, today this simplicity appears challenged in Scan-dinavian publics. In Give-a-Goat, the triangulation—inclusion of a third party in the gift relationship—operates as a skeptimental mutation in the sentimental, economic gift form.[5] The third-party gift registers an openness, and perhaps an outright wish, to count, to keep accounts, and to give in other ways than those we understand to be the dominant calculation methods of, respectively, humanitarianism and the cold market.

Some years ago, in 2011, Danish UNICEF promoted their catalog of "World Gifts" with a picture of vaccines bound with gift ribbon and the heading "Let an undernourished three-year-old have your friends' Christmas gifts this year."[6] Norwegian UNICEF's online store also brings us close to the life and death of "the others": Here, typical world gifts are polio vaccines, malaria medicine, HIV tests, rehydration powders, and other life technolo-gies.[7] At the time of writing, a survival pack for an undernourished child costs 209 Norwegian kroner, or approximately $20.[8] By inviting you to let a disadvantaged child "have your friends' Christmas gifts this year," UNICEF is addressing their Scandinavian constituencies on terms stipulated by bio-politics and paternalism. They highlight the social capital and power of the benefactor while disappearing the others' agency. These are still the terms of humanitarian markets. But are these appeals not also whispering, Take something from the structurally privileged (you and your friends), and give to the poor (the undernourished three-year-old) to whom you, in fact, owe something? And is it not also *this* privilege-sensitive imperative to which the humanitarian benefactor responds when giving world gifts?

If it feels right to give a goat or a vaccine as third-party gift, rather than a conventional humanitarian donation, then it must be because it also feels right to relinquish something: to allocate in a slightly different way. Human-itarian reason is about relieving suffering, reducing poverty, and saving lives; it does not in itself prompt us to establish a connection between our prosperity, our way of life, and their poverty. The third-party gift does, however, establish exactly this kind of connection. There is something about the third-party gift, specifically its element of renouncement, that implies ethical claims distinct from the humanitarian claim to relieve suffering and save lives. While I do not wish to recuperate this gift genre as a new revolutionary form of exchange, I will suggest that it is the *redistributional feel* of the genre that makes it relevant to skeptimental publics. The goat's meaningfulness for Scandinavian publics can be found, in my opinion, in the skeptimental constellation: The third-party gift is a humanitarian commodity that can be interpreted as a more-than-humanitarian economic form. This n+1 gift phenomenon provides the sensibility of privilege with a moral-economic form for addressing a sense of debt and guilt that is not necessarily addressed by the traditional humanitarian relationship: a form that distributes in a way that extends beyond the perimeters of humanitarianism, even though it still pertains within humanitarian advocacy.

Debt Economy

In all respects, the Give-a-Goat genre we have just reviewed resembles the opposite of debt: While debt takes and takes, the goat is a gift that never stops giving in the form of kids and milk. Prima facie, humanitarianism and indebtedness are structured around two diverse economic relationships and rationales. The logic of debt is the logic of the loan, in which something that is "given" is expected to be returned, with interest, at a later date. The humanitarian logic, conversely, is the ideal structure of the gift, in which something given is not expected to be returned. Here, however, reservations come thick and fast. Firstly, the "philosophical" reservation that gifts are always part of a cycle of exchange and thereby of an economy;[9] secondly, the "political" reservation that humanitarian help is typically given as bilateral and multilateral aid to which conditions and obligations are attached, particularly since the structural adjustment programs of the 1980s.

However, behind the central structural differences between debt relationships and humanitarian relationships, we must take note of an obvious uniformity: Both types of relationship are asymmetrical.[10] The creditor lends something to the debtor because he has something the debtor does not have. Similarly, the humanitarian benefactor gives something to the beneficiary because the benefactor has something the beneficiary does not have.

Inequality is, so to speak, a condition for both these relationships. While the question of which of these relational logics—that of the humanitarian "gift" or the loan—is the most problematic in an egalitarian perspective is up for discussion, such deliberations are not central here.[11] Rather, the following sections examine ways in which to understand debt, gifts, guilt, and accounting as phenomena that structure the relationship between rich and poor, structurally privileged and underprivileged, North and South—phenomena that increasingly borrow from one another's methods of calculation.

In *The Making of the Indebted Man* (2011), the Italian philosopher Maurizio Lazzarato describes debt as the absolute central mechanism in modern-day capitalism. According to Lazzarato, the creditor-debtor relation is today the most universal and most fundamental power relation. Why? Because everyone is included in it. To live you must become a debtor. If you are too poor to borrow, you must nonetheless contribute to the repayment of public debt. Lazzarato speaks of the debt economy as a mode of enforcing a neoliberal political program. Debt is both an apparatus that produces capital and an apparatus that produces specific power relations and subjectivities. Lazzarato here reminds us, via Nietzsche's *On the Genealogy of Morals*, that "guilt" as concept and as moral-affective phenomenon is rooted in precisely the relation of debt where someone owes someone else something. The debt relationship is thus subjectivizing, writes Lazzarato in agreement with Nietzsche, because by activating memory, responsibility, and feelings of guilt it also creates a particular morality. In this manner, the neoliberal debt economy produces a specific economic subjectivity. With his or her debt, this "indebted man" has had to shoulder the risks that have otherwise primarily been the responsibility of state and capital. Indebted man is therefore also someone who sees herself as a form of capital, which must be continually optimized, reinvested, and all in all, worked upon. As aids to this brutal, yet eternal, processing of the self, the debtor has the secularized versions of original sin dispositions: guilt, shame, bad conscience, sense of responsibility, and a certain gloomy relation to the future.

Lazzarato makes the important point that, under neoliberal capitalism, indebted man has become such a generalized form of subjectivity that this form permeates all the positions in a social ensemble: "All the designations of the social divisions of labor in neoliberal societies ('consumer,' 'beneficiary,' 'worker,' 'entrepreneur,' 'unemployed,' 'tourist,' etc.) are now invested by the subjective figure of the 'indebted man,' which transforms them into indebted consumers, indebted welfare users, and, finally, as in the case with Greece, indebted citizens" (Lazzarato 2012, 38). Lazzarato's discussion of the relationship between creditor and debtor places sympathy unreservedly with the debtor. Creditors, for him, are the more conglomerate, anonymized specimens: the International Monetary Fund (IMF), for example, or the World Bank, private investment companies, banks, "the neoliberal political program," and, in the case of Greece, former German Chancellor Angela Merkel and the Eurozone. Lazzarato does not refer to the plausible situation of being creditor and debtor at one and the same time. Why not? In Lazzarato's analysis, the inequality and dominance characterizing the relationship between creditor and debtor is today the primary inequality, and therefore, I imagine, he is not interested in the other inequalities and power relations that are still organizing the social ensemble. "No distinction exists," according to Lazzarato, between working people and unemployed people, consumers and producers, pensioners and recipients of welfare benefits: "Everyone is a 'debtor'" (2012, 7).

Lazzarato's is a sweeping theoretical trajectory possessed of great conceptual clarity, notwithstanding its risks of rendering invisible those power formations not eliminated by debt economy, including humanitarianism. We are the 99%, we are the indebted, went the mobilizing debt-activist rallying cry in 2011. But what is the implication in economic and subjective terms when the 99%, the debtors, are also creditors and donors, in some cases mediated by the very same institutional structures to which they are accountable as debtors—the state, for instance? Nor were or are all the citizens of Greece exclusively debtors in the austerity plans imposed on them; they are also gift-givers, perhaps even creditors.[12] Many Greek citizens are actively engaged in humanitarian organizations, donating and sharing necessities such as medicine, clothes, and food not only with one another but also with the refugees who have arrived in the country in recent years. Presumably, at least some Greek citizens do the same as other European and North American citizens: lend small amounts of money in microloans to millions of impoverished people elsewhere in the world as a way to assist development. In other words: Subject positions such as creditor, gift-giver, and debtor are often overlaid in more complex ways than Lazzarato's account of the neoliberal debt economy is able to explicate. Indebted man may well be debtor and creditor simultaneously. Of what significance is this observation for the particular subjectivity that Lazzarato describes? How are guilt, shame, and responsibility distributed and navigated when debt economy is not an exclusive technique of power and subjectivization but operates in conjunction with, for example, humanitarian gift-giving?

The Greeks learned that your creditor can also be your humanitarian benefactor when, in 2015, having voted no to the Eurozone's proposal for an economic bailout involving more austerity measures, they suddenly became the object of the EU leaders' humanitarian feelings. The then-president of the European Parliament, Martin Schulz, was now talking about a humanitarian aid program for the compromised Greek population. From one day to the next, the Eurogroup chose to interpret "debt crisis" as a "humanitarian crisis." One omnipresent moral imperative, *You must repay your debt*, was seemingly superposed by a different, yet equally omnipresent moral imperative, *We must alleviate the suffering of the vulnerable*. The language of debt was replaced by the language of humanitarianism, and the debt economy was overlaid with what I shall call humanitarian economy, two diverse ways of accounting and being held accountable.[13] In this humanitarian reinterpretation of the economic crisis, what happened with the guilt? Was the Greek moral debt doubled? Or was the Greek guilt, if not the debt, simply disappeared? Conversely, did the humanitarian language used by the Eurogroup acknowledge a form of guiltiness or responsibility for the situation?

Two Subjectivities

Let us return to Lazzarato's account of the debt economy. In *Governing by Debt* (2015), Lazzarato described American students as a social group paradigmatically subject to the neoliberal political program and to the debt economy that Lazzarato sees as its preferred strategy. In this view, the students' considerable indebtedness is an example of the neoliberal strategy employed since the 1970s, when the right to acquire an education was replaced by the right to contract debt. With the increased individualization of debt in the form of student loan debt—and thereby individualization of the risks associated with borrowing—resources previously spent by the state on education have been released to the wealthiest households via, for example, lower taxes (Lazzarato 2015, 68). According to Lazzarato, indebtedness, as we have seen, is a tool used to exercise control, and in the American students, too, credit and loans engender a particular sense of shamed and guilty subjectivity: "Debtors interiorize power relations instead of externalizing and combatting them. They feel ashamed and guilty. The only time that American students began to free themselves from the guilt and responsibility that afflicts them was perhaps, fleetingly, during the Occupy Wall Street movement: three months of revolt and thirty years of payback" (Lazzarato 2015, 70). By acquiring debt, the students pledge their behavior and their future. They learn, in Lazzarato's view, to behave like the good *homo economicus*; they become, in other words, accustomed to perceiving themselves as human capital, as individual businesses.

In *Poverty Capital: Microfinance and the Making of Development* (2010), the development scholar Ananya Roy describes the American students in different terms. In short, *Poverty Capital* is about what Roy refers to as the democratization of capital and development, respectively. In this context, democratized capital means that financial products also become accessible to the poor of the world, a process involving a steady flow of philanthropy, investment, and return payment between the global North and the global South. With the title *poverty capital*, Roy is pointing out that this democratization of capital involves both the capitalization *of* the poor and, to a great extent, capitalizing *on* the poor. Democratization of development in this context means that, today, ownership of development practices and humanitarian tools extends well beyond, for instance, the World Bank, individual nation-states, or NGOs. Development and humanitarian aid are now part of everyday life in the West and for the people living in it: When we participate in the returned bottle deposit donation scheme, sending the money to a remote but good cause, when we volunteer for ActionAid Sweden, and when we lend a small sum of money to a female microentrepreneur in Guatemala, we are enacting this democratization of development and humanitarian aid. This is where the American students enter the picture: They are "world citizens" of a sort, defined by their awareness of poverty in the global South and awareness of their own capacities for making a difference. They are "a generation of world citizens eager to tackle the urgent problem of persistent poverty, brimming with enthusiasm as they spend their summers in Guatemala to Ghana" (Roy 2010, 4). Poverty and suffering are insistent topics in the public domain, in relation to which the American students manifest a form of global conscience. This global conscience is not abstract, argues Roy. On the contrary, it permeates everyday life; as an example, Roy mentions a young student "who works tirelessly to raise money for anti-malaria bed nets for African families, dollars converted into lives saved, an equation made possible through selfless volunteerism" (2010, 12).

So, we are here presented with two contrasting descriptions of American students as a specific social group. Firstly, the student as indebted subject, full of guilt, bad conscience, and a canceled future (Lazzarato). Secondly, the student as humanitarian subject, full of drive, global conscience, and enthusiasm about the future (Roy). How are these two pictures, these two subject models, related? Assuming that both are valid, how can we interpret their coexistence? Can the debt economy described by Lazzarato as the capitalism of our time animate debtors and humanitarian subjects alike?

On the one hand: yes. Given that Roy's book addresses debt, it would seem obvious to link her account of the democratization of capital and development with Lazzarato's account of the neoliberal debt economy. The financial instrument exemplary of poverty capital's mode of operation is, seen through Roy's lens, microcredit—that is, the popular loan model linking private individuals, small businesses, and investment companies in the North with primarily female microentrepreneurs in the global South. As a nonprofit development tool, microcredit was originally conceived and put into practice in the South by the Bangladeshi economist Muhammad Yunus. However, Roy observes that microloans have now become a domain operated primarily by commercial banks, investment firms, and money markets in the global North, for which *the bottom billion* is a colossal, but still dormant, market that microcredit has the ability to rouse. Capital to impoverished people, but also capitalization on the poverty of the impoverished and their ostensibly creative and entrepreneurial striving toward a better life.

Thus, one may argue that the success of microcredit proves Lazzarato's thesis that debt is today universal. The global South is the Wild West of the debt economy: more market, more work, more consumption, more debt, and increased numbers of manageable debtors. When indebted American students use a lending platform such as Kiva to give small loans to garbage sellers in Pakistan, it could be argued that they are simply doing what they know best: participating in the debt industry by which they themselves are ensnared. They multiply the debt, behaving in exactly the way the debt economy and the neoliberal project have invited them to. With microloans, the power asymmetry, which in Lazzarato's opinion is defining for the relationship between creditor and debtor, is institutionalized as a geopolitical power asymmetry. Microcredit is simultaneously an example of a humanitarianized debt market on which the debt economy appropriates humanitarian morality and affectivity, while humanitarianism adopts the debt economy's mode of subjectivization and structure of incentive.

On the other hand: no. The cooperation of debt economy and humanitarian sensibility does not immediately entail that the former explains or generates the latter. The commitment to saving vulnerable lives, antipathy to poverty and suffering, great expectations of humanitarian technologies, and the repertoire of moral sentiments that animate Ananya Roy's American students and manifest a sentimental fantasy of an alternative, good capitalism—these moral stances and affective orientations would not seem to grow from the neoliberal debt economy described by Lazzarato. The imperatives, actions, and affects are of a different kind but perhaps no less key to the moral and political order than is the debt economy. It can indeed be argued that the current humanitarianism and neoliberal debt economy share the postpolitics of the 1970s as context for their genealogies. This results, however, in a narrowed analysis, as it does not take into account the longer parallel genealogies of capitalism and humanitarianism and thus does not contribute to an understanding of the sedimentation of humanitarianism as commonsensical moral compass: The imbrication of humanitarianism and social reform movements, and with sentimental popular cultures and their hopes for global reciprocity, has modulated the moral landscape of humanitarianism in a way distinct from that of the debt economy. If the debt economy does not explain or cause humanitarian sensibility, however, how, then, can we describe the relationship between what Lazzarato calls "debt government" (Lazzarato 2015) and what Fassin calls "humanitarian government" (Fassin 2012)?

Debt and Gifts in Haiti

A month or so after the 2010 earthquake in Haiti, an article by Naomi Klein was published in *The Nation* under the title "Haiti: A Creditor, Not a Debtor" and the subtitle "It is we in the West who owe it reparations." Klein's point is primarily that, in the light of the earthquake, institutions such as the IMF, the World Bank, and the Inter-American Development Bank (IDB) ought to cancel the enormous debts that have shackled Haiti since it gained its independence. They indeed ought to, but Klein's point is that the very idea of Haiti as a debtor nation should be flatly rejected. How could Haiti be a debtor nation, asks Klein, when so many people in the West have profited so much from two hundred years of interest on illegitimate debts, including a debt to France for having "stolen" slave owners' land and (human) property? Klein suggests it is more a case of the West owing reparations to Haiti. Haiti is but one of many examples of the way in which relations between the global North and the global South are shaped by debt. Klein reminds us why we should continue to ask who is actually the debtor and who the creditor in these global debt relations. We are the debtors, says Klein, thereby intervening in the debt economy by questioning its method of calculation.

My interest here concerns the link between this debt relation and the humanitarian relation serving to structure the relationship between North and South, between rich and poor countries. After the earthquake, Haiti was the object of an astounding humanitarian mobilization. Many governments and humanitarian organizations contributed with food, medical supplies, personnel, and troops; France and the United States in particular seemed to be vying to outdo each other in terms of humanitarian aid given to a country they have each, in their own way, oppressed and exploited for centuries, not least through indebtedness. Colloquially, humanitarian donations are commonly and skeptically referred to as "indulgences," a means of begging for the remission of guilt and sin. Is that what was at work in 2010? According to Didier Fassin, the humanitarian commitment was certainly profitable for France and the United States: "For a fleeting moment we had the illusion that we shared a common human condition. We could forget that only 6% of Haitian asylum seekers are granted the status of refugee in France . . . or that thirty thousand Haitians were on the deportation lists of the U.S. Immigration and Customs Enforcement Agency" (Fassin 2012, xi). If the humanitarian aid provided was a form of atonement, then it was, according to Fassin, a superficial one. And while sending humanitarian aid, the powerful member countries France and the United States endorsed the IMF's provision of *emergency loans* to Haiti rather than *grants* that would not entail repayment. In this crisis situation, two economic and moral primary forms, those of debt and gift, again overlapped—not unlike the situation in Greece.

Above, I described how, via microloans to small entrepreneurs in impoverished countries, the debt economy takes on the moral and affective language of humanitarianism, while, conversely, humanitarianism adopts the mode of subjectivization and incentive structures of the debt economy. In the case of Haiti and other heavily indebted nations, indebtedness and debt reduction alike are handled in a moral vocabulary similar to that of humanitarianism.

Just after the 2010 earthquake, Haiti received an IMF emergency loan of $100 million. Debt activists from, for instance, Jubilee Debt Campaign (now Debt Justice) criticized the IMF for offering loans rather than funds with no repayment requirement—that is, loans rather than "gifts." The then–managing director of the IMF, Dominique Strauss-Kahn, defended the action by saying it was simply quicker to organize a loan for Haiti: "And so, the question was: were we going to do nothing—or give a loan?" Strauss-Kahn explained. "We decided to give a loan—but a zero-interest loan, with a long grace period."[14] The IMF then called on donor countries to cancel this and older debts in future. Here we should note that both incurring debt and debt cancellation can be rendered humanitarian phenomena: for example, Strauss-Kahn describing a loan from the IMF as a humanitarian loan, an emergency loan. At the same time, the pressure that debt activism today exerts on international creditors to cancel debt generally also implies a humanitarianization of the language of debt, since debt cancellation is typically framed as a kind of humanitarian gift.[15] Debt cancellation may therefore share some of the atonement functions identified by Fassin in humanitarian assistance.

The purpose of these examples from outside the Nordic region is to emphasize the ways in which debt government and humanitarian government operate by means of one another. On the face of it, debt and gift seem to involve dissimilar economic imaginaries, dissimilar ways of managing accounts, dissimilar concepts of the "good," and dissimilar affective dispositions. While humanitarian economies and their logic of giving seem very different from the methods of calculation in debt economies, today we nonetheless see a particular political division of labor between them, and their ways of counting and managing accounts might come to validate and supplement one another. Again, my point is that the apparently incompatible economic and subjective positions of debtor, creditor, and gift-giver are, in practice, often morally and politically combined and entangled in ways that are worth bearing in mind as we return in chapter 9 to the suspicion of sentimental economies in Scandinavian publics.

Earlier in this chapter, I presented descriptions of American students as reported by Maurizio Lazzarato and Ananya Roy, respectively. Lazzarato described the student as a debt subject, full of guilt, bad conscience, and a canceled future. By contrast, Roy described the student as a humanitarian subject, full of drive, global conscience, and enthusiasm on behalf of the future. One motivating factor for writing this chapter was an impression that neither of these descriptions fit the students I meet in my capacity as lecturer at a Danish university. While Danish students also seem weighed down with a sense of guilt and complicity, their experience of being in debt is primarily based not on financial indebtedness—which in Denmark, as in the rest of Scandinavia, is mainly mediated by the welfare state—but on their experience of being unduly privileged by an unjust world order. They are, so to speak, indebted subjects, but their sense of guilt is of a different nature from that described by Lazzarato. At the same time, Scandinavian students' commitment to humanitarian reason is rarely quite as optimistic as in Roy's version. They do not see charity as a convincing response to their collective, indistinct impression of owing on the global balance sheet, and their incentive to humanitarian measures is not particularly strong. This is indicative of the critical sensibility these students share and, I am arguing, of the reorientation underway in humanitarian sensibility. This reorientation may, as we have seen, be described as a skeptimentalization of humanitarian sensibilities.

9.

The Art of Guilt-Tripping

IF, IN THE financial world, morally virtuous products such as microloans are also deployed in an attempt to reestablish the credibility and relevance of late capitalism and its debt economy, then the arts and culture of skeptimental publics frequently show signs of the opposite logic, insofar as artistic and cultural works may gain credibility and relevance in such publics by drawing on that which may be considered immoral. For instance, the immoral can be a way of injecting relevance into art projects that engage with relations to the global South, a way of signaling distance from an ethically good and perhaps even "humanitarian" art upon which the skeptimental public looks with distrust. In these kinds of skeptimental artworks, the artist sometimes invokes or reenacts colonial histories or positions, which then form a background against which to reflect on the guilt, the debts, and the accountability of art and on the ways in which art also capitalizes on inequality. In chapter 6, we saw Renzo Martens's colonial-satirical work on image economies, and in chapter 7, we listened in on the artist-subject of *My African Letters* consulting her own "colonial guilt" about exploitation of the others "for the sake of art." In this chapter, we shall take a closer look at the scandalous strand of skeptimentality as a key mode of Nordic contemporary works of art for engaging their skeptimental publics.

One of the most talked about art events in Norway in the 2010s was the restaging of "Kongolandsbyen" (the Congo village), presented in the Frogner Park in central Oslo in May 2014 for the celebration of the two hundredth anniversary of Norway's constitution. In 2011, the Swedish artist Lars Cuzner and the Norwegian-Sudanese artist Mohamed Ali Fadlabi received funding from KORO, Norway's national body for art in public space, to create an artistic reenactment of a hugely popular 1914 live human exhibition of sixty to eighty African women, men, and children, which was at the time included in the official program for the celebrations marking the centenary of the constitution.[1] The artists' stated aim was to disturb the "image of Norwegian goodness," and the "aren't we grand for being more equal than everyone else" attitude, which they saw as characteristic of the Scandinavian welfare states more generally: a distinct "Scandinavian style superiority" (Overgaard 2014; Cuzner, n.d.). To *The Washington Post*, Cuzner and Fadlabi thus explained that "it is entirely essential to understand that the currently accepted narrative of a morally superior Scandinavia is directly tied to the scientific ethnic superiority of the recent past; they both describe a people winning the race of evolutionary development" (Taylor 2014).

In the years between 2011, when the debate about the planned restoration of the so-called Congo Village gathered pace, and 2014, when Cuzner and Fadlabi's exhibition finally opened, the exhibition concept seemed to change several times. Thus, the public conversation about the project evolved around a series of never fully answered questions: What did the artists hope to achieve? Would they actually exhibit people from Africa in the Frogner Park? Would the audience also be refashioned according to the 1914 historical context? And were, in fact, the public discussions *about* the exhibition plans intended to be the actual work of art? The artists' responses remained open-ended right up until the opening of the exhibition. This consisted of a tall red entrance portal to the Kongolandsbyen as well as fourteen uninhabited thatch-roofed huts, which together appeared as an open, historical backdrop with which today's Oslo citizens were invited to engage. No human beings were exhibited.

The 2014 replica was titled *European Attraction Limited* after the company responsible for the Congo Village at the 1914 Jubilee Exhibition. These kinds of live human exhibitions were not unusual at the time. In fact, live ethnographic displays were "an exhibition practice typical all over the Western world in the nineteenth and early twentieth centuries" (Baglo and Stien 2018, 166).[2] Scholars such as Cathrine Baglo, Hanne Hammer Stien, Anne Folke Henningsen, and Rikke Andreassen have examined the Nordic versions of this historical exhibition practice, emphasizing in particular the racial hierarchies that the exhibitions helped both to establish and, sometimes, to challenge in Scandinavia, as well as the experiences, motivations, and stories of the people who actually participated in the exhibitions. "The exhibitions were not just disciplinary demonstrations of power," Baglo and Stien argue; "they were also places for cultural encounters, identity formation, and for experience" (2018,

172).[3] Present-day criticism of this historical exhibition practice, concentrating on colonial power relations, dehumanization, and the making of a civilized whiteness, has, according to Baglo and Stien, sometimes obscured the motives of the people participating in the live exhibitions, who have been viewed as passive objects of the white European gaze. It is for this reason that Baglo and Stien conclude that Cuzner and Fadlabi's *European Attraction Limited* "contributed to flattening historical complexity and consequently perpetuated the perception of the original inhabitants of the Congo Village as well as contemporary Africans as passive subjects without agency" (2018, 181).[4]

Yet the public criticism of the 2014 Congo Village took on other aspects of the project too. Antiracist organizations and commentators protested against the prospect of African people being put on display for white entertainment and self-exploration. Sam Chimaobi Ahamba, head of African Youth Norway, found in the project a "reproduction of the stigmatization we saw in 1914" (Nordenborg and Trulsen 2011). Furthermore, critics asked whether a reenactment of the 1914 Congo Village was in fact a suitable way of addressing continued structural racism in the Nordics. Why didn't the artists focus instead on current institutions such as "refugee camps, asylum centers—or barren settlements of foreign workers, insofar as economic immigrants . . . are our time's version of the participants in the ethnographic caravans"? (Petersen 2013). To *This Is Africa*, Muauke B. Munfocol, a Norwegian of Congolese descent, expanded on this sense of misplaced attention: "One might wonder why at such a time, rather than putting its efforts to acknowledge the existence of racism, paying reparations, and changing the historical-political and cultural relationship to other non-white countries, the Norwegian government chooses to finance a project that reaffirms their part in a global white domination system where black people are dehumanised spiritually, economically, socially and culturally" (Mwesigire 2014).

The question of state funding proved counterintuitive to commentators, considering also the professed aim of the project. If the object of criticism was a Norwegian "goodness regime," the art critic Stian Gabrielsen wonders, "is it not a problem to have the Norwegian state fund the project, and to have the project be part of the celebrations of the anniversary of the Norwegian constitution?" (Gabrielsen 2014). Surely, Gabrielsen suggests, the exhibition could be read as playing into, rather than opposing, an image of extraordinary Norwegian goodness: "Rather than chastising a nation that has repressed its own past, Fadlabi and Cuzner act as henchmen for staging

Norway as a nation that addresses and marks a break with its racist past, a nation which, in all its humility, is critical of any portrayal of itself as thoroughly and entirely good." Here Gabrielsen voices a familiar caution against too easily identifying an "againstness" in cultural productions hoping to constitute a criticism of a "system," in this case an alleged Norwegian goodness regime. In part 4 of this study, I take a closer look at theoretical and literary considerations of the possibility of "being against" a system from which the critical subject benefits. For now, I want to emphasize, as I did in my discussion of Radi-Aid in chapter 5, that the widespread notion of a Norwegian goodness regime invites politically diverse criticism of the "regime" in question while simultaneously *capturing* some, but not all, forms of criticism and in effect framing them as complicit with the regime. In the Norwegian context, "goodness" has indeed become a sticky and hypersuspect signifier.

In Cuzner and Fadlabi's Congo Village, we find an example of the scandalous strand of skeptimentality. We shall see another example in a moment, with Kristian von Hornsleth's *Hornsleth Village Project Uganda*. In ways similar to Hornsleth's art project, *European Attraction Limited* embodies the idea that scandal is a relevant riposte to what appears sentimental—in this case the "image of Norwegian goodness." This scandalous thread in the cultural politics of skeptimentality seems to draw sustenance in particular from racialized encounters between an allegedly white "we" and its others, whether these others appear in or out of the North European societies. It is as if the Scandinavian sensibility of privilege discovers, over and over again, the scandal of racial inequality and violence and then responds to it by turning out scandalous works of art for the skeptimental public to chew, if not choke, on. Frequently, such cultural productions verge on the privilege genre I call the artful guilt trip. To this privilege genre, racial scandal, not sympathy, is a preferred mode of engagement. In this vein, examining Afro-Nordic art histories, the art historian Nina Cramer has pointed out that when "Blackness in the artistic field enters the attention of mainstream media, it is often invoked in sensationalized ways as scandal" (Cramer 2025). Here Cramer mentions Cuzner and Fadlabi's *European Attraction Limited* along with examples of Nordic "blackface aesthetics" and "hyperracial performance." She goes on to argue that "this association with scandal overshadows sustained research and nuanced narratives of Blackness in the Nordic region" (Cramer 2025).

Before turning to the *Hornsleth Village Project Uganda*, let me address another correspondence between *European Attraction Limited* and Hornsleth's work. The question of art's freedom and autonomy under conditions of unjust privilege is raised by both of these projects as well as by other cultural texts in my archive. In the introduction, we listened in on the Norwegian poet Cathrine Grøndahl's "Prisen for et dikt" (The price of a poem), in which the poem inquires into its own costs and the debts it owes to others; this problematic of art checking its privilege, as it were, structures several of the artworks under study in this book. Certainly, issues of artistic freedom, including the right to represent under conditions of unjust privilege, are hardly a North European issue alone. In North America, a series of principled discussions about the artistic freedom to represent (and capitalize on) violence against black lives thus erupted once again with the inclusion in the 2017 Whitney Biennial of Dana Schutz's painting *Open Casket* (2016), an abstracted oil painting based on the open-coffin photographs of the body of Emmett Till, the black child who was abducted and lynched in Mississippi in 1955. The artist Hannah Black pinpoints the matter at hand in her open letter to the curators of the biennial, arguing that Schutz's painting had to go. Maintaining that "it is not acceptable for a white person to transmute Black suffering into profit and fun, though the practice has been normalized for a long time," Black challenges the notion of artistic freedom as universal right. "Although Schutz's intention may be to present white shame," Black contends, "this shame is not correctly represented as a painting of a dead Black boy by a white artist— those non-Black artists who sincerely wish to highlight the shameful nature of white violence should first of all stop treating Black pain as raw material. The subject matter is not Schutz's; white free speech and white creative freedom have been founded on the constraint of others, and are not natural rights. The painting must go" (Black 2017).

For Baglo and Stien, *European Attraction Limited* raises a variant of this concern about white creativity advancing at the expense of others. "What was the cost," they ask, "for this white, Norwegian 'we' to have the opportunity to see itself in a new critical light?" (Baglo and Stien 2018, 181).[5] These are, then, some of the questions continuously raised by art and culture in the scandalous-skeptimental mode: What is the critical value, if any, of an artistic project activating racial hierarchies in order to educate a white public about the history and predicament of its privileges? How can one evaluate the aesthetic or pedagogic significance of Nordic art against its debts, of which the art in question speaks so loudly, to other communities? According to which logics of accountancy could we calculate such value? This pointing, hesitantly or forcefully, to art as an art of privilege, an art of performing privilege and hierarchy, sometimes shamefully so, is by now an integral part of the predicament of privilege and its aesthetic of complicity.

Brand Aid Art

The Danish artist Kristian von Hornsleth's *Hornsleth Village Project Uganda* (2006) was, according to the artist himself, both an art project and a commercial transaction, more specifically a "business deal" made between the artist and Buteyongera, a small village in Uganda. In 2006, the same year as DanChurchAid sold its first goats, Kristian von Hornsleth made a deal with the Ugandan village leaders that one hundred villagers would all take *Hornsleth* as their first given name. The basic idea of the art project was a transaction: the assumption of an artist's name for a farmyard animal. As certification of the name change, the villagers were issued new, official ID cards, and each person was then photographed holding their new ID card, bringing about a series of one hundred portraits, which the artist defined as "an original artwork." The villagers' return on the deal was a domestic animal, such as a pig, and the idea was, according to the artist, that "5,000 people will in five years have received an animal from this project if it runs as planned."[6] The subtitle of the artwork is "We want to help you, but we want to own you," while other recurring slogans of the project are "Stop donations, start free trade!" and "Don't worry, this is art." The project thus presented itself, with varying emphases in varying contexts, as a combination of development aid, trade, and art—or perhaps it was more a case of rendering visible the coincident economic logics in these domains.

Branding was a fundamental principle in *Hornsleth Village Project Uganda*. Buteyongera was branded as the Hornsleth Village; the new names the residents were given belonged to the same artist brand. In a sense, the villagers were thus branded as art objects, which in mediated, photographic form could be exhibited as such and sold on the market as art commodities. Yet branding was not only pivotal in the Uganda project; it is a central element of most of Kristian von Hornsleth's work. For many years now, Hornsleth has been writing the logo HORN$LETH across brightly colored collages, paintings, and other objects, which often include "transgressive" images or text fragments assembled in ways designed to provoke the privilege-sensitive and egalitarian imagination by confronting it with its own purported hypocrisy.

COVID-19 face masks, skateboards, vodka, dildos, and caps printed with the HORN$LETH logo are all available for purchase. Recurring slogans on the branded art commodities include "Fuck the poor," "Fuck you art lovers," and "Fuck Socialism." The primary ambition of the HORN$LETH brand would thus seem to be the identification and display of hypocrisy in present-day "politically correct" agendas in and outside the art world, in a boundary-pushing way.

Seen in this light, I would suggest we view *Hornsleth Village Project Uganda* as a form of "brand aid art." *Brand aid* is the helpful term coined in *Brand Aid: Shopping Well to Save the World* (2011) by Lisa Ann Richey and Stefano Ponte for "branded" development interventions that provide aid for both development and commodity brands: "Brand Aid is the combined meaning of 'aid to brands' and 'brands that provide aid.' It is 'aid to brands' because it helps sell branded products and improve a brand's ethical profile and value. It is 'brands that provide aid' because, like other cause-related marketing initiatives, a portion of the profit or sales is devoted to helping others. As a response to the crisis of legitimacy in international aid to Africa, Brand Aid also helps to rebrand aid itself and aid to Africa in particular" (Richey and Ponte 2011, 10). *Hornsleth Village Project Uganda* can usefully be described as brand aid art given that the project is an art brand bringing about development aid in the form of pigs and goats while also being "art-brand aid" by contributing to the production and sale of HORN$LETH-branded art commodities, among these the portraits and other objects related to the Uganda project. It is brand aid *art*, also, because it critically exposes a phenomenon, that of brand aid, which it simultaneously exemplifies: that is, it is an artwork that makes use of its status *as* artwork to display and radicalize relations between branding and development aid as they take shape in brand aid's particular form of win-winism. Furthermore, it could be argued that *Hornsleth Village Project Uganda*, as response to a perceived crisis of legitimacy in socially engaged art, was an attempt to rebrand art itself, and intervention art in particular, by promoting a more skeptimentally scandalous profile of this art. Accordingly, *Hornsleth Village Project Uganda* is one of several instances of contemporary art playing a part in the brand aid phenomenon and, more generally, in the "age of poverty"—which is Ananya Roy's name for the new millennium's preoccupation with poverty (Roy 2012).

In the previous chapter, I described the Give-a-Goat initiative as a skeptimental mutation in the humanitarian gift relation and, consequently, in the sentimental economy in which humanitarian gifts circulate. *Hornsleth Village Project Uganda* was a rather maximalist mutation in sentimental economic reason and its wish to replace an exploitative economy with a caring one—so much so that it would perhaps be more precise to speak of scandalous negation rather than skeptimental mutation. The project aimed at rendering visible the circumstance that sentimental economies are merely an alibi for exploitation by other means. In Hornsleth's work, this negation of the aspirations of sentimental economies is evinced as a scandalous performance of the "cold economy" and its transactions, which the artwork finds to be concealed behind humanitarian gestures and costumes: In *Hornsleth Village Project Uganda*, the exploitation economy between North and South is displayed *and* sustained; the conventional racial hierarchies are displayed and sustained; white economic supremacy is displayed and sustained. If the third-party gift registered a certain interest in counting, accounting, and giving by methods different from those we understand to be employed by, respectively, the market and humanitarianism, the *Hornsleth Village Project Uganda*, as brand aid art, instead reenacts and intensifies the method of calculation it seeks to criticize: *doing art* is *doing good* is *doing well*. Hence, *Hornsleth Village Project Uganda* is not a work purporting to be transformative. As is generally the case in skeptimental scenarios, both the pleasure of feeling morally elevated by participating in humanitarian economies and the pleasure of feeling sentimentally transformed by a work of art are obstructed.

Artful Guilt Trips

Hornsleth Village Project Uganda thus exemplifies both the art genre I call (following Richey and Ponte) brand aid art and the more socially familiar privilege genre I call the artful guilt trip. According to skeptimental structures of feeling, moral sentiments are fundamentally ambivalent, I have argued, inasmuch as here a morally "good" feeling of caring typically incites a "negative" metaresponse, because the moral feeling also smacks of something immoral. At any time, therefore, moral sentiments might change indicator and become indicative of a certain immorality in the feeling subject. Often, this perceived immorality is linked to experiences of either guilt or shame, or a combination of the two; a sense of guilt and complicity is what "negatively" disturbs sentimental personhood and politics. In what I call artful guilt trips, however, the sense of guilt plays a role slightly different from that played in the other examples of skeptimental privilege genres we have seen in this book's archive. The conventions of the artful guilt trip signal both a recognition of guilt and a skeptimental distrust of guilt as moral feeling due to its presumedly purifying effect. Hence, in this particular privilege genre, it is often the guilt itself that is cast as a self-charitable moral feeling, the immoral shadow-side of which the genre then addresses.

In this genre of the artful guilt trip, what, then, is the skeptimental "negative" metaresponse to the impression of guilt, perceived now as a self-ennobling and therefore suspicious feeling? A "positive" response would be guiltlessness, inasmuch as getting rid of the guilty feelings would be a kind of self-care. The literary scholar Frode Helland has suggested the term *aggressive guiltlessness* to characterize the force with which the issue of guilt toward minorities and immigrants is at times dismissed in the Norwegian public. Aggressive guiltlessness is, Helland proposes, an element in the ideological mobilization to defend privileges: "There is today an ideological struggle for hegemony concerning questions about guilt and responsibility; if our privileges are a result not only of our brilliant endeavors, but rather of exploitation and asymmetrical power relations, then our privileges must also be partly illegitimate" (Helland 2016, 32).[7] Aggressive guiltlessness thus shows itself as a forceful corroboration of the notion that the collective Scandinavian subject has actually earned its privileges and does not therefore owe anyone anything.

Returning to the artworks under study here in part 3—*My African Letters*, *European Attraction Limited*, and *Hornsleth Village Project Uganda*—we see the differences between what Helland calls aggressive guiltlessness and what I call the artful guilt trip. In the Scandinavian languages, guiltlessness is literally "guilt freedom" (*skyldfrihet*): that is, freedom from guilt. Yet *Hornsleth Village Project Uganda*, for instance, does not purport to be free from guilt. On the contrary, this art project trades in guilt, and it also offers a more reflexive relation to the meaning of freedom than aggressive guiltlessness. On one hand, the work clearly sides with freedom and liberal-mindedness: With the slogan "Stop donations, start free trade!" the work seems to advocate the economic kind of freedom we call free trade while exposing the hypocrisy of an "unfree" development aid that ties recipient countries to reforms, debts, and "recipient mentality." On the other hand, the work also ridicules the idea of free trade between free traders, meaning traders who are free to enter voluntarily into a given transaction: To exchange a name for a pig, across North and South, is a scandalizing way in which to question the terms of "free trade." Furthermore, the fact that this exchange-exploitation occurs in the name of art is a scandalizing way to question, also, the ways in which art, including the Uganda project itself, intervenes in and capitalizes on the apparatus of development aid.

The artful guilt trip differs, then, from an aggressive insistence on guilt-lessness, with which it can be confused: In the artful guilt trip, the skepti-mentalizing metaresponse to the sense of guilt is not guiltlessness, I would suggest, but crisp additional guilt. This is a genre for recording and trading in "white" shame and guilt, while simultaneously generating extra guilt as "crit-ical" surplus value—that is, as a kind of bonus. From the expression *guilt trip*, we assume that an individual or collective subject is "getting high" on guilt and in so doing seems to be somehow saved from the guilt—coming out on the other side of it, so to speak. Or, alternatively, we assume that the guilt trip is a "bad" trip that results in "getting low" in the sense of being paralyzed, overwhelmed by bad conscience, and unable to take action. In this respect, the *artful* guilt trip is notable for being a genre that neither makes a claim to guiltlessness nor lacks agency. Rather, the primary affective convention of this privilege genre is a kind of *guilty agency*. Here the agential meanings of the term *trip* are indicative. To go on a trip abroad, a business trip, is thus a key part of Hornsleth's Uganda project, as is the case in other skeptimental artful guilt trips, such as the Danish journalist and filmmaker Mads Brüg-ger's film *Ambassadøren* (The ambassador, 2011) and Renzo Martens's *Enjoy Poverty*. Both of these projects boasted a form of artful Afrosploitation in their engagements in deliberately skewed versions of business adventures with Congolese partners. Consider also the second installment of the doc-umentary *The Five Obstructions* (2003) by the Danish filmmakers Lars von Trier and Jørgen Leth, in which Leth travels/guilt-trips to Mumbai. Finally, Cuzner and Fadlabi also included in their enterprise a trip to the African continent, just as they included a devious business adventure called "Euro-pean Attraction Limited Tours," which offered "refugee tourism in Europe," meaning trips to refugee camps.

A genre of tripping must have a subject who "trips." In the case of the art-ful guilt trip, this is often the prominent characterological form of a "white colonial master." In both Martens's *Enjoy Poverty* and Brügger's *Ambas-sadøren*, the main characters, the artists-documentarists-humanitarians-businessmen, are quite literally outfitted like colonial masters. By contrast,

Ejlerskov's artist-I only by introspection finds herself to be, in fact, assuming the affective and economic attitude of a "colonial businessman." As character, the white colonial master is a means by which the affective juxtaposition central to the genre—a sense of guilt *and* agency—assumes a form that embodies the various connotations of "the trip," including of course "power trip." In all the artworks examined here, the white colonial master is, as a subject position taken up by the artist, thus a means by which to register a historical relation of guilt while also, against this backdrop, taking the artistic freedom to *act*, in the present, like a neocolonial artist, a neocolonial humanitarian, and a neocolonial businessman.

In this manner, colonial debts and guilt *are* entered into the accounts, but debts and guilty relations are also rejuvenated. There is thus also a markedly rhapsodic quality to the way in which the genre responds to guilt, something of a "The (white) king is dead—long live the king" approach to colonial and postcolonial histories. In *Hornsleth Village Project Uganda*, the figure of white colonial master is important to the artful articulation of the amalgamated economic-moral rationalities of the three domains mobilized by the project: market, development aid, art.[8] Hornsleth's artwork says something to the effect of "The free art is actually unfree—long live free art; the free market is actually unfree—long live the free market; the guiltless subject is actually guilty—long live the guiltless subject" and so on.

Usually, a skeptimental public is well practiced in recognizing and mistrusting the rhetorical-affective conventions of the confessional guilt trip. The artful guilt trip, by contrast, provokes fair amounts of critical wavering, even paralysis. In the case of art, this critical-interpretative standoff is typically due partly to questions regarding the status *as* art of the artwork in question, as was the case with both *European Attraction Limited* and *Hornsleth Village Project Uganda*. Yet the artfulness of this privilege genre is a matter not only of how works of art actualize the genre but of the more general sense of something strikingly artificial and *constructed* about the way in which the genre enacts the guilt trip. It is this artful processing and regeneration of guilt that ensures the continuation of the prominent role played by the genre in skeptimental publics.

One feature of skeptimental humanitarianism is that the issue of guilt and debt has generated a critical mutation in the sentimental economies. The cultural texts examined here in part 3 display variations on this skeptimental mutation. Humanitarian organizations generally market their products *as if* charity could patch the deficit in the global balance sheets on which the predicament of privilege turns, and innovations such as third-party gifts are accordingly a kind of skeptimental updating of humanitarian discourse and practice. We saw in Ditte Ejlerskov's *My African Letters* how a social-economic genre such as the advance fee scam, with its apparently straightforward division of guilt and innocence (financial scammers are guilty; victims of financial scams are innocent) mutated in its encounter with the predicament of privilege, so that innocence transformed into an impression of guilt. Finally, *Hornsleth Village Project Uganda* corroborates one of this book's fundamental assumptions: Humanitarian sensibility and its moral-economic forms no longer do the kind of cultural work presupposed by vernacular and academic discourses on these forms. In skeptimental publics, sentimental humanitarian economy is rarely cause for ennobling moral-affective uplift. By contrast, distrust of the sentimental and its economic forms may give rise to skeptimental transgression in the form of immoral scandal.

Why is the artful guilt trip as cultural genre relevant to skeptimental publics? Because, I suggest, these publics do not know on which basis they should answer the question this genre asks in so mannered a fashion: Is this okay? The skeptimental public is in doubt. In a privilege-sensitive era, in which global inequality disrupts the egalitarian imagination and muddles any sense of proper accounting, skeptimental publics are characterized by an absence of methods of counting, calculating, keeping accounts, and gift-giving perceived as relevant and "fair." Certainly, artful guilt trips such as the ones examined here are not mock-ups of a more egalitarian idea of accounting and accountability, and they only superficially purport to be so. Rather, in my understanding of this privilege genre, it is more a matter of raising a number of basic questions about how to account for debt, guilt, and our methods of calculation—questions to which a skeptimental public does not know the answers and for which it does not even really have a shared language: Which type of distribution is win-winism really? Which type of exchange, if any, is (not) okay? What do freedom, liberal-mindedness, and voluntariness actually mean in an unequal world? What is the moral and economic value of guilt and debt, and how can one make them somehow count? The artful guilt trip is a privilege genre that resonates with a skeptimental public, which nebulously senses that deep global inequality constitutes a problem for principles cherished in liberal market democracies, including the concept of advantageous free trade between equals, but which does not yet seem to have a common ethico-political language for this experience. In this historical situation, the mode of scandalous skeptimentality comes in handy for flaunting ways of (ac)counting.

With its barren mode of critique, a scandalous-skeptimental project such as *Hornsleth Village Project Uganda* reminds us that the sentimental has frequently been, and sometimes still is, a forceful form of social critique.[9] This is one of the surprises awaiting anyone who becomes acquainted with the Americanist tradition of sentimentalism studies. In *The Female Complaint*, Berlant describes, for instance, sentimentality as a critical aesthetic and ethico-politics. At times, the sentimental can even be a revolutionary rhetoric, Berlant notes, as in the case of *Uncle Tom's Cabin*; this rhetoric, however, most often wraps up its proposals for change in entertainment genres, so that they do not make quite so much noise: "Sentimentality, after all, is the only vehicle for social change that neither produces more pain nor requires much courage, unlike other revolutionary rhetorics" (Berlant 2008, 66). At first glance, sentimentality does not rhyme with criticality. But the kind of criticality we associate with egalitarian social movements and their intellectual histories so often contains sentimental elements that the negation of sentimentality may at times seem synonymous with the negation of criticality, too. So which forms might critique assume in publics so suspicious of ideas of the moral good—as is the case of skeptimental publics? If, as pointed out by Lousley, one attribute of the sentimental humanitarian subject is a desire for playing a role in social change, how, then, is this desire administered in the skeptimental public? As a way of responding to these questions, part 4 focuses on a particular genre of critique under conditions of complicity—what I call hypocrisy literature.

Part 4

On Critique

10.

Under Conditions
of Complicity

THE SKEPTIMENTAL STRUCTURE of feeling that I have described contrasts
with feelings of envy—an affective structure described by Sianne Ngai as a
kind of "deficit feeling," an affective interpretation that registers inequality
from below. While envy frequently identifies and centers on a factual relation of inequality, Ngai points out, we nonetheless typically write it off as
subjective pettiness: "Envy has been subjectivized or psychologized in a way
that perpetually renders the objectivity of its object (inequality) vulnerable
to epistemological doubt. And even when the relation of inequality which
envy discerns is a brute fact and not a matter of individualizing psychological
'perspective'" (Ngai in Rasmussen and Sharma 2017). Given that the unequal
distribution of opportunities, to which envy responds, is a fact—be it wom-
en's envy of male privilege or the migrant's envy of Western citizen status—
we can, according to Ngai, see the subjectivization and psychologization of
envy as a form of affective management: a form of control. Therefore, to gain
a better idea of the political rather than the purely psychological implications
of envy, Ngai asks for "an amoral reevaluation of envy" (Ngai in Rasmussen and Sharma 2017). Ngai observes that envy, when examined without the
considerations of morals, "has the potential to become a feeling that binds
subjects together in their sense of mutual antagonism to those who possess
what they do not." From Ngai's vantage point, then, envy is a matter of two
interconnected key theories of what we generally understand as politics: "the
formation and making visible of collectives and collectivity" and "the construction of the enemy." Seen in this light, Ngai points out, framing envy as
an apolitical affect is a form of affective discipline; seen amorally, however,
envy can be recognized as a politicizing emotion, one which provides the

envious with occasion to articulate an "us" in the face of a structurally privileged antagonist.

Ngai describes envy as the only negative emotion in the affective repertoire of the subject of advanced capitalist society that proceeds from his or her acknowledgment of social or distributional inequality. Also subjects of late capitalism, the classically privileged and their sensations of complicity and "privilege-guilt" register distributive inequality too—but they do so from "above." I am opening this chapter with Ngai's arguments about envy as political affect because, on the one hand, envy and privilege-qualms are socially opposing emotions (or, more precisely, they are directed toward the same privileged position but from, respectively, below and the privileged position itself) and, on the other hand, they have shared fates in terms of their evaluation as critical or political emotions. As often as privilege-guilt may be dismissed as narcissism, the asymmetrical relations of wealth and power to which the Scandinavian sensibility of privilege responds are also generally "a brute fact and not a matter of individualizing psychological 'perspective.'" And so, we might ask, is not the continuous subjectivization, psychologization, feminization, and belittling of the individual and collective experience of complicity and privilege-guilt a form of affective disciplining? Certainly, privilege-qualms would seem, like envy, to be antithetical to the grand "political" and "critical" affects of, say, anger and indignation. Yet, could privilege-qualms, considered amorally, nonetheless be an element in "the formation and making visible of collectives and collectivity," which according to Ngai is the case with envy? And, if so, for whom would that be an objective? And who, if anyone, is "the enemy" of those privileged subjects who find themselves complicit in late-capitalist systems of exploitation? These are the types of question motivating both this part of the book and the coda that follows it.

These chapters deal with critique produced by the complicit subject: critique under conditions of complicity. The conditions of (im)possibility for this form of critique encompass the historically sedimented "global maldistribution of symbolic and material resources," a maldistribution that favors the critical subject herself—just not in terms of critical value (Gilroy and Gilmore 2020). The type of critique I shall be looking at here can be recognized by the critical subject's particular position of enunciation: This subject sees herself as complicit in and privileged by the unjust system to which she attempts to respond critically. We can also recognize this form of critique in the specific form of address by which the privilege-sensitive subject tries to speak critically to other systemically privileged persons rather than to or on behalf of those un- or underprivileged by the system. Herein lies the close affiliation between this form of critique and the rhetorical genre that Bruce Robbins in *The Beneficiary* (2017) identifies as "the discourse of the beneficiary," to which I return in the following chapters.

Lastly, we should note that the form of critique I am aiming to pin down is generally criticized for being pseudocritical, if not downright uncritical. Importantly, it also criticizes itself: The guilt-feeling critic looks uneasily at her glass house, asking herself how on earth she could indulge in stone throwing. To "throw stones" is a cheap metaphor for critique. Still, this remains a central question pertaining to the meditations in skeptimental publics on the conditions of possibility for critical speech: How can you throw stones when you live in a glass house and are acutely aware of it?

As we have seen in the previous chapters, a sense of guilt is often the "negative" metaresponse to a "positive" feeling of care, sympathy, or compassion that converts a sentimental structure of feeling into what I am describing as a skeptimental structure of feeling. However, as we saw in chapter 9's analysis of Kristian von Hornsleth and the privilege genre I call the artful guilt trip, the sense of guilt can itself be identified as a sentimental affective pattern. In such cases, guilt is tagged as a backhandedly self-ennobling feeling that, in order to be palatable in a skeptimental public, must therefore be rendered an object of critical mutation.

It is this understanding of guilt as a sentimental emotion—the category of shallow guilt ascribed to bleeding hearts and guilty liberals—that the moral philosopher Sandra Lee Bartky discusses in her personal essay "In Defense of Guilt," the central argument of which is that the depiction of guilt common to moral psychology is inadequate in a political context. The political guilt Bartky is interested in does not accord with "the normal distinction between having done something wrong and having done nothing wrong." I may see myself as guilty, says Bartky, "by virtue of my relationship to wrongdoing, a relationship that I did not create but have not severed, either" (Bartky 2002, 141–42). She examines two slightly disparate forms of "political" guilt, both of which can be found in the Nordic sensibility I call the predicament of privilege: "guilt by complicity" and "guilt by reason of privilege" (Bartky 2002, 134–35). According to Bartky's classification, these two forms differ in respect of their objects: "acts and policies of government" in the former, "the structure of an entire social totality" in the latter (2002, 141).

In the left-wing American political culture Bartky herself encountered in the late 1960s, and which the essay looks back upon with a critical gaze, "guilty liberals" were just as despised as were "bleeding heart liberals" on the American right-wing flank. Guilty liberals were hypocrites because, unlike the radical group of which Bartky saw herself as a member, they were unwilling to forgo privilege "in order to make the kinds of sacrifices that social revolution was supposed to require" (2002, 133). "Radicals, we believed, have a tough and complex analysis—a class analysis accompanied perhaps by considerations of gender or race. Radicals permit themselves certain emotions, to be sure—outrage at the action of right-wing dictators, joy at the prospect of the triumph of socialism. We did not permit ourselves guilt. Guilt was for liberals. Liberals had only a few woolly minded ideas about the efficacy of electoral politics, 'bourgeois right,' and—guilt, an unclean emotion in which, like self-pity, some are thought to wallow" (2002, 133).

Such cultural notions of the privileged guilty hypocrite are familiar to Nordic publics today. Usually, these notions are underpinned, Bartky points out, by a gendered subtext of "tender" versus "tough"—and, we might add, "sentimental" versus "unsentimental." The fact that we typically psychologize and femininize the sense of guilt is, in Bartky's analysis, one of the reasons we fail to notice that guilt can be a political fact and that the sense of guilt is a political affect.

The issue of critique under conditions of complicity is pivotal to the predicament of privilege, and contemporary Scandinavian culture, in particular its literature, is a privileged place to monitor both reservations about and attempts to actually devise this kind of critique. In discussing the critical relevance of privilege-guilt, the following chapters also draw upon thinkers such as Bruce Robbins and Sara Ahmed, who, like Bartky, albeit in other contexts, have dwelled meticulously on variants of the question, When and how is self-criticism by the unjustly privileged critically relevant—and when is it not? Even Bartky, in her magnificent defense of guilt, warns that the systemically privileged worry *too much* about the degree of their complicity, because that kind of scrutiny may very well become a new "back-handed way of keeping ourselves still in the center" (2002, 148). Versions of this reservation—which I conceptualize in this book as a skeptimental reservation about the self-ennobling element of a structure of feeling, in this case guilt, experienced as sentimental—are omnipresent in discussions about the political relevance of feelings of complicity and their public representation. A truly resounding defense of guilt and complicity as critical-political attitudes is a rare thing.

The next two chapters examine the self-professed hypocrite, and particularly his endeavors to speak critically about and from his position of privilege. I call these endeavors hypocrite critique and, when it comes to the literature, hypocrisy literature. Whereas sentimental literatures are characterized by an aesthetic of sympathy, hypocrisy literature, which has absolutely no intention whatsoever of being sentimental, is characterized, conversely, by a skeptimental mutation in the aesthetic of sympathy, which by virtue of this very mutation becomes instead an aesthetic of complicity. Hypocrisy literature is a privilege genre, thematically characterized by the way in which the texts outline the contours of an unjust global system from which they themselves—the texts, their narrators, their authors, and their readers—gain privilege. Hence, this literature underscores the extent to which it is *of* this system. While these chapters are primarily concerned with Danish hypocrisy literature, this skeptimental genre will be recognizable to other Nordic publics and beyond. What interests me in particular about hypocrisy literature as a privilege genre are the critique-conceptual pointers, or rather questions, it raises, but I also look at the genre's formal concerns, including the way in which hypocrisy literature formulates and mediates an "I" and a "we," respectively.

11.

Hypocrisy Literature

AS A LITERARY label, *hypocrisy literature* was coined in 2014 upon publication of the first volume of the Danish poet Victor Boy Lindholm's "hypocrite trilogy."[1] However, the predicament indexed by what I term hypocrisy literature is not exclusive to Lindholm's poetry or to contemporary literature more generally. Rather, the hypocrite is a transgeneric character, and his or her attempt at shaping a critical discourse about his or her hypocrisy generates a number of closely related privilege genres: what we might call hypocrisy documentary, hypocrisy performance art, hypocrisy public discourse, and so forth. The salient features of hypocrisy discourse are its indications, assumptions, or descriptions of a global system that continues to produce relatively affluent lives; a juxtaposition of these lives with oppressed, precarious lives; and a portrayal of globally privileged subjects living with the knowledge of benefiting from and contributing to this unjust world order. In hypocrisy narratives, figures such as miners, child laborers, sweatshop laborers, and refugees frequently serve as tropes for life on the flip side of the system.

According to the *Oxford English Dictionary*, hypocrisy has to do with pretense, dissimulation, insincerity, and double standards. A hypocrite is someone "who falsely professes to be virtuously or religiously inclined; one who pretends to have feelings or beliefs of a higher order than his real ones; hence generally, a dissembler, pretender."[2] In everyday discourse, we tend to go along with this dictionary definition, understanding hypocrisy as identifying a fraudulent relationship between a self and its social context. Yet such formulations are not particularly accurate in capturing the kind of hypocrisy narrated by Scandinavian hypocrisy literature. The hypocrite portrayed in contemporary hypocrisy fiction and the broader archive of hypocrisy genres does not generally dissimulate, or if he or she does dissimulate, it is not the dissimulation itself that is central to the hypocrisy at hand. Rather, in these narratives, hypocrisy involves a self's relationship to itself: A moral consciousness regards its own immorality with aversion, apathy, or both.

As an example of this consciousness at work, consider Mette, the female protagonist in the Danish author Kirsten Hammann's 2004 novel *Fra smørhullet* (From the land of milk and honey). In the following scene, Mette has been watching a TV broadcast about the pursuit of Saddam Hussein; she takes a short break in order to visit the bathroom, where she mercilessly kills a crane fly: "Most likely, the crane fly doesn't mind being squashed and drowned and chemically attacked. But Mette has a bad conscience anyway. She's disgusting. Sits eating candy to images of the war in Iraq and has a minor existential crisis about killing a crane fly. Pathetic. Hypocrisy, they call it" (Hammann 2004, 239).[3] If we think of the third-person narrator as Mette's critical self-evaluation, then what Mette is detecting in herself and names *hypocrisy* is not dissimulation. Rather, it is the fact that she is capable of doing something—enjoying candy while watching a real war—that she, according to her own ethics, ought not to be capable of. Mette becomes aware there is something filthy inside her, that she is disgusting, via the exposure of an unacceptable inconsistency in her affective register: She cannot stomach that she has killed a crane fly, but she *can* watch a war being waged in her name. So, for starters, we may say that the hypocrisy in hypocrisy literature is the experience of an affective, moral, or political inconsistency that upsets the hypocrite. Or, better: Hypocrisy is the judgment passed by a critical consciousness on its own moral inconsistency.

Fra smørhullet and Kirsten Hammann's subsequent novel *En dråbe i havet* (A drop in the ocean, 2008) are exemplars of hypocrisy fiction. Both novels center on female protagonists who observe the inconsequence of their own lives with alternately listless and desperate distaste. The critical evaluation of self is animated by the protagonists' identification of the contrasts between gross world poverty and their own materially, if not emotionally, satisfied way of life—and especially by a nagging sense that the latter is contingent on the former. In *Fra smørhullet*, the superego-like narrator explains the material well-being of the "spoiled" protagonist Mette and her Northern European contemporaries: "On a global scale, too, Mette's done well. Okay, more than well: born white, in the 1960s, in a suburb of Aarhus, Denmark, Europe, right up in the north among the former imperialists with their colonies down where the blacks live. Lovely cheap sugar and coffee, because the Negroes were so good at working without pay" (Hammann 2004, 97).[4] Self-depictions soaked with such coarse sarcasm are particularly conspicuous in Hammann's hypocrite fiction, and they are also a recurrent feature in hypocrisy literature more generally.

The coarseness is perhaps designed to let the reader understand that Mette, and the privilege-sensitive subjectivity she represents, does not base her sense of complicity on a scrupulously precise analysis of exploitative planetary patterns and their histories. If anything, Mette—who is incidentally also an artist—sounds like Ditte Ejlerskov's artist-I from *My African Letters* whom we met in chapter 7 and who was consumed by an equally diffuse "colonial guilt." Both of these works thus catalog a debtor subjectivity that seems to know enough about the complexion of the world to feel guilty but knows too little to be able to present a "tough" class analysis qualifying as properly political and (self-)mobilizing discourse.

The sarcastic self-depiction in the passage quoted above relates to a factually somewhat blurred but affectively concise understanding of how colonial history impacts Mette, her contemporaries, and their privileges. Yet the unfair world order of which Mette knows herself to be a beneficiary, relating more to the unfinished business of such histories, cannot be adequately explained by colonial histories alone. Thus, the object of Mette's most pressing sensations of guilt and complicity is not the past but her everyday encounter with political arrangements and global markets. The protagonist of Hammann's novel *En dråbe i havet*, whose name is also Mette, is possibly familiar with Scandinavians' high scores on the international Happiness Index; in the following passage, we hear more from the hypocrite's superego and its idea of the true meaning of Scandinavian happiness: "Mette has no idea what she's talking about when she says she is happy. She ought to say that she's happy about being so filthy rich and powerful that she can screw over the poor while slurping underpriced South American orange juice and telling Sofie never mind about losing her beep-beep game at preschool, 'we'll just buy a new one.'That's what she's really happy about!"(Hammann 2008, 77).[5] In other words, Hammann's two Mettes face the same predicament: While behaving in the most ordinary way possible, they find themselves treading on the global poor. Injustice, and their complicity with it, appears systemic: The filth is located at the heart of everyday life because, regardless of how powerless they may feel, they are "so filthy rich and powerful."

Hypocrisy literature thus presents us with a subject who has come to identify herself as a global problem. In Victor Boy Lindholm's poetry collection *Guld*, the structures of global inequality saturate not only the body politic but also the individual human body. The poetic self unremittingly discerns this structure in himself, as when he "draws breath via the mines in congo" or declares that "I have microchipflashcardbloodstainedchildlabor in / my body / I have africa as a structure in my eye" (Lindholm 2014, 13, 63).[6] This "I" talks about the mineral resources in his iPhone, about himself as mineral, about child labor, about the gold, the guilt, the hypocrite inside him while sipping Mountain Dew on the Adriatic coast. Lindholm's hypocrite self-identifies as a hypocrite because he hesitantly challenges unsavory things, which he nevertheless continues to enjoy and from which he benefits. The "I," sometimes called Victor, wishes to apologize for his geopolitical belonging: "some day world / I'd like to say sorry on europe's behalf / sorry for the good vibe" (Lindholm 2014, 55).[7] But elsewhere he states: "im so sorry / but im not" (59).[8] The tone is not sardonic, as it is in Hammann's novels. To the consciousness portrayed here, the preoccupation with complicity seems to be part of an everyday reflexive routine.

I read this literary privilege genre as a contemplation of what critique under conditions of complicity might look like. Hypocrisy literature is a cultural response to a specific historical situation in which the Nordic middle classes suspect that they live their lives at the expense of others. But it is also a response, I submit, to a change in the collective ideas about what constitutes critique at all. As an attempt to form a critical discourse, hypocrisy literature is shaped by reservations about the propensity of "critique" for routine skepticism, ordinary superciliousness, and metaphysical positioning. In other words, the will to self-implication, which is so pronounced in hypocrisy literature, is a response to the acknowledgment of two kinds of complicity: one having to do with distributive justice, the other having to do with our ideas about the politics of critique. In hypocrisy literature, we see these two kinds of complicity merge to attain a common language.

Each in its own way, the literary works touched upon in these chapters raise questions about the critical relevance of literary renderings of unearned privilege, hypocrisy, and complicity. Am I critical? this literature asks, often anxiously so. The poetic subject in Victor Boy Lindholm's *Guld* does not seem to think highly of his own criticality. Nor did the literary critics. One critic found the consciousness expressed in Lindholm's poetry to be fashionably guilty and argued that in *Guld* the suffering of others mainly functioned as ornament (Ernst 2014, 10). Another literary critic considered the poems' political engagement to be mere garnish, while to yet a third, the declarations of hypocrisy seemed simply too premeditated and therefore exculpatory (Bukdahl 2014, 16; Frantzen 2015, 10). In other words, the critics detected a certain dissimulation or hypocrisy in the tone, style, and sensibility of Lindholm's debut collection (see also Thomsen 2016; Friis 2015). By thus emphasizing authenticity and sincerity as the main problems with Lindholm's *Guld*, this type of literary criticism lingers, I think, in a terrain from which hypocrisy literature itself in fact endeavors to depart. I am suggesting that dissimulation and feigning are not the principal features in the portrait of hypocrisy offered by hypocrisy literature: The experience that turns you into a self-professed hypocrite is not the acknowledgment of your own insincerity; it is, rather, the acknowledgment that sincerity will not save you from complicity.

One of the literary critics who found Lindholm's *Guld* to be pseudo-critical summed up an apparent trend among Danish poets: "Politics has become a tic in the young generation, every third line is breaking news about the injustice of the world" (Bukdahl 2014).[9] Instead of commitment, we get "excuses for lack of heartfelt, committed indignation."[10] The reviewer in question also detected this garnish-engagement in a poetic analysis written by the Danish poet Olga Ravn, in which Ravn had mixed fragments from an article about refugees living in an asylum center with observations about her own life in Copenhagen. According to the critic, Ravn's text opens with the line "I've never spoken with a refugee."[11] The critic challenged the methodology: "Then do so, poet, you just have to get on a bus!" (Bukdahl 2014).[12] In a critique-conceptual sense, "getting on a bus" is an image of a no-nonsense critique—of critical *action* rather than shamefaced navel-gazing about the absence of action. This image of critique as an efficient act, and one totally within reach of the privileged writer or critic, haunts hypocrite narratives and criticism of the hypocrite's speech alike. The privilege-sensitive subject hopes to be able to "make a difference," but of what can this "making" consist?

On Being Against

In Sara Ahmed's early work on antiracism, whiteness studies, and shame, we find an incisive investigation into the critical relevance of publicly displaying one's unearned privilege and into the issue of when critical speech counts as an act. In the following I regard Ahmed's investigation of what is at work in whiteness studies as a contribution to a more general consideration of the systemically privileged's options to critically confront the system by which they are privileged. According to Ahmed, one fundamental assumption in whiteness studies, which must be understood as an offshoot of the study of race and racism, is that understanding the production of racial privileges is a prerequisite for understanding racism: Where and how does this privileging happen? In this, a central endeavor is to render visible the production of racial privileges, based on the assumption that visibility will challenge these privileges. It is this assumption—that to render privilege visible is to challenge it—that Ahmed examines.

There are two elements in Ahmed's discussion of the critical relevance of critical whiteness studies to which I would like to draw our attention. First, Ahmed reads whiteness studies and its self-reflexivity as part of a more general "politics of declaration" that designates situations in which someone admits "to forms of bad practice, and in which the 'admission' itself becomes seen as good practice" (Ahmed 2004, para. 11). In stating that I am white, I perhaps implicitly mean that I am white in a slightly better way—a nonracist way—than other white people.

Second, Ahmed argues that we can never be sure that antiracist discourse constitutes an antiracist speech act in the Austinian sense.[13] According to Ahmed, most often white antiracism is "non-performative," which is to say that to declare oneself an antiracist does not constitute an antiracist *act* against the social hierarchies established in and through racism. To believe that antiracist speech is a political act is not merely to overestimate the power of speech, Ahmed warns us; it is also "a *performance* of the very privilege that such statements claim they undo" (2004, para. 54; emphasis added). Ahmed offers the example of white subjects confessing to feelings of shame: "Declarations of shame can work to re-install the very ideals they seek to contest. . . . The presumption that saying is doing—that being sorry means that we have overcome the very thing we are sorry about—hence works to support racism in the present. Indeed, what is done in this speech act, if anything is done, is that the white subject is re-posited as the social ideal" (Ahmed 2004, para. 27). To say that we are ashamed of racism might enforce racism, Ahmed argues, because what we rely on when we imagine our speech to be political action is a fantasy of transcendence. And, she suggests, this fantasy of transcendence—the idea that our discursive declarations may overcome that which otherwise seems to hold us—may in itself be a symptom of white privilege. In this manner, it is by subscribing to this fantasy that critical white-ness studies risks further consolidation of the power of the white subject.

Ahmed gives an example from her own antiracist work, illustrating that critique is not guaranteed to do what it says. At the British university where she was employed, Ahmed was involved in the formulation of a race equality policy. The race equality policy was in fact a performative action, she infers, but indeed an unintentional performance on her part: The strategy of document-ing racism at the university became a measure of the university acting well by making such a policy. Ahmed is here posing a variant of the pivotal question in this chapter: "The critique I am offering, as a Black feminist, is a critique of something in which I am implicated, insofar as racism structures the institu-tional space in which I make my critique, and even the very terms out of which I make it. In the face of how much we are 'in it', our question might become: is anti-racism impossible?" (2004, para. 46). Ahmed answers in the affirmative. To doubt that antiracism is possible in light of our complicity in the racist distribution of resources is, she writes, to doubt black politics and the historical fact of political agency: "Surely the commitment to being against racism has 'done things' and continues to 'do things'" (2004, para. 47).

So, antiracism has indeed achieved something, and opposition of this kind continues to achieve something. Yet for critical whiteness studies, Ahmed does not consider the relevant assignment to be reiteration of antiracism utterances in the hope that they will *perform* something: "Whiteness studies should instead be about attending to forms of white racism and white privi-lege that are not undone, and may even be repeated and intensified, through declarations of whiteness, or through the recognition of privilege as privi-lege" (2004, para. 58). To my mind, Ahmed risks undervaluing the potentially mobilizing effects of such utterances, rendering her interpretation too pessi-mistic overall. On the one hand, white antiracist speech is nonperformative, Ahmed suggests, because the conditions that would allow such speech to do what it says are not in place. On the other hand, white antiracist speech *is* performative, only its performativity falls on the wrong side, so to speak, in the sense that such utterances risk doing what they say they will not do. Hence, it remains unclear if Ahmed thinks that white privileged subjects (even hypothetically, over time, and so forth) can or cannot *do* something to reduce racism and white privileges.

Importantly, clarifying this issue is not Ahmed's concern. Rather, she is occupied with drawing attention to the nontranscendental terms of critique:

"The messy work of 'againstness' might even help remind us," Ahmed suggests, "that the work of critique does not mean the transcendence of the object of our critique; indeed critique *might even be dependent on non-transcendence*" (2004, para. 47; emphasis in original). This latter description of critique as messy, as being necessarily formed by an intimate relationship with what you are against is, I believe, a fruitful opening to our further exploration of the type of critique under conditions of complicity I call hypocrisy literature.

In Ahmed's reservation about well-meant admissions of privilege, we recognize the reservations central to the scholarship on sentimentality and humanitarianism about the purifying functions of sympathy. In terms of criticality these reservations translate into reservations about the assumption that critique should somehow transcend its object and, in Ahmed's terminology, undo that which has been done.[14] Ahmed shares this reservation with Scandinavian hypocrisy literature, which is immensely aware of the limitations of its agency: firstly, because it is literature, and as such used to immense humility with regard to its own political and critical relevance; secondly, because it is not a sentimental literature of sympathy but a skeptimental literature of complicity, and as such does not subscribe to the idea of art as transformative event and terrain for affective, moral, and political reform. This latter idea is, as we have seen, central to the multibranched sentimental tradition we can, with Lauren Berlant, designate the *"Uncle Tom* tradition."* As we shall see, hypocrisy literature knows only too well that it does not transcend its object, this object being both a global system and the hypocrite's entanglements with it.

Skeptimental Beneficiaries

In Hammann's novel *En dråbe i havet*, the writer Mette Mæt asks herself which kind of action can qualify as critical action in relation to the global inequality and injustice occupying her thoughts. She had initially considered various forms of humanitarian ingenuity, such as setting up a fund called "A Drop in the Ocean" or writing a novel with some pages only accessible by pulling out an inserted Giro payment slip, but she then discarded these ideas as being too frivolous. On the fiftieth anniversary of the Treaty of Rome, Mette reads an open letter signed by nine European "wise old men" condemning the leaders of Europe for ignoring the genocide in Darfur, Sudan. At first she is fired with indignation and is jubilant that these world-famous men are speaking out about the situation. But her enthusiasm is quick to wane because she is well aware that "27 heads of government couldn't care less about a handful of intellectuals sounding off with no fear of repercussions" (Hammann 2008, 181).[15] At other times, Mette wonders if critical reflection in itself might perhaps count as action. Her husband, Martin, does not believe in the efficacy of sudden outbursts of collective action. Rather, he believes in the long haul of raising awareness, and "Martin can get her to believe she's part of a movement even though she doesn't do anything" (Hammann 2008, 153).[16] Nonetheless, Mette is not totally convinced, and she gradually even loses belief in acts of empathy, in her ability to write the book that will rouse her readers from the somnambulism of complicity. Mette herself has absolutely no critical share in the two images of global justice that prove most durable in the novel. One of these images is her fantasy of a global reshuffle: a global domicile rotation along the lines of job rotation; the other is an image of angry underprivileged hordes streaming in from the global South and demanding their fair share of everything.[17]

Hypocrisy literature documents the Scandinavian sensibility of privilege, generally describing it as ordinary. However, this literary privilege genre also contributes to the fact that the predicament of privilege appears in public culture *as* an ordinary problem, because hypocrisy literature is busy portraying the hypocrite as a character in whom readers can recognize themselves. If this literature is to be believed, then the hypocrite's experience of moral-political inconsistency and complicity is a commonsensical and everyday experience, "everyday" in the sense both of being common and of being tied to the practices of everyday life. In this manner, recognizability forms part of this literature's meditation on what critique under conditions of complicity might look like. Recognizability, rather than, say, alienation, variation, or historicization, is an unusual strategy for cultural critique, and neither hypocrisy literature's characters, writers, nor readers seem at all convinced that an account of the recognizable can qualify as critique. In other words, we are dealing with a literature that doubts its own criticality and more specifically doubts the critical value of generating recognition. And vice versa: We are dealing with a literature suggesting that being in doubt about one's own criticality is very much part of recognizable life as a hypocrite.

Let us hear a little more about this predicament of criticality from a writer and a character. In an interview on the publication of her novel *To the Modern Man* (2022), the Danish writer Kristina Nya Glaffey described collective hypocrite-life and the somewhat humble prospect this life offers of being able to "act upon" the hypocrisy:[18]

> I think a lot of people will be able to recognize themselves in the book [*To the Modern Man*]—whatever their gender—perhaps it can make us stop and wonder if it might be in somewhat bad taste to walk straight from a demonstration on City Hall Square in support of Syrian refugees to a bar on the corner for a glass of white wine once you've grown tired of standing up. That's life in our society, full of hypocrisy and contrasts, and it's not a pretty sight, but it's hard to give up the privileges you have—for me, too, and all sorts of other people. So then the least you can do is have a bit of a laugh about it—laugh and face your own hypocrisy. At least it's in minimally better taste to have some kind of self-irony than to be devoid of any. (Carlsen 2022)[19]

This is indeed a modest critical horizon for a privilege-sensitive discourse seemingly motivated by global injustice.

Eighteen years prior to the publication of Glaffey's novel, Kirsten Hammann's female protagonist Mette in *Fra smørhullet* metareflects on the effect of the novel she is appearing in and its recognizable depiction of life as privileged hypocrite: "What if you could write a novel about someone like Mette. Then, reading about her charitable outlook, superegoism, dreams of change, and extreme laziness, a lot of people could loll back even more comfortably and feel both recognized and understood. 'Wow, that's me in a nutshell,' you could say. 'I feel there's so much wrong in the world, but I simply can't work out what I can do about it. Are there really so many of us that feel like that? We mean well, but we're powerless.' And that's it. Just recognition and then down to the shops" (Hammann 2004, 186).[20] This is, then, an important question posed by hypocrisy literature: What effect can be generated, if any, by the representation of the predicament of privilege as a recognizable, commonplace Scandinavian sensibility? I return to this question in chapter 12.

To gain a broader context for hypocrisy literature and the questions about critique that it raises, I propose adding twenty-first-century Scandinavian hypocrisy fiction to the primarily Anglo-American twentieth-century cultural history of the discourse of the beneficiary offered by Bruce Robbins. In Robbins's definition, the discourse of the beneficiary is characterized by a specific rhetorical situation in which a subject who benefits from global economic inequality writes or speaks to other such beneficiaries about the injustice of the privileges they have in common, thus "denouncing a system which one finds unbearable but to which one nevertheless continues to belong, from which one continues to derive certain benefits and privileges, and from which one may have no possibility of making a clean break" (Robbins 2014, 259). Robbins's 2017 book *The Beneficiary* offers an intellectual history of this discourse and the transnational egalitarianism, or "materially invested cosmopolitanism," in which it endeavors to partake. Works by thinkers such as George Orwell, Jean-Paul Sartre, and Naomi Klein feature in Robbins's many examples of the beneficiary's discourse.

In Robbins's opinion, the genre's transnational sphere of interest and focus on economic justice are particular qualifying factors in viewing the discourse of the beneficiary as "a more serious kind of cosmopolitanism than most of the varieties we have come to know" (2014, 259). With reference to, among other texts, Jean-Paul Sartre's preface to Frantz Fanon's *Les damnés de la terre*, a devastating critique under conditions of complicity in French imperialism, Robbins argues that the transnationalism found in the discourse of the beneficiary is more ambitious than a humanitarian transnationalism. Here, and as we saw in chapter 3, Robbins emphasizes what he takes to be a central discrepancy between humanitarian discourse and the discourse of the beneficiary:

> Humanitarian discourse forbids the positing of a causal logic between
> the situation of the haves and the situation of the have-nots. As a
> humanitarian, you can make your addressees feel guilty, but you can't do
> so by saying . . . that distant others are miserable because they them-
> selves are much better off. An analysis that makes this causal link is
> doing something more ambitious than humanitarianism even if it is not
> doing the sorts of things we might expect from directly political speech,
> like communicating directly with the victims of economic inequality
> in search of a hypothetical alliance against what we have come to call
> globalization. (Robbins 2014, 262)

Hence, to Robbins it is the notion of being "causally responsible" for the fates of distant others that makes the discourse of the beneficiary stand out from the history of humanitarianism (Robbins 2017, 3).

One of the things that makes Robbins's work on the discourse of the beneficiary particularly relevant for our discussion of critique under conditions of complicity is his focus on various theoretical attempts at discrediting this rhetorical genre as indulgent, merely ethical, politically trivial, a manifestation of self-flagellation, bourgeois guilt, and so on and so forth. To a large extent, Robbins defends the genre, arguing that it has "a certain mobilizing potential" and viewing it as "a useful experiment in stretching the political, an experiment in fashioning a politics of global economic inequality" (2014, 259). Robbins particularly defends the discourse of the beneficiary against intellectuals who "speak the language of politics but, demanding above all else moral purity as judged by today's standards, are unprepared for any of the messiness of historical struggle" (2014, 253).[21] Against this form of unrealistic and therefore, according to Robbins, *a*political idealism, he argues that "no political action however revolutionary, can be solely and successfully carried out by people who lack any trace of power or privilege. To demand purity from political actors is to take oneself out of politics" (2014, 258). However, Robbins also has his own reservations about the potential critical-political effects of the genre. The discourse of the beneficiary cannot, he concedes, be described as properly political. It is more of an "ethico-political amalgam" and a "proto-political discursive hybrid" (Robbins 2014, 259–62).

While it is not entirely clear to me upon which assumptions of the "properly political" these reservations are based, let us nonetheless take note of Robbins's designation of the discourse of the beneficiary as "proto-political." Scandinavian hypocrisy literature, and hypocrisy discourses more generally, are closely related to this discursive genre identified by Robbins. In the contemporary Nordic context, however, the discourse of the beneficiary is not the prerogative of intellectuals. Rather, mediated by cultural privilege genres, it forms part of a prevalent historical common sense evidenced in popular culture and public discourse alike.

Whatever the extent of their differences, none of the reservations about the political value of hypocrite critique we have seen playing out in the writings of Bartky, Ahmed, and Robbins is alien to Scandinavian hypocrisy literature. In this literary genre we see a critical consciousness treading water, because the experience that is fundamental to it, the impression of complicity and hypocrisy, cannot be transcended or ignored, cannot in any

radical way be made relevant as efficient critical discourse. These reservations are thus part of a critique under conditions of complicity. Among
other features, it is the attention to, or even embrace of, these reservations
that makes hypocrisy literature a skeptimental rather than a sentimental
literature.

12.

Crisis and Collectivity

IN AN ESSAY on the credit crunch of 2008 and the ensuing ten years of recession, John Lanchester describes the numbness he encountered in the immediate aftermath of the crisis, the banking bailout, and the austerity measures imposed on societies across the Western world. However, at some point along the line, Lanchester recollects, this numbness was transforming into public rage fueled by the realization that the financial systems themselves would in fact be protected from the consequences of the preceding years of predatory lending and debt swopping. "That impunity," Lanchester writes, "the sense that these things had consequences for *us* but not for the people who caused the crisis, has been central to the story of the last ten years" (2018, 5; emphasis added). This "us," which Lanchester evokes here, is the *we* of the "99%." It is an "us" formed by righteous indignation over the unjust national and transnational inequalities laid bare and exacerbated by the economic crisis. Furthermore, it seems to be an "us" that is easily identifiable, an "us" that is itself even aware of who it is. In a vein similar to the envious *we* outlined by Sianne Ngai (see chapter 10), Lanchester's furious *we* seems to be a recognizable political collective with a clear antagonist: in this case, the 1%.

I am interested in this "we," the contours of which can seem so self-evident, because this imagined collective holds such a different place in the popular imagination from that of the systemically privileged hypocrites. The 99% is a coherent political subject to the extent that it finds unjust benefits on the other side, with its antagonists (and due, perhaps, to its politically valued rage). By contrast, the hypocrites find unjust benefits within their own quarters; they are on the wrong side of blame. The two collective social formations are, to some extent, however, overlapping collective subjects: the global middle classes living in the Western world. Contrary to the "us" casually evoked by Lanchester and others, the self-professed hypocrites have not yet come to figure in public culture as a coherent political subject. The predicament of privilege is, if we are to believe Scandinavian hypocrisy literature, experienced as a private and idiosyncratic problem, not a massifying one. According to this literature, along with the more extensive archive of this book, the hypocrite has no sense of being part of any collective, certainly not a political collective. Nonetheless, one of the effects of the literary repurposing of hypocrisy and complicity in Scandinavian hypocrisy fiction is, I suggest in this chapter, that political questions of a collective hypocrite-"we" are coming to the fore in Scandinavian (literary) publics.

Literature preoccupied with migration to Europe after the Arab uprisings is one forum in which to learn more about the skeptimental aesthetic of complicity central to Scandinavian hypocrisy fiction. The egalitarian imaginary's confrontation with refugees tramping the highways of Nordic welfare states in September 2015, and the ensuing crises of national self-images, triggered a great deal of cultural response. Hence, there is a considerable archive of literary works by Scandinavian authors addressing this charged state of affairs: writers such as Henrik Nordbrandt, Tomas Espedal, Julie Sten-Knudsen, Morten Søndergaard, Ursula Andkjær Olsen, Victor Boy Lindholm, Peter-Clement Woetmann, Peter Laugesen, Negar Naseh, Madame Nielsen, Johannes Anyuru, Vigdis Hjort, and Ida Jessen.[1] Inevitably, this literature engages with humanitarian crisis. But most often it also speaks of a crisis *in* humanitarianism, not only because it registers some of the decidedly antihumanitarian sentiments showcased by what came to be known discursively as "the refugee crisis," but also because of the perplexity about how to respond and take responsibility that is given form in these works. In taking a hypocritical consciousness as its starting point, this archive probes relevant strategies for literary engagement under conditions of complicity. It thus demonstrates various modes of what Ahmed calls the "messy work" of againstness (2004, para. 47).

The Danish author Peter Højrup's novel *Til stranden* (To the beach, 2017) portrays a group of white middle-aged Danish friends and their kids vacationing on a Turkish island at a time when refugees are arriving in lifeboats. A Syrian boy is found dead on the Turkish coast not too far from where the friends are spending their holiday, the novel thus pointing us to the event of Alan (often reported as Aylan) Kurdi's death in September 2015. But Højrup's work is not disaster writing or atrocity fiction. Instead, we hear a lot about familiar relationship problems between couples, friends, parents, and children, as these problems are processed by a shared and emblematically ordinary upper-middle-class consciousness. The problems experienced by this consciousness are effectively framed as first world problems, but without the tonalities of irony and sarcasm one might have expected in a literary scenario such as this.

Much of the little that goes on in *Til stranden* is about trying to stop feeling overwhelmed, just for a moment: The narrative quietly articulates the experience of witnessing an unjust, and as such depressing, world order and not having the energy to figure out how to respond to it. The novel addresses the friends' encounter with the actual refugee situation happening around them. But to an even greater extent, it addresses the sedate privilege-sensitive crisis-awareness in which Alan Kurdi is but one flash point in a network of significance that, for the novel, also includes poverty, child labor, destitution, sweatshop labor, systemic inequality, and other signs of "the system." The narrative registers the friends' anxieties, hopes, impulses, and stray associations, often with mediating recourse to the plight of others, as in this conversation between Linn and Betty:

> Well we've got love too, Betty says, yes, Linn says, yes, it's really not true that it's all just wickedness, but we're witnessing it; every day we have to look at children suffering and dying without being able to do anything about it, and even if you try to do something, you realize that behind the first wretchedness ten thousand others lurk. It's overwhelming, not that I think that's any excuse for sitting on your hands. Hermann spent three weeks in South Sudan with Doctors Without Borders. Is he a doctor, Betty says. No, a dentist, Linn says, *Dentists Without Borders*, then they have a little laugh about that, then they sit for a little while. (Højrup 2017, 103)[2]

This conversation also gives us a sense of the narrative style of *Til stranden*: dialogue and monologue alike are reported without quotation marks or question marks, in what therefore reads like a collective stream of consciousness that tends to disorient the reader.

The confrontation of this privilege-sensitive and overwhelmed sensorium with refugees arriving on the island gives rise to a trope of complicity, frequently recurring in this literary archive, we might call swimming in the same sea in which other people are drowning (see, for instance, Højrup 2017, 129, 151, 174, 180). In several ways, *Til stranden* nods to Virginia Woolf, and especially *To the Lighthouse* and *The Waves*, but what is most striking about its relationship to Woolf is that waves, as a motif and metaphor for the movements of consciousness, have lost whatever innocence and cleansing effect they may once have had. "The beach where I usually swim," says a woman who is visiting the group of friends after the drowned child has been found on the beach, "now I can never go in the water again, the beach turns my stomach, the sea makes me think of death" (Højrup 2017, 129).[3] Elsewhere, one of the friends, a chef called Ib, is watching a Turkish couple and their children playing in the sea: "Why don't they do something, thinks Ib, why are they swimming and having fun when people are drowning in the very same water. In an attempt to deflect the question about why he doesn't do anything himself, he pays a considerable sum of money to a relief agency once every three months, sometimes more often if he's overwhelmed by the news coverage . . . and anyway no one's situation is improved by us going around feeling bad about the wretched state of the world. He tells himself this kind of stuff, without really believing it" (Højrup 2017, 151–52).[4] In *Til stranden*, the waves flowing over consciousness are full of death, apathy, and a sense of hypocrisy.

The trope of swimming in a sea of dying people also sets the scene for a lengthy reprimand on the theme of complicity made by one of the friends, Ernst, addressed to the others. I shall dwell a little on this scene because, among other things, its combination of pompous hypocrite-indignation with the instant puncturing of this indignation is a constant in hypocrisy literature. The scene begins with a figure of innocence, a child, asking an innocent question: "and Wilma said, so are the fish full of bread when you pull them out, and Ernst said, yes, the fish are full of bread and dead refugees" (Højrup 2017, 173).[5] Ernst then launches into an angry rant, too long to quote in its entirety; here is a sample:

All that nasty war pouring out of your screens, kids bleeding from eyes and ears, kids with arms and legs blown off, you can't bear the sight of it, so you rush to give a hundred-kroner note to a relief agency and reward yourselves with some new clothes, because you're so clever, because you're just such humanitarians, what you forget to take into account is that the clothes are made by child laborers, sitting chained to the wall in some filthy factory in the third world, all because it's most cost-effective, all because you don't want to pay what things cost, but you still expect the best quality at a bargain price. (Højrup 2017, 176–77)[6]

Ernst is berating his friends for not being willing to face up to their own hypocrisy. Yet he is himself included in the very hypocritical life he is talking about. Most of all, therefore, Ernst is acting as the self-appointed superego of the group of friends, and he does indeed sound very similar to the superego-like third-person narrators in Kirsten Hammann's hypocrisy novels. This is, then, how the hypocrite-superego speaks, often simplifying "the vectors of guilt at the planetary or local scale" (Robbins 2014, 261). Ernst's tirade is the discourse of the beneficiary in an almost farcical mode of sublimity. When his girlfriend Betty asks what he is talking about, Ernst responds, "I'm talking about all of it" (Højrup 2017, 176).[7]

Ernst's reprimand of the complicit includes several condensed "commodity recognition scenes" like the one included above. "Commodity recognition scenes are," Robbins writes, "epiphanies in which some familiar consumer good is suddenly recognized as coming from a distant place of origin and from the labor, perhaps the coerced or otherwise unpleasant labor, of the distant inhabitants" (2014, 267; see also Robbins 2017, 51–74). Pointing to the cultural practice of looking behind commodities to the histories of their production—a cultural practice that, in the terminology of this book, we could also describe as a privilege-collaging, skeptimental gaze on one's surroundings—Robbins identifies a range of commodity recognition scenes in prose by authors such as George Eliot, Virginia Woolf, and Adam Smith. Often comprising long lists of modes of specialized labor and sites of coproduction, commodity recognition scenes are staples of the discourse of the beneficiary, and, Robbins suggests, they typically evoke a kind of "capitalist sublime" (2017, 54).

In these chapters' literary sources we have seen several examples of commodity recognition. In these scenes, what seems sublime to the hypocrite-subject is largely the sense of entanglement, via one's consumption, in a system one abhors. In Scandinavian hypocrisy literature, this form of "entanglement sublime" does not, however, offer any sense of transcendent guilt. This is ensured by the skeptimental mutation, which manifests itself in hypocrisy literature as a puncturing—be it an ironic, comic, or resigned puncturing—of the pomposity of privilege qualms. Indeed, while Ernst's tirade might seem

to be bordering on a self-ennobling sense of transcendence, the sublima-
tion of guilt and complicity is effectively countered by Højrup's distinctive
narrative style, which sees to it that Ernst's lecture is repeatedly interrupted
by the almost comically puncturing interjections and quoted responses of
his confused friends. In what follows, we first hear Ernst and then hear the
baffled responses of two of his verbally abused companions: "You're floating
around in your ridiculous inflatable swim ring, with your drink, and people
are drowning left, right, and center, he said, and it's not that they're out of
sight, it's that you've chosen not to see them. I haven't actually got a swim
ring, I said. We're just on vacation, said Ib" (Højrup 2017, 174).[8]

Narratively speaking, this is not a moment of transcendence. If Højrup's
novel, in general, contemplates the encounter between an overwhelming
sense of guilty relationality and notions of everything in life that ought to
be straightforward and simple, this problem is transfigured in the narrative
structure into a play of the high-flown and the flat. What we witness in this
scene, then, is not an awed response to the rendering of a sublime system of
global, capitalist entanglement. Rather, in terms of emotion and style, it is a
sort of stupefying slapstick.[9] This coexistence of high-flown and disarming
affective tonalities is a distinctive feature of skeptimental hypocrisy literature.
The puncturing of the high-flown is a tonal aspect of the skeptimental mutation in the aesthetic of sympathy.

Everyday Crises

In Lone Aburas's 2017 novel *Det er et jeg der taler (Regnskabets time)* (It is an I
speaking [The hour of reckoning]), we get to know an individual consciousness
that is explicitly situated in contemporary Copenhagen and furiously preoccupied with all manner of structurally unjust issues—especially the hypocrisies
generated by Scandinavian-style racism, imperialism, and neoliberalism. The
book is no more than forty-five pages long, thus resembling the form of the
political pamphlet, and its self-declared "agitprop" genre immediately raises
questions about literature, commitment, and action. While it thus picks up on
the theme of Aburas's previous novel, *Politisk roman* (Political novel, 2013), *Det
er et jeg der taler* has no patience for fiction, it tells us. "Bloated and satiated
with literary conscience," the first-person narrator—an author-I resembling
Lone Aburas herself—wants to "write a text that is free from fictions and
heaving insight" (Aburas 2017, 45).[10] The subtitle, *Regnskabets time* (The hour of

reckoning), is a precise label insofar as what goes on in the book is an impatient and complex settling of accounts. Reprimands are handed out liberally to politicians, intellectuals, and daycare workers alike, but the narrator also admits to owing several difficult debts herself.

Halfway through the book, refugees start featuring as addressees and recurring points of reference, first introduced by the seemingly casual subordinate clause "and now springtime is already here and the refugees are again drowning in the Mediterranean" (Aburas 2017, 27).[11] In *Det er et jeg der taler* we find several of the condensed commodity recognition scenes that primarily function in hypocrisy literature to denote unfathomable disparity and the overwhelming sense of entanglement in the system that is responsible for it. We also find variants of the complicity trope of the sea that we saw in *Til stranden*. Consider this example: "I hate hating so much, and that you can get pizza made with Mediterranean water down in the old Meatpacking District, given the situation" (Aburas 2017, 35).[12] Like the poem-subject that speaks in Norwegian poet Cathrine Grøndahl's "Prisen for et dikt" (The price of a poem, 2008), the writerly narrator of Aburas's agitprop pamphlet tends to find her own poetic endeavor perverse, given the situation.

What is the refugee crisis doing in *Det er et jeg der taler*? First, it adds significantly to the urgency of the accounts to be settled, to the historical time of the subtitle's hour of reckoning: Payback time is our time! Second, it transforms *Det er et jeg der taler*, which had been busy pointing at the hypocrisy and shamelessness of other people, into a case of hypocrisy literature, a literary discourse of the beneficiary. With the trope of migration, the literary tone of anger and moral self-confidence is complemented with an exhausted and sorrowful rendering of the puncturing fact of experiencing complicity. Now, for all its resoluteness, *Det er et jeg der taler* is also beset with the hypocrite's repertoire of "ugly feelings": "I don't want to benefit from the misfortune of others. I don't want to use suffering for anything other than what it is, but even buying organic in the grocery store, taking expensive yoga classes down on trendy Ryesgade feels like a felony" (Aburas 2017, 33).[13]

This is a moral consciousness looking aghast at its own immoral conditions of existence, according to which even small and "positive" elements of everyday life constitute an offense to someone somewhere. In *Det er et jeg der taler* we again find the skeptimental puncturing of high affective intensity: The subject who hates also feels chronically guilty (albeit not for hating). As an affective index, then, *Det er et jeg der taler*, like other works of hypocrisy literature, confirms Bartky's observation that "the recognition that one is guilty of complicity is not incompatible with righteous indignation or with feelings of solidarity with the victims of injustice" (2002, 135). In this manner, the experience of complicity portrayed by *Det er et jeg der taler* is an only apparently paradoxical structure of feeling in which terror, anger, and hate are coupled with exhaustion, shame, and guilt. For all its agitation and its calls for action, Aburas's pamphlet testifies most profoundly to an obstructed political, if not literary, agency.

Let us include in this archive of hypocrisy fiction, also, the Swedish author Negar Naseh's novel *De fördrivna* (The displaced, 2016), closely related in many ways to Højrup's *Til stranden*. The narrative of *De fördrivna* plays out in Sicily, where the Swedish couple Miriam and Filip spend their parental leave with their little daughter, having left the cold of Stockholm for the heat, the sea, and the solitude of Southern Italy. Filip, an artist, works in the studio on the grounds; Miriam, an anesthesiologist, is to return to work on her thesis on pain relief as soon as Filip takes over parental leave. To Miriam, spending her sleep-deprived days in the heat with an abundance of alcohol and concern for her daughter's well-being, however, these plans all feel very far away. The mood of *De fördrivna* is at once lazy and tense, and the tension rises when Ashkan and Erika visit from Stockholm. Ashkan is Filip's good friend and, like Ernst in *Til stranden*, a committed photojournalist with a keen interest in the refugee situation in the Mediterranean. Refugees now begin to haunt the conversations between the four friends, whose stay in Southern Europe is a matter of both business and pleasure. During their stay in Sicily, Ashkan wants to visit Lampedusa to photograph the island's cemetery for refugees.

The collective, discursive negotiation of the predicament of privilege depicted in this novel is absolutely recognizable from the wider archive of hypocrisy literature. Miriam just can't stomach Ashkan "lecturing" her on her "white melancholy," but his lecture makes an impression on her nevertheless: She feels judged, becomes unsure of whether or not her way of life is okay, and maybe she really *did* need to read that book about the refugee situation Ashkan talks so much about? (Naseh 2016, 68–71). This anxious communal dance around questions of knowledge, nonknowledge, commitment, and the scant possibility of living a justified life is a familiar social situation in and outside of Scandinavian hypocrisy fiction alike.

Yet in its portrayal of Filip, the novel's third-person narrator offers an account of a disposition far less familiar to the cultural archive of the predicament of privilege. Consider, for instance, this insight into Filip's calm attitude upon contemplating his friend's critical assessment of his way of life: "He [Filip] has no problem with Ashkan judging Filip and looking down on his bourgeois way of life, something Filip has been aware of for a long time now. On the contrary, he thinks it is quite a relief that someone reacts to how he lives his life and to the great privileges that condition his existence. It's nice to be reminded of that. He forgets it easily" (Naseh 2016, 132).[14] Filip, this representative of the creative upper middle class in equality-loving Sweden, has "no problem" with "the great privileges that condition his existence"! In Ruben Östlund's *The Square*, we saw a very different representation of a Stockholm art scene preoccupied by demonstrating social commitment in artistically clever, and thus skeptimental, ways.

The literary scholar Åsa Arping remarks about Filip's disposition, "His basic attitude remains that he is worthy of his success and privileged life" (Arping 2022, 182). I agree with Arping when she suggests that Filip, with "his consistent refusal to let himself be convinced to act in the service of 'goodness,'" represents a contrast to the humanitarian disposition that Ashkan and, increasingly, Miriam come to embody in *De fördrivna* (2022, 83).[15] However, the contrast (to a humanitarian disposition) represented by Filip does not represent the ordinary skeptimental modification of sentimental humanitarian reason that is my focus in this study. Rather, Filip's joyful and unequivocal embrace of his privileges is depicted as being so foreign to the social milieu with which the novel is engaged that his comportment comes across as almost sociopathic.

Filip's way of standing outside of his own time, as it were, is hinted at by the narrator in several instances. For instance, Filip and Miriam are not too pleased with the publication of a significant artist interview featuring him in a notable art magazine. Both discern in it an underlying criticism "against Filip's lack of awareness of his own position." Reading the interview, its framing of him as an artist seems to them to convey that he "appeared incapable of comprehending the power he possesses" (Naseh 2016, 169).[16] Thus, in the interview's interpretation of Filip, Miriam and Filip both detect something socially disagreeable—"his cluelessness" (169).[17] What I want to emphasize here about *De fördrivna*, then, is that the novel's sketch of a Scandinavian subject position seemingly untouched by the predicament of privilege describes a position that appears, contextually, to be socially clueless.

It Is a We Speaking

In this part of my study, my assumption has been that the predicament of privilege is also a predicament of criticality. We have seen that hypocrisy literature is concerned with the recognizable everyday aspects of the predicament of privilege and that giving a recognizable account of this predicament of privilege is even a method of this literature. We saw that hypocrisy literature's demonstrative doubt about the critical value of generating this recognizability indicates that being in doubt about one's criticality is part of the recognizable picture of life as hypocrite. However, the literature's keenness for the recognizable is also a way in which to focus on the predicament of privilege not as simply an idiosyncratic and private predicament but as a communal predicament—or, better, a predicament of community.

Surely, a recognizable predicament is not necessarily a communal predicament. Conversely, a communal predicament should be made recognizable as such in order to be experienced as being communal. In this sense, the literary representation of the predicament of privilege as a common condition is a way of drawing out the contours of a collective subject that has not really found its voice outside of this literary genre. In hypocrisy literature, however, this collective hypocrite subject is also brought out through complicit narrative styles: narrative forms that collectivize the complicity in various ways; narrative forms that implicate narrators, other characters, readers, as well as authors, in the hypocritical character's experience of his or her hypocritical life. While hypocrite narratives often start from a clearly situated protagonist's sense of hypocrisy, this literature also endeavors to engender correlations between the individually situated subject and a more inclusive subject, a situated *we*. This literary endeavor to involve, include, and implicate only rarely refers to a preexisting "we" but, rather, narratively collectivizes the complicity. To round off this chapter, let us look at a couple of examples.

In both of Kirsten Hammann's novels about Mette, *Fra smørhullet* and *En dråbe i havet*, complicity is also a problem of form. The literary historian Dan Ringgaard (2009) has discussed two distinct narrative moves in these novels, which I suggest we regard as two central elements in the novels' literary work on complicity and hypocrisy. Firstly, Ringgaard points to Hammann's characteristic way of letting her characters express themselves through the vocabulary and phrasing of a third-person narrator. Central to this narrative move, Ringgaard argues, is the impression that the narrator has covered the distance to the narrated person so that "narrator and narrated can be present at the same time" (2009, 76).[18] It is this simultaneous presence of the third-person narrator and Mette that we encounter as the hypocrite subject's superego. Thus, the overall tone of irony, belittling, and angry desperation in these novels appears to be a composite affect shared by Mette and the narrator. Employing my own conceptual framework, we may say that this distinct literary strategy makes the narrator an accomplice: someone who is complicit with what is being narrated. Secondly, Ringgaard notes that the protagonists Mette and Mette are more ordinary as characters than the protagonists in Hammann's earlier works, such as *Vera Winkelvir* (1993), *Bannister* (1997), and *Bruger De ord i kaffen?* (Do you take words in your coffee?, 2001). There is something distinctively "familiar and common finding its voice through Mette, who then speaks through the narrator," Ringgaard writes (2009, 76).[19] As he sees it, Hammann has thereby gained access to layers of collective consciousness. I agree, and I would suggest that, given something common and familiar seems to be speaking through Mette and Mette, they are thus also speaking about an *us*. We might say that Hammann's novels treat their readers as being no less complicit than their characters and their narrators.

In *Til stranden*, Peter Højrup has built up several layers in the narrator's representation of the thoughts and exchanges within the group of friends. One example is the integration of different tenses in a single representation of thought, as here in Linn's reflection on Ernst's complicity rant: "Drunk fool, I thought, thinks Linn" (Højrup 2017, 178).[20] However, stratification in the narrative integrates not only various specifications of time but various subject positions, too. Three of the five friends have previously lived in a commune together, and in general *Til stranden* takes an interest in the collective novel and the ways in which this genre effects a collective consciousness. On one hand, the book is divided into sections with headings such as "Herman, sunset" or "Linn indecisive," signaling perhaps, on the face of it, that the narrated experiences of hypocrisy are "a matter of individualizing psychological 'perspective'" (Ngai in Rasmussen and Sharma 2017). On the other hand, it is as if the narrative rounds up the individual characters in all sorts of ways; not only do they exist as a group at the same time and place but they also seem to exist in a communal, skeptimental consciousness. Quoted speech embedded in quoted interior monologue is a favorite device in Højrup's reproduction of dialogue and thought. An example from another passage recalling Ernst's tirade: "Why do you care so much about food, he said to me, thinks Ib and glances at a sparrow, which has landed on the cake plate. Why do you care so much about wine and about cars and shirts and ridiculous suits that cost a fortune, Ernst said and pointed at me, Herman thinks" (2017, 175).[21] This multiplication of the layers of narrative reporting has the effect of tangling the individual characters and their points of view, generating, as it were, a social ensemble intimately implicated in each other's thinking, sensing, and doing.

Another example of the organizing of various consciousnesses, stances, subject positions, and attitudes in one single narrative stream is found in the Danish author Hanne Højgaard Viemose's hypocrite novel *HHV, Frshwn: Dødsknaldet i Amazonas* (HHV, Frshwn: The deathfuck in Amazonia, 2019), which along with Viemose's previous books *Hannah* (2011) and *Mado* (2015) compose a trilogy about the persona Hanne Højgaard Viemose. The way in which the trilogy approaches the matter of an individual's boundaries is another story altogether: in *HHV, Frshwn*, for example, the protagonist, the authorial narrator Hanne, also goes under the names Hannah, Anita, Hanuta, Hanella, Hinterbella Hüüfgarden Viemoza, h, Ana Viemoza, and Ana Doloroza. Here the boundaries of the mind, the body, and the nation-state are each porous in their own, yet often overlapping, ways. For instance, at the beginning of the fifth chapter, the point in time is specified thus: "As I've said, it was that crazy autumn when the refugees came wandering up the southern Danish highways, I'd just been let out of the psych unit, was trying to get an everyday life up and running, keep the anxiety at bay, and walking was part of my new routine" (Viemose 2019, 89).[22]

In December 2016, the protagonist spends Christmas with her family in Reykjavik, Iceland, but is "in a dreadful mood, can't think about anything except the kids burning in Aleppo," and she slips away from all the Christmas palaver and goes to a demonstration in support of the people under siege in Syria (Viemose 2019, 143).[23] After the demonstration, during which the hypocrite-I cannot avoid doubting the point of "50 people in the dark and rain on a little dark square in a downpour on a little island in the North Atlantic" and is again overpowered by "the burning kids' screams, rage and impotence," the narrative is suddenly taken over by an exchange between the first-person and a skeptical interlocutor, who has no name and is not really one of the novel's characters (Viemose 2019, 144–45).[24] The dialogue ends:

Why won't you talk about anything?
What do you mean?
Refugees.
Makes me so tired.
. . .
It's a shame you stood there crying in the rain.
Stop it.
It's a shame it was dark, so no one could see your tears.
Pff.
But still, it's great you're writing a book about it. (Viemose 2019, 148)[25]

As we have seen from previous examples, skeptimental scenes are characterized by a situation in which the reflexive moment in the experience of a touching object manifests itself not as a hot tear but rather as a distrustful nagging. Something apparently morally important is experienced as morally embarrassing. The dialogue just quoted expresses a skeptimentalization of the Hanne-subject's distraught and solicitous empathy insofar as here the experience of solicitude stimulates a "negative" metaresponse in the narrative. In this manner, the skeptimental structure of feeling is indicated narratively by the polyphony of this skeptimental ambivalence.

In hypocrisy literature, I am arguing, complicity and collectivity are always also formal issues. We see this reflected, for instance, in Hammann's doublings of Mette the hypocrite, in Højrup's layering of interjections, and in rendering common the otherwise markedly individual point of view in Aburas's *Det er et jeg der taler*. We have also noted how the ambivalence underpinning skeptimentality shows up in hypocrisy literature as multivoiced narrative, in the sense that two or more positions of enunciation are active in a single voice. In this manner, skeptimentality comes to the fore as a shared sensibility: One result of these narrative styles is that discrete positions, consciousnesses, and attitudes commingle into a shared "hypocrite subjectivity."

To my mind, then, critique under conditions of complicity, the trajectory of hypocrisy literature, comes to be a matter of facilitating questions not so easily posed outside this literary genre: What do hypocrites want? If these globally privileged subjects could in fact articulate a "we," a collective subject responding to their shared sense of injustice, what, then, would be their political aims? As I see it, this is one reason why hypocrisy literature is critical: In probing the collective organization of "hypocrites," it also provokes questions about the dormant and unconventional political possibilities of privilege-sensitive publics.

The Unfinished Business with Inequality

IN THE INTRODUCTION to his book *A Brief History of Equality* (2022), Thomas Piketty sums up some of the main lessons from the economic and social history he has been unearthing, including his overall argument that the world has seen a "long-term movement toward equality" since the latter part of the eighteenth century. According to Piketty, this movement is mainly the result of "conflicts and revolts against injustice"—that is, revolts against inequitable institutions supported by the dominant classes. "Generally speaking," Piketty writes, "the most fundamental transformations seen in the history of inegalitarian regimes involve social conflicts and large-scale political crises. It was the peasant revolts of 1788–1789 and the events of the French Revolution that led to the abolition of the nobility's privileges. Similarly, it was not muted discussions in Paris salons but the slave revolt in Saint-Domingue in 1791 that led to the beginning of the end of the Atlantic slavery system" (Piketty 2022, 10). While, in Piketty's view, continued social struggles over power relationships do not in themselves suffice to build egalitarian societies, the historical lesson nevertheless remains clear: The abolition of unjust privileges is in general forged from below, by the unprivileged, not through the quiet conversations of the classically privileged.

I begin this coda by referring to this historical lesson as summed up by Piketty not to dispute it but, rather, to put into stark contrast one last time the fuzzy political subjectivity of the globally privileged *and* privilege-sensitive subject of this book: the middle classes of twenty-first-century Scandinavia. As we have seen, the predicament of privilege is often encountered as a moral and affective problem—or, more precisely, as a crisis in the affective logic of the moral sentiments. However, in examining the predicament of privilege in some detail, I have wished to bring about an *a*moral reevaluation of this predicament and the skeptimental qualms at its heart. By tracing the dilemmas and trouble that the predicament spells for the ways the subject feels, sees, (ac)counts, and critiques, I have wanted to take seriously these privilege-qualms, the material relevance of which is, in general, written off in both public and private discourse. In ways parallel to the feeling of envy, which has been significantly reassessed by Sianne Ngai, privilege-qualms have, like envy, been "subjectivized or psychologized in a way that perpetually renders the objectivity of its object (inequality) vulnerable to epistemologic doubt" (Ngai in Rasmussen and Sharma 2017). Articulations of discontent with being unjustly privileged are most often derided as either self-congratulatory or self-flagellatory, or both. This is the case even though the relation of inequality to which privilege-qualms respond is "a brute fact and not a matter of individualizing psychological 'perspective'" (Ngai in Rasmussen and Sharma 2017).

The concept of "skeptimentality" has played an important part in my analysis of the predicament of privilege and the cultural articulations to which it gives rise. Skeptimentality names a mode of responsivity that both departs from sentimentality and maintains a connection to it as its modification or interruption. In Nordic public arenas, I have argued, the noble moral sentiments have a propensity for changing sign and appearing to be indicative instead of something *im*moral in the feeling subject, be this subject an individual or a collective. Unlike the "positive" metaresponse we associate with the sentimental mode, in skeptimentality the "negative" metaresponse instead indicates that to feel morally good, for instance about "doing good," is in fact morally embarrassing. Skeptimentality thus names a certain moral embarrassment. And this embarrassment concerns a perceived sentimental (and thus self-charitable) charge in the ways in which the subject relates to global inequality and to her own place and part in this unequal world.

I regard this modification in sensibility as politically relevant because, as Judith Butler reminds us, "new moral sentiments are bound up with new moral judgments" (Butler 2013, 103). To humanitarian (sentimental) sensibilities, global economic hierarchies may seem politically unproblematic and thus acceptable. Here the focus is on helping, typically by donating, and as we saw in the discussion in chapter 3 of *Danmarks indsamling*, it is not exceptional to think that the better off you are, the more you are able to help.

To skeptimental sensibilities, however, global economic hierarchies pose a problem. In this manner, skeptimental sensibility marks, I have argued, an interruption in humanitarian sensibility and its forms of care, whose contingent nature is thus intuited. This is, in my opinion, one of several reasons why the skeptimental sensibility of privilege and its feelings of inequality deserve our attention.

While writing this book and considering the political significance of the predicament of privilege, I have found Ariella Aïsha Azoulay's book *Potential History: Unlearning Imperialism* from 2019 to be good company. Admittedly a far more radical framework for engaging with unearned privilege than the skeptimental publics of Norden might warrant, Azoulay's depiction of a political principle of differentiality with which the privileged classes must reckon is nonetheless an apt portrayal of the differential principle perceived, alleged, and to some extent resisted by skeptimental publics. Still a template for political regimes today, "the differential principle" was, Azoulay argues, invented and instituted historically with colonial and imperial forms of exploitation based on a fundamental "differential body politic." One key argument in *Potential History*, as in Azoulay's writing in general, is that this differential principle cannot be dismantled by focusing on "dispossessed and oppressed groups" alone. "Unlearning the effects of differential rule," Azoulay contends, "means accounting for its abusiveness to the entire body politic, including citizens who constitute the privileged groups" (2019b, 37).

This assumption leads Azoulay to a critical discussion of the ways in which "the privileged groups" care for others, including humanitarian forms of caring. She writes:

> Members of the privileged class may be concerned about oppressed groups and even express solidarity with them, but they are prompted to shape such concern and solidarity as a humanitarian care for the lives and fates of the oppressed, and not as an objection to and rejection of the political regime under which they, too, are governed. Acts of solidarity, humanitarian assistance, and protest against abuse and the dispossession of others tend to fall short of a struggle against the principle of differential rule, if there is no claim to radically reconsider the structure and meaning of citizenship and no call to dismantle the major principles underlying a differential political regime (Azoulay 2019b, 37).

I have two reasons for referring here at length to Azoulay's critique of humanitarianism for its tendency to circulate a political principle of difference. Firstly, while the predicament of privilege and the skeptimental sensibility at its center does correspond to a sense of being subjected to, in being privileged by, differential rule, it only rarely amounts to "a struggle against the principle of differential rule." As we have seen, privilege sensibility does not in and of itself give rise to egalitarian or anti-imperial modes of responding to inequality. Rather, it sometimes triggers a bolstering of the differential principle and its effects. We saw this dynamic laid bare perhaps most evidently in Kristian von Hornsleth's *Hornsleth Village Project Uganda*, but this side of the skeptimental coin will be readily evident to anyone familiar with twenty-first-century Scandinavian public culture. While an altogether more radical side of that coin could have been unearthed by focusing more exclusively on cultural texts indicating that this is *not* okay, I have wanted in this study to identify and name the broader, and thus nonradical, *collective* sensibility that includes a wide range of responses to the central question, Is this okay? This remains, then, the inescapable equivocality of the skeptimental sensibility of privilege: In terms of transnational egalitarianism and solidarity, the prospects of skeptimental publics are, as you might expect, bound up with the ways in which such publics do not merely mistrust the sentimental charge of the humanitarian sentiments but also oppose the principles of differentiality that continue to structure the global hierarchies in which they find themselves.

Secondly, I wish to highlight a valuable position on sympathy detectable across Azoulay's work, and one that has been important to my study of late-humanitarian culture too. Humanitarian forms of care are insufficient, Azoulay seems to imply, not primarily because they are based on the moral sentiments of compassion and sympathy. Rather, they remain insufficient because they offer no objection to the political principles of differentiality and inequality that lie behind the dispossession, oppression, poverty, violence, and crises that animate humanitarian response. I take this distinction to be crucial for any discussion of solidarity and egalitarian ambition. With the concept of skeptimentality I have wanted to engage critically with this assumption prevailing within academic and public discourse alike: that the moral sentiments operate according to a self-charitable sentimental logic. This assumption is at best too unsubtle for our analytical purposes, and in the distinct conjuncture of twenty-first-century Scandinavia (as in other privilege-sensitive publics) it is simply ill-suited to make sense of the pre-dicament that privilege poses here. These acknowledgments are relevant, I suggest, not merely to the study of privilege-sensitive contexts but also to a more general reevaluation of sympathy and its "family of fine sentiments" (Solomon 2004).

Lauren Berlant's sentimentality trilogy has been important to *The Predicament of Privilege*. In this work, Berlant diagnosed sentimentality as unfin-ished business in US culture. In my study, the relevant unfinished business is the business in Norden with inequality. In sentimental publics, Berlant showed, sympathy and compassion for subaltern subjects function as "great equalizers" producing *a sense of* equality and universality—if, in reality, such equality is materially nonexistent. By contrast, a skeptimental public is a pub-lic that suspects that inequality is a precondition for the sentimental sense of equality. Skeptimental publics are thus different from sentimental ones, I have argued, in that they carry reservations about the politics of sentimen-tality according to which good, authentic feeling is the core of a just society. Members of skeptimental publics typically perceive expressions of morally virtuous sentiment as elements in asymmetrical power relations; to an egal-itarian imagination preoccupied with evaluating privilege, such expressions thus appear suspect. Yet, this skeptimental pause before sentimental politics, including the politics of humanitarianism, does not in itself call forth what Piketty calls "a new egalitarian coalition" (2020, 41). Rather, the discontent with the sentimental register has brought a vacuum in which the skepti-mental public now lacks a "positive" affective, moral, and political language for representing and intervening in inequality. If what Paul Gilroy calls "the hostility to sympathy" is, in terms of transnational egalitarianism, unpromis-ing, then where, we are left to ponder, might skeptimental publics take their caring moral sentiments after the discrediting of humanitarian reason.

In part 4, I asked about the kind of collective organization that the self-professed hypocrites and others struck by the predicament of their privilege could possibly forge. Could these globally privileged populations articulate a "we," a collective subject acting on their shared sense of injustice? What, then, would be their political aims? And who or what would be the antag-onist of this "we," if anyone or anything? Answering these questions would require imaginative work beyond the scope of this study, but I raise them to hone in, again, on the latent and deeply unconventional political prospects of skeptimental, privilege-sensitive publics.

In fact, John Lanchester, in the essay I referred to in chapter 12, offers one such image of the globally privileged as a political subject acting against their relative global privilege. Privilege is a relational condition, Lanchester points out in the essay; he goes on to relate the circumstance, highlighted by economists such as Branko Milanović, that while Western publics have to various degrees struggled with austerity measures in the aftermath of the 2008 credit crisis, the percentage of the world's population that lives in absolute poverty (as defined by the United Nations) decreased significantly over the same decade. While living standards of the lower and middle classes in "the developed world" seem to have flattened or even declined, the number of people living in poverty in "the developing world" has more than halved. Here, Lanchester refers, like Piketty, to the so-called "elephant curve" of global inequality in the period between 1980 and 2018. Overall, this period saw a revival of national and regional inequality nearly everywhere, including in the regions of North America and Europe, thus "reversing the historic trend toward ever greater equality" (Piketty 2020, 33). Yet according to the elephant curve, two groups in particular benefited from economic growth in this period: the groups below and above the global middle classes. This is how Piketty sums up the trend: "Inequality between the bottom and middle of the global income distribution has decreased, while inequality between the middle and top has increased" (2020, 26).

This fact leads Lanchester to a vision of a compound Western "we," a collective subject simultaneously globally advantaged and nationally disadvantaged, and whose agency reflects this politically ambiguous position. "What if," Lanchester asks hypothetically, "the governments of the developed world turned to their electorates and explicitly said this was the deal? The pitch might go something like this: We're living in a competitive global system, there are billions of desperately poor people in the world, and in order for their standards of living to improve, ours will have to decline in relative terms. Perhaps we should accept that on moral grounds: we've been rich enough for long enough to be able to share some of the proceeds of prosperity with our brothers and sisters" (Lanchester 2018, 8). The electorate's answer to this grand scheme, Lanchester imagines, would be something like, Okay, fine, but we are game only if the rich in our own societies, the 1%, will experience as large a decline as we will.

Importantly, this image of political capacity conjured up by Lanchester presupposes a convergence in the popular imagination of two collective subjects: the 99% and the relatively globally privileged. According to this image, they are a single collective subject. For this composite "we" to accept a flattening or even a decline in living standards (and thus to act collectively on the predicament of privilege), they would need, Lanchester envisions, concessions from the few, the 1%. With this fantasy, Lanchester thus offers up a political vision in which two systems of distributive justice, or two sides of the political brain—the national-regional side and a global side—inform each other. It assumes that the (re)distribution of resources will need to be thought along these different axes simultaneously.

In this manner, Lanchester takes seriously a certain will within the global North, or at least a tolerance, for transnational economic equality and justice. By locating this redistributive impetus with "the governments of the developed world," however, Lanchester arguably amplifies beyond reason the fantastic element of his vision. Why not uncover this impetus among the relatively privileged populations themselves? My study allows us to take into consideration as a social fact the sensibility of privilege among these populations. It allows us to consider their sense of indebtedness and their impatience with sentimental forms of care that seem only to reinforce the global inegalitarian regime. For instance, the choir of hypocrites that we met in part 4 would seem to suggest that an untapped egalitarian drive of this kind may be real even if we tend to regard it as fiction.

Integrating, in a manner akin to Lanchester's vision, transnational egalitarian narratives with national narratives would be one way of addressing and responding to the fundamental misalliance between the two distinct Scandinavian discourses on privilege I identified in the introduction: two different ways of thinking and feeling about privilege, both of which organize Scandinavian senses of self and collective agency. According to one of these two frameworks, the discourse of benevolent internationalism, Nordic global privileges and the asymmetric relationships to which they refer are in fact *unproblematic*. According to the other interpretative framework, the discourse of the Nordic welfare model, privileges are always, in principle, a *problematic*. My suggestion was that the particular Scandinavian configuration of the predicament of privilege results from the deep-seated mismatch between these two different cultural and political interpretations of privilege, both of which play a constitutive role for prevailing self-images of Scandinavian societies. The Nordic sensibility of privilege is a response to the global inequality regime in which we now live. More specifically, it is a response to a failure of these two political discourses and systems of distributive justice to form, in a globalized world, an egalitarian narrative that speaks to both sides of the political brain and its senses.

Piketty would agree, I think. In an era of globalization, he argued in *Capital and Ideology*, the "frame within which political action is imagined must be permanently rethought," and the context of social justice "must be explicitly global and transnational (2020, 41). It is, exactly, the failure of post-war social democracies (and to Piketty, Sweden is "the quintessential social democracy") in Europe and the United States "to devote sufficient thought to alternative ways of organizing the global economy and transcending the nation-state" that bears much of the responsibility for the inegalitarian pressures of globalization and the return of inequality since the 1980s (2020, 39–40). Northern Europe has not escaped this development toward more inequality, although, according to Piketty, "the European social-democratic model seems to offer greater protection than other models (especially the meager American social state)" from these inegalitarian pressures (2020, 491). Prominent among the ideological failures of social democracies, Piketty suggests, is their "inability to conceptualize or organize progressive taxation and redistribution at the transnational level. During the period of successful redistribution at the national level, social democrats largely avoided this issue. To date they have never really grappled with it even at the level of the European Union, much less globally" (2020, 40). In sum: Social-democratic societies gave up the demand to redistribute wealth and income; they gave up on updating their egalitarian narratives.

It is not overly speculative, I suggest, to understand the skeptimental sensibility of privilege as a response to this ideological failure of the social-democratic model to grapple harder with income and wealth redistribution at especially, but not solely, the transnational level. As I suggested in the preface—referring to Piketty's claim that "no human society can live without an ideology to make sense of its inequalities"—the cultural work carried out by skeptimentality consists, precisely, in trying to make sense of privilege and inequality in a global context (2020, 1034). My study suggests that if sentimental humanitarianism was a preferred such ideology in the latter part of the twentieth century, to the skeptimental publics in Norden the alliance between the Nordic welfare state model and the "Scandinavian humanitarian brand" no longer gives the impression of an egalitarian coalition (Bengy Puyvallée and Bjørkdahl 2021).

In the Scandinavian societies, the history of the welfare state and the profound self-understanding as extraordinarily egalitarian societies give eminent legitimacy to the preoccupation with nonhierarchical social formations. This is one of the reasons why the culture of this region provides us with such a distinct profile of the predicament of privilege and its skeptimental ways. Skeptimental culture serves to indicate the unfinished business with inequality in the region. By paying closer attention to this culture—and the ways of feeling, seeing, (ac)counting, and critiquing it renegotiates—one can at least begin to probe the complex, sometimes feeble, sometimes robust, attachments of privilege-sensitive publics to egalitarian notions of distributive justice not met by the postwar social-democratic ambitions and even less acknowledged by the present political field.

Notes

PREFACE AND ACKNOWLEDGMENTS

1. I do not, however, employ Piketty's term *inequality regime*, by which he means "a set of discourses and institutional arrangements intended to justify and structure the economic, social, and political inequalities of a given society" (Piketty 2020, 2). In Piketty's terms, an "inegalitarian ideology" is a theory that explains and naturalizes the social inequalities between the different social groups in the regime in question (2020, 14).
2. Piketty would not necessarily agree, however, that humanitarianism is in fact an inegalitarian ideology.

INTRODUCTION. IS THIS OKAY?

1. See Neutral's "Certified Responsibility" web page, accessed May 2023, https://neutral.com/pages/certificates: "It doesn't save the world. It doesn't make us better. But it's reasonable. And that makes it okay."
2. The historical shifts in meaning between emotional terms such as *sentimentality*, *sentiment*, and *sensibility* will not be important to what follows—they have been analyzed by, among others, Janet Todd in *Sensibility: An Introduction* (1986, 6–9). Like Todd, Julie Ellison stresses both the interchangeability and the historical development of terms: "In its day, 'sensibility' was part of a cluster of closely related terms. 'Sensibility,' 'sensitivity,' 'sympathy,' and 'sentiment' were often interchangeable. These words could be used as synonyms *and* they could mark real distinctions" (Ellison 2012, 37). Importantly, Ellison also describes a shift early in the eighteenth-century Anglo-American political tradition, not primarily between the differences in meaning of the various terms but rather between, on the one hand, an understanding of sensibility as something characterizing relationships between socially equal persons and, on the other hand, an understanding of sensibility as something characterizing "scenarios of inequality" (Ellison 1999, 6). My study of Scandinavian privilege sensibility is, in extension of this last tradition, about the affects of inequality.
3. "Dette diktet sysselsetter / en dagmamma fra Marokko / og en vaskehjelp fra Polen / Det snakker for 350 kr timen / på bekostning av / små barn og fattige kvinner / som ikke kan språket / Hvis dette diktet virkelig setter så stor pris på ord, / bør det vel gi dem videre til andre? / Ikke bare stå der og prate / men gi det norske barnet et barnerim / passe det marokkanske / så moren kan lære

seg norsk / og betale vaskehjelpen for å lese Wislawa Szymborska på polsk" (Grøndahl 2009, 65). Unless otherwise noted, translations into English of texts in Swedish, Norwegian, and Danish are mine.

4. For an analysis of "Prisen for et dikt" and other privilege-sensitive poems in Grøndahl's oeuvre, see Linhart 2017.

5. I am grateful to the literary historian Isak Winkel Holm for this observation. Lauren Berlant's concept of genre is important for my use of the term. "Genres," Berlant writes in *Cruel Optimism*, "provide an affective expectation of watching something unfold, whether that thing is in life or in art" (2011, 20).

6. In fact, Fassin emphasizes that humanitarian reason is not only active in designated humanitarian domains but also, he shows, traverses the domestic management of asylum and immigration in France and scenes of epidemics, disasters, and conflicts in places like South Africa, Venezuela, and Palestine. In his book *Moral Abdication: How the World Failed to Stop the Destruction of Gaza*, Fassin hones in on the current war on Gaza and challenges the inclination in mainstream media to describe the situation as a humanitarian crisis. In this case, to speak of a humanitarian crisis is to "avoid naming things for what they are, by designating the effects without stating the cause; and to justify a demand for 'humanitarian corridors and pauses' while permitting the continued bombardment of civilians in apparent respect for international law" (Fassin 2024, 86).

7. Fassin describes moral sentiments as "the emotions that direct our attention to the suffering of others and make us want to remedy them" (2012, 1).

8. It is customary to distinguish between a longer and a shorter history of humanitarianism, the first of which "relates to the emergence of moral sentiments in philosophical reflection, and subsequently in common sense, in Western societies from the eighteenth century onward" (Fassin 2012, 4). For a deeper genealogical framework, including "aspects of ancient traditions of charity," "the history of European imperialism," and "the Enlightenment and the nineteenth-century idealization of progress," see Craig Calhoun's "The Idea of Emergency" (2010, 53). For a mapping of three distinct phases of humanitarianism, see Michael Barnett (2011). For a critical perspective on "the Europe-centered depiction of the origins of humanitarian law and the international refugee regime, the foundations of humanitarian reason, and the basis of professional expertise," see Arzoo Osanloo and Cabeiri deBergh Robinson (2024, 5).

9. To name only a few, see Hunt 2007; Festa 2006; Feldman and Ticktin 2010; Roy 2010; Barnett 2011; Weizman 2011; Chouliaraki 2013; Malkki 2015; Puar 2017; Moyn 2012; Ticktin 2011; Davey 2015; Abu-Lughod, Hammami, and Shalhoub-Kevorkian 2023; Osanloo and Robinson 2024.

10. Calhoun writes of this development that "the field of humanitarian response to emergencies entered a phase of dramatic growth amid the waning of 1960s-era protest politics. Many of the early protagonists were activists from the left who

grew disillusioned with more conventional programs for political and economic change. Humanitarianism was in a sense a way to retain the emotional urgency of 1960s politics, but in a form not dependent on any political party, movement, or state" (Calhoun 2010, 49). For detailed delineations of this late-modern humanitarianism, see for instance Eleanor Davey, *Idealism Beyond Borders: The French Revolutionary Left and the Rise of Humanitarianism, 1954–1988* (2015).

11. In *Casualties of Care* (2011), Ticktin studies the politics of compassion that marked the governing of immigration in France in the 1990s and 2000s, focusing in particular on the rise and fall of the so-called "illness clause," which stipulated that, at a time in which immigration policies were tightened, immigrants affected by serious illness could be granted temporary resident status.

12. See "The Creeping Criminalisation of Humanitarian Aid," *The New Humanitarian*, June 7, 2019, https://www.thenewhumanitarian.org/news/2019/06/07/creeping-criminalisation-humanitarian-aid.

13. The ACLU's full coverage of immigrants' rights and border patrol abuses ("ICE and Border Patrol Abuses," accessed March 2023) is available at https://www.aclu.org/issues/immigrants-rights/ice-and-border-patrol-abuses. See also the *Intercept* coverage of lawsuits against border enforcement agencies, which, according to the complaints filed, direct "surveillance, detention, intrusive searches accompanied by excessive physical restraint, and intensive interrogation at the border" against individuals "because of their lawful humanitarian activities." https://theintercept.com/2019/10/17/aclu-lawsuit-cbp-ice-journalists/.

14. In this vein, Fassin identifies a "double register of humanitarianism," in which humanitarianism in poor countries deals with mass initiatives for large populations, while the humanitarianism exercised in rich countries deals with the individual asylum seeker and his or her sympathy-eliciting story. For this double register to work, Fassin points out, the boundaries between the two worlds must be tightly sealed (2012, 253).

15. The advertisement announced to its Middle Eastern readers that, among other tightenings, "the Danish parliament has just passed a regulation to: Reduce the social benefits significantly. The social benefits for newly arrived refugees will be reduced by up to 50 percent" (Gormsen 2015).

16. "En mekanisme for overførsel af asylansøgere fra Danmark til Rwanda." The statement is available at the Ministry of Immigration and Integration: https://uim.dk/nyhedsarkiv/2022/september/danmark-og-rwanda-enige-om-faelles-erklaering/ (accessed March 2023).

17. This is a point made in various ways in the literature on humanitarianism. The literary historian Bruce Robbins's development of this point in his 2017 study, *The Beneficiary*, has been especially pertinent for my own thinking about the Scandinavian case. I thus return to Robbins's discussion of the "discourse of the beneficiary" in the chapters to come; see, especially, part 4.

18. For studies paying attention to the relations between the eighteenth-century sentimental novel and the emergence of human rights and humanitarian sensibility, see, for instance, Hunt (2007) and Festa (2006). For studies of the (Anglo-)American sentimental tradition, see studies by Glen Hendler (2001), Kyla Schuller (2018), Lori Merish (2000), Julie Ellison (1999), Lauren Berlant (2008), and June Howard (1999). While some of this literature is interested primarily in discussing sentimentality as a gendered cultural mode, most studies of American sentimentalism also examine its links to the abolitionist movement and the emergence of humanitarian sensibilities. Notably, Fassin designates our own historical period, the one of humanitarian government, as one "conducive to sentimentality" (2012, 5).

19. Sentimentality is often analyzed as what Raymond Williams calls a "structure of feeling" (Williams 1977; Hendler 2001; Howard 2020). I return in chapter 1 to the relevance of this concept for my way of conceptualizing skeptimentality.

20. I have learned to think about affective metaresponse in this way from Sianne Ngai, *Ugly Feelings* (2005; see, in particular, 6–11).

21. A politics of compassion, philosopher Alain Badiou argues in *Ethics* (2001 [1993]), regulates the global distribution of agency by distinguishing compassionate subjects from the objects of compassion, and in turn promotes the moral superiority of the Western responsible subject, who is capable of sympathetic feeling. Badiou asks, "Who can fail to see that in our humanitarian expeditions, interventions, embarkations of charitable *légionnaires*, the Subject presumed to be universal is split? On the side of the victims, the haggard animal exposed on television screens. On the side of the benefactors, conscience and the imperative to intervene. And why does this splitting always assign the same roles to the same sides?" (Badiou 2001, 12).

22. We may dismiss such humanitarian practices as self-deluding, politically flawed, narcissistic, and downright silly, but they nonetheless imply, Malkki insists, a kind of imaginative politics. Rather than focusing on the realpolitik and broader ideology of humanitarianism, Malkki studied Finnish Red Cross aid workers and Finns who knit soft toys for needy children in the developing world.

23. There is extensive scholarship on this discourse of Nordic exceptionalism. Some strands of this literature contest the objective validity of the Nordic brand, while others focus more on the status in world politics of the reputation-building of the Nordics. The Norwegian historian Terje Tvedt's work on the intellectual, cultural, and political history of Norway's "do-gooder regime" has played a prominent role in the study of Nordic exceptionalism (see, for instance, Tvedt 2002; 2018), as has the work of the Norwegian social anthropologist Marianne Gullestad. I return to these bodies of work in part 2.

24. Narratives of an innocent Scandinavian colonialism have been allowed to go rather unchallenged until the last two decades or so. Such narratives remain active in public discourse on the relationship of Denmark(-Norway) and Sweden to their former colonies, trading posts, and possessions in West Africa,

the Caribbean, Bengal, Greenland, Faroe Islands, Iceland, and North America, respectively. The idea of a *mission civilisatrice* seems characteristic also of Finland's self-image as a colonizer, internally, of its Sámi populations (Naum and Nordin 2013; Loftsdóttir and Jensen 2012; Keskinen, Skaptadóttir, and Toivanen 2019). The fact that both Denmark and Sweden were active in the transatlantic slave trade and exploited slave labor on the plantations in their possession is still a disputed problematic when raised in Nordic public culture (Nonbo Andersen 2017).

25. According to Esping-Andersen, the historical forces behind the Nordic welfare regimes include social democracy's capacity to shape a middle class devoted to universal welfare and income equalization. While political dominance in continental Europe before World War II was largely a question of rural class politics, the postwar consolidation of welfare states in turn depended on the alliances of the new middle classes: "The Scandinavian model relied almost entirely on social democracy's capacity to incorporate [the middle classes] into a new kind of welfare state: one that provided benefits tailored to the tastes and expectations of the middle classes, but nonetheless retained universalism of rights" (Esping-Andersen 1995, 31). See also Arter (2016), especially part 6, and Baldwin (1990).

26. For two methodologically distinct studies of the cultural foundations of the Norwegian and Danish welfare states, respectively, see Nina Witoszek's *The Origins of the "Regime of Goodness": Remapping the Cultural History of Norway* (2011) and Lasse Horne Kjældgaard's *Meningen med velfærdsstaten: Da litteraturen tog ordet—og politikerne lyttede* (2018).

27. A growing body of literature regards the Nordic welfare states as postimperial societies shaped by particular practices of subordination of indigenous peoples and ethnic minorities within the region as well as of populations in the Danish and Swedish colonies and possessions (Keskinen, Skaptadóttir, and Toivanen 2019; Naum and Nordin 2013; Loftsdóttir and Jensen 2012; Adler-Nissen and Gad 2014; Einhorn, Harbison, and Huss 2022; Nonbo Andersen 2017; Rud and Ivarsson 2021). See also Grete Brochmann, Anniken Hagelund, Karin Borevi, Heidi Vad Jønsson, and Klaus Petersen's *Immigration Policy and the Scandinavian Welfare State 1945–2010* (2012).

28. In fact, this distinction is not as clear-cut as suggested here: Norway, for instance, formed part of the imperial authority of Denmark-Norway until the Napoleonic wars, becoming the first successor state in the region upon independence in 1905. For an overview of the "making of modern Scandinavia" see Arter (2016), especially part 1, in which Arter discusses specifically the case of "the two mainland Nordic 'colonies' of Norway and Finland." For a comprehensive study of the Finnish case, sitting restlessly between imperial powers while also "colonizing internally" ethnic minorities, see *Finnish Colonial Encounters: From Anti-Imperialism to Cultural Colonialism and Complicity* (Merivirta, Koivunen, and Särkkä 2021).

29. For examples of this research, see also Oxfeldt (2016b); Oxfeldt and Bakken (2017); Dancus, Hyvönen, and Karlsson (2020); Oxfeldt, Nestingen, and Simonsen (2017); Körber (2018); Oxfeldt and Sharma (2018).
30. "Forstå kunstens, estetikkens og retorikkens rolle i å formidle skyldfølelsene."
31. "Hvorfor er det lige præcis den racistiske provokation, som 'frihed' i disse år bedst bevises igennem?"
32. According to this narrative of racial exceptionalism, "racism is a term reserved to describe acts of discrimination based on a belief in the biological difference and inferiority of people of other 'races,'" as Danbolt puts it; this "restricted and biological and intentionalist conceptualization of racism" contributes to the idea that racism "proper" is that which exists far removed in time and/or space (Danbolt 2017, 108).
33. "Med kampagnen vil vi også sige til danskerne, at det er OK at nyde et godt og trygt liv herhjemme med god samvittighed. Så længe man også af og til kigger op og ikke lukker døren for de mennesker, der bor i en verden, der hverken er tryg eller god."

CHAPTER 1. SKEPTIMENTALITY

1. "Nu kan det fanme være nok! Fordel så verdens velstand, så alle kan få! Hvorfor skal de, som var heldige at blive født på den rige jord, egentlig have lov til at blive boende?"
2. "Hun ved godt, det er latterligt og bare for at købe aflad, men det var alligevel vigtigt for hende at bevise over for sig selv at hun ville sætte handling bag ordene."
3. Solomon's own position on the sentimental logic of moral sentiments is that, while "tender emotions" such as sympathy and compassion are indeed pleasant to hold, because "we feel good about ourselves when we experience the tender emotions, and we feel even better when, reflectively, we perceive ourselves as the sort of people who feel such feelings," this doubling of moral-emotional uplift should be seen not in itself, he argues, as self-indulgence but rather as a form of reflection that is, he suggests, a precondition of an "examined life" (2004, 11–12).
4. One could argue that this kind of ambivalence is present already in any judgment of an object as being a sentimental one. As an instance of *judgment*, sentimentality seems to hinge on a reflexive relay between feeling moved by the object before us and then feeling, mildly or resolutely, repelled or manipulated by the now recognizably sentimental convention that caused the movement in the first place. This is what Jennifer L. Fleissner hints at when noting that "if the sentimental text *did* simply carry out its ends—if one were deeply moved by it, period—one would not use the word *sentimental* to characterize it; the use of the word automatically implies some distance from the sentimental effect" (Fleissner 2004, 166). In a similar vein, June Howard has pointed out that ascriptions of sentimentality "mark moments when the discursive pro-

cesses that construct emotion become visible." This is true, Howard suggests, for expert judgments and vernacular remarks alike (Howard 1999, 69). As a judgment, sentimentality thus involves an awareness of the social and aesthetic conventionality of what seems intimate and personal in our response.

5. The Law of Jante was devised by the Danish-Norwegian author Aksel Sandemose in his 1933 novel *En flygtning krydser sit spor* (A fugitive crosses his tracks). The basic premise of the ten rules is that the individual is nothing special; it is a cultural code of conduct aimed at safeguarding the greater good: It's not about you.

6. Other aspects of Williams's definition are less important to this book, including his emphasis that structures of feeling are social formations that are not yet articulate or manifest, but rather "emergent or pre-emergent" and "at the very edge of semantic availability" (1977, 132, 134).

7. In fact, as Sianne Ngai has pointed out, Williams did not really analyze emotion or affect but instead mobilized "an entire register of felt phenomena in order to expand the existing domain and methods of social critique" (Ngai 2005, 360).

8. As Sandra Lee Bartky notes, "The recognition of unearned privilege does not inevitably engender guilt feelings in the heart of the one privileged. The response might well be anger, or dismay. . . . My role in the maintenance of an unjust social order is a fact, *whether I recognize it or not*. Guilt, then, need not be felt as emotions are typically felt: it is an existential-moral condition that can be, but need not be accompanied by 'feeling guilty'" (Bartky 2002, 142; emphasis in original).

9. This is the case with landmark studies such as Didier Fassin's *Humanitarian Reason* (2012), Miriam Ticktin's *Casualties of Care* (2011), and Lynn Festa's *Sentimental Figures of Empire in Eighteenth-Century Britain and France* (2006), but it is true also for more positive assessments of humanitarian sensibility such as Lynn Hunt's *Inventing Human Rights* (2007) and Liisa Malkki's *The Need to Help* (2015). In his study of humanitarian iconography, Fuyuki Kurasawa employs the term *humanitarian sentimentalism* to account for a predominant "sentimentalizing mode of representation of humanitarian crises" (Kurasawa 2013, 206).

10. Julie Ellison even suggests that scholarly work on sentiment "has been a disproportionately American enterprise, carried out by American critics with reference to American literature" (Ellison 1999, 7).

11. I am thinking here of (Anglo-)Americanists such as June Howard, Julie Ellison, Saidiya Hartman, Laura Wexler, Dana Luciano, Elizabeth Freeman, Lauren Berlant, and Kyla Schuller, who have, each in their own way, contributed to our understanding of the importance of sentiment, sensibility, and sentimentality to the nineteenth- and twentieth-century North American publics. Scholarship on eighteenth-century France thus plays a decidedly smaller part in my study, although the work by Lynn Hunt and Lynn Festa

has been important to my examination of the sentimental constellations that sustain humanitarian sensibilities.

12. For a discussion of the nature of sympathetic identification, see literary historian Glenn Hendler's *Public Sentiments* (2001). The affective power of sympathetic identification, writes Hendler with reference to the nineteenth-century American sentimental novel, relies on a "fantasy of experiential equivalence" (Hendler 2001, 7).

13. *The Female Complaint* forms part of Berlant's national sentimentality trilogy, which includes also *The Anatomy of National Fantasy* (1991) and *The Queen of America Goes to Washington City* (1997). The primary focus in *The Female Complaint* is North American "women's culture," arguably the first identity-driven intimate public in the United States; since the 1830s it has functioned as a subcultural sphere in which women have cultivated and repaired their sense of belonging in a society, in which they actually were, and are, underprivileged. In Berlant's interpretation, sentimentality is thus a politics of suffering, which has its shared origins in the abolitionist protest culture and in the conventional, mass-produced "women's culture." In *The Queen of America Goes to Washington City*, Berlant addressed the general "intimization"—and thus also depoliticization—of the public sphere in the United States in the wake of President Ronald Reagan's moral-patriotic nationalism and the Bush administrations' "compassionate conservatism." Intimate publics are publics that provide people with a sense of emotional community, of being able to recognize and be reflected in one another's experiences, aspirations, worries, good fortune, and misfortune. In an intimate public, the individual's subjectivity feels general—one assumes that everyone is experiencing the same feelings. Just like other publics, an intimate public is mediated and structured by commodities, which circulate among strangers and facilitate intimate *insider*-talk, often a form of self-help interaction. In intimate publics, in other words, intimacy is mass-mediated. I discuss, in Danish, Berlant's work on "intimate publics" in Sharma (2019a).

CHAPTER 2. SKEPTIMENTAL PUBLICS

1. For instance, the Danish historian Thorkild Kjærgaard diagnosed a "false colony ideology" (*falsk koloniideologi*) that, according to him, potentiates those who feel guilt: "It has annoyed me as historian that today there is an insistence on speaking about Greenland as a colony. This started in the 1960s, as the result of anti-imperialist and anticolonial ideas. At that time, there was *political potential in claiming guilt about something*. Greenland was therefore fashioned as a Danish colony, and the Inuits, being the 'indigenous population,' were given the role of the oppressed and a people who should break free" (Baeré 2018; emphasis added). "Som historiker har det irriteret mig, at man i dag insisterer på at tale om Grønland som en koloni. Det er noget, der er kommet i 1960'erne som resultat af antiimperialistiske og antikolonialistiske ideer. På det tidspunkt var der politisk potentiale i at påstå, at man havde skyld over for

nogen. Derfor opfandt man Grønland som dansk koloni, og inuitterne fik som 'oprindeligt folk' rollen som undertrykte og som nogen, der skulle frigøre sig."

2. *Den Danske ordbog* (*DDO*, The Danish dictionary), specifies that the term *godhedsindustri* (benevolence industry) has been in use at least since 1995. *Den Danske ordbog* (online version, accessed May 8, 2025), under "godhedsindustri." Anker Brink Lund and Gitte Meyer (2016) list *godhedsindustri* in their lexicon of civil society on the grounds that what was originally meant as a derogatory term can also be used constructively in appealing to the benevolence industry to "make an effort to be better at sifting the good from the industrial. By, for example, generating realistic expectations rather than airy promises of the moon and the stars" (anstrenge sig for at blive bedre til at skille det gode fra det industrielle. Blandt andet ved at generere realistiske forventninger frem for luftige løfter om guld og grønne skove).

3. He did so in his much-discussed "open your hearts" speech (*öppna era hjärtan*); see, for example, the editorial in *Dagens Nyheter* newspaper, August 17, 2014 (in Swedish).

4. In this manner, it could be argued that *The Square* records the antihumanitarian turn we have seen in Nordic policy in the wake of the asylum crisis in 2015 and reflected in the alliances forged between Sverigedemokraterna (the Sweden Democrats) and other Swedish right-wing parties to produce new proposals for integration policies.

5. These fundamental questions also inform the notorious scene in which a performance artist imitating an ape harasses guests at a gala dinner held for the Swedish cultural aristocracy—a scene that will not, however, play a role in my analysis of the film.

6. In Östlund's work, as in the historical reality of Scandinavian publics, the concrete housing projects as symbol of the welfare-state promise of space for everyone embodies disappointment; the concrete apartment block has now become "ghetto" and, as such, the object of white middle-class fear and disdain. In a key scene, the Tesla-in-apartment-block scene, *The Square* goes along both with and against this fear of the projects.

7. Andreas Önnerfors offers a critical interpretation of the current invocations of the "political master concept *folkhemmet*" in Sweden, where it "informs a vision of the future *as* the past, a presumed golden age of purity undisturbed by 'the foreigner,' its diverging body, and its mentalities": "Since the origins and heydays of *folkhemmet* are placed in the period before the advent of mass migration to Sweden, my claim is that the concept is of exceptionally salient value in contemporary Swedish retrotopian political rhetoric" (Önnerfors 2022, 60–61).

8. According to Östlund's production company, *The Square* (*Rutan*) is an artwork originally created by Ruben Östlund and Kalle Boman for the city of Värnamo, Sweden, in 2015. See Melanie Goodfellow, "Ruben Östlund's Production Company Issues Apology to Argentinian Artist Cited in *The Square*," *Deadline*,

March 28, 2023, https://deadline.com/2023/03/ruben-ostlund-apology
-plattform-produktion-artist-lola-arias-the-square-1235310802/.

9. A speculative and scandalous approach in a mode similar to this particular
advertising strategy can, in reality too, be effective when addressing a skeptimental public—as we saw in 2017, for instance, when the then–Danish minister for
immigration and integration marked the tightening of new immigration curbs
with a celebratory cake. This type of racialized nationalism can find legitimacy
in the skeptimental structure of feeling, which in a number of instances seems
happier with the morally unseemly than with the "morally appropriate."

10. Later Christian does give the woman money, but this is mostly a case of relieved
guilt at having got his wallet back, on account of the threatening letters.

11. Christian ends up using violence against the boy, pushing him down a flight
of stairs. Afflicted by bad conscience, Christian then has to search for a cleaner
conscience by rummaging through a nasty pile of trash to find the boy's cell
phone number.

12. "Det, der gør filmen så frygtelig, er, at den for 117. gang optegner det samme
satiriske portræt af den privilegerede og elitære Generation X og deres åh-så-
tomme-og-kunstige-luksusliv. Vi gider ikke se på dem mere.... De tiggere, der
omgiver hovedpersonen og forgæves forsøger at råbe den privilegerede verden
op, hives aldrig for alvor ind i handlingsrummet. The Square foregiver—lige-
som så mange Generation X-forfattere—at være moralsk indigneret. Men i
virkeligheden er den hypernarcissistisk i sit fokus på, hvad det vil sige at være
en postmodernistisk, postironisk 45-årig person."

13. A standard definition of the hypocrite is "one who pretends to have feelings or
beliefs of a higher order than his or her real ones." *Oxford English Dictionary*
(online version, accessed May 8, 2025), under "hypocrite."

14. This immanent risk is implied also in Nikolaj Lübecker's interpretation of
Play, in which Östlund (according to Lübecker) needed first to stimulate the
stereotypes in order to incite "the race reading on which he wants us to reflect"
(Lübecker 2015, 108).

15. This is implied also by Lindqvist's contrasting of Andersson's films to the
"unrelenting naturalism, extreme close-up shots, and emotional high drama" in
the work of Danish director Susanne Bier.

16. "Operations," Boliden, accessed April 2025, https://www.boliden.com/operations/.

17. "Trial over Spanish Ecological Disaster Starts, 25 Years on," France 24, April 7,
2023, https://www.france24.com/en/live-news/20230704-trial-over-spanish
-ecological-disaster-starts-25-years-on.

18. Environmental Defender Law Center, accessed April 2025, https://edlc.org/.

CHAPTER 3. PRIVILEGE MONTAGE

1. The "Donor Without Borders" campaign epitomizes what the media scholar
Lilie Chouliaraki, in her 2013 study *The Ironic Spectator*, calls posthumanitarian communication. Chouliaraki employs the term *posthumanitarianism* to

signify a range of restructurings of humanitarian solidarity under conditions of neoliberalism—emotional, communicative, and ideological restructurings, the result of which is a solidarity meant to be of immediate benefit to the humanitarian benefactor. Posthumanitarian communication includes current "reflexive styles of appealing," in which the humanitarian benefactor is invited to reflect upon the contrasts that structure the relationship between herself and the beneficiary (Chouliaraki 2013).

2. "Med kampagnen vil vi også sige til danskerne, at det er OK at nyde et godt og trygt liv herhjemme med god samvittighed. Så længe man også af og til kigger op og ikke lukker døren for de mennesker, der bor i en verden, der hverken er tryg eller god."

3. "I Danmark er vi heldige, men sådan er det langt fra alle steder i verden. Der er sult, der er sygdom, der er krig, der er børn, der dør, der er mennesker på flugt. / Ja, og de har brug for vores hjælp."

4. "Lille land, stort hjerte."

5. "Vi er ligeglade med, om I donerer jeres penge til *Danmarks Indsamling*, fordi I gerne vil vinde premierne eller om I gør det af jeres gode hjerte."

6. "De vidste nemlig godt at det er svært at være verdens lykkeligste land, mens resten af kloden bløder. / Det var ikke, fordi de var perfekte, men de var virkelig i orden."

7. "Der er nogen, der synes, det er en ulækker måde at samle ind på. Men det vil jeg da skide på. . . . Jeg samler ind, som det passer mig."

8. By including a sketch that stands up for the morally inappropriate, *Danmarks indsamling* is also signaling, perhaps, that the show stands up for "the people" against the class-suffused "political correctness" of the elite. This framing then implicitly assumes that moral inappropriateness *is* actually characteristic of "the little man." This assumption is, however, thoroughly ridiculed by the personas adopted by the same comedy duo, Rytteriet, in their better known and equally skeptimental satire based on two wealthy and snobbish men who excel in "unlikable" and "morally inappropriate" jokes at the expense of the underprivileged members of society.

9. "Underholdningsprogram med rørende indslag."

10. Festa coined the literary trope *sentimental ventriloquism* to refer specifically to the metropolitan novelist or narrator speaking on behalf of the natives, the wretched, the poor, and the enslaved (Festa 2006, 12). However, sentimental ventriloquism is an apt description also of the focalizer's task in humanitarian communication.

11. Elaboration of sexual violence against women and children is a recurring story in many of these program items. Amid all the evocation of a shared humanity, the black man thus nevertheless figures, ghostlike, as perpetrator. For case studies and critical discussions of the tendency of humanitarian aid and communication to fetishize sexual violence, see Abu-Lughod, Hammami, and Shalhoub-Kevorkian (2023).

12. For matters addressed by the movement, see "Tidehvervs anliggende" (in Danish) on the periodical's website (accessed April 2025): https://tidehverv.dk/tidehvervs-anliggende-topmenu-41.

13. The *Tidehverv*-ian criticism of humanitarianism and human rights frequently takes the parable of the Good Samaritan (Luke 10: 23–37) as pretext for an understanding of "neighbor," which, according to the pastors and writers of the movement, contrasts sharply with the "sentimental" exegesis of the gospel underlying the lazy understanding of charity exhibited by the benevolence industry (and the established Danish church). To Krarup, Christian charity can never be formalized in social and political manifestos, because the real charitable deed is the exigency of the moment, free of policy statements and idealism. In a published sermon, for example, Krarup states, "Neighbor means the nearest. . . . The man on the other side of the globe is not my neighbor. The woman in a faraway country is not my neighbor." (Næste betyder den nærmeste. . . . Manden på den anden side af jordkloden er ikke min næste. Kvinden i et fjernt land er ikke min næste" [Krarup 2009, 171–72]). See Sharma (2017) for an analysis of *Danmarks indsamling*'s take on the parable.

14. "Hjælp børn uden hjem."

15. These car advertisements in the humanitarian format are a conspicuous example of what Lisa Richey and Stephano Ponte (2011) call brand aid: branded development interventions that not only give aid to development but also give aid to commodity brands. In chapter 3, I discuss the phenomenon of branded aid as well as its avatar in the art world, what I call brand aid art.

16. "Årets kjole til barnebruden / CE-mærket sminkesæt til den unge prostituerede."

CHAPTER 4. HUMANITARIAN SPECTATORSHIP

1. "De sad under de sene nyheder og så togene standse ved Padborg station og flygtninge løbe ud over markerne i et land de ikke kendte, et land de var bange for, *deres* trygge land hvor ingen skulle være bange. En ung mor løb med en lille dreng i den ene hånd og en rullekuffert i den anden, hun kunne ikke klare begge dele og gav slip på sin søn. En kvinde slog sig i ansigtet, små børn skreg fra det dybeste mørke, og store knægte løb som kalve. Lisa og Frederik tog hinandens hænder. De sad i deres stue og så ikke kun på fjernsynet, de så også på stuen og på hele deres hjem, på stuerne og værelserne hvor de boede."

2. As summed up by Rebecca A. Adelman and Wendy Kozol, "critical conversations about ethics and spectatorship that turn on analyses of images of spectacular harm often take the shape of a recursive debate about whether or not such images can inspire their spectators to awareness, sympathy, or action" (2014). The groundbreaking work in the field by Judith Butler (2009), Ariella Azoulay (2008; 2015; 2019b), and Eyal Weizman (2017), especially, marks a welcome break with received notions about the politics of visuality.

3. While Sontag's final book, *Regarding the Pain of Others* (2003), is concerned mostly with war photography and its modern history, in giving the book its

epigrammatic title Sontag also coined an umbrella term for a range of inqui-
ries into visual politics more broadly conceived, including the visual politics of
humanitarianism. In the latter part of the book, especially, Sontag scrutinizes
strongly held assumptions, including her own such assumptions in earlier
writings on photography, about the waning affects and effects of atrocity imagery in an era of apparent image bombardment. Wendy Hesford (2011) charts
crucial strands in the field of visual human rights studies that Sontag's work
helped establish; Sharon Sliwinski (2011) discusses the aesthetic encounters
between spectator and image that have shaped the history of human rights and
humanitarianism; Susie Linfield (2010) tracks the history of the hostility to the
medium of photography, which she finds to be reflected also in Sontag's work;
Mark Reinhardt profiles the "challenge to the aestheticization of suffering
in photographic representation" that "runs through much twentieth-century
criticism" (Reinhardt 2007, 14).

4. As far as we feel sympathy as spectators, Sontag suggests, "we feel we are
not accomplices to what caused the suffering. Our sympathy proclaims our
innocence as well as our impotence" (2003, 102). In a similar vein, the art
historian T. J. Demos writes that in a state of sympathy we tend to fashion a
false "proximity to the victimized that grants spectators distance from complicity in the wider situation of generalized economic inequality" (2011). For
all the lamenting of the sympathy-indulgent, innocent-feeling spectator, the
research literature also contains a considerable catalog of her guilty pleasures,
which include voyeuristic appetites, a taste for brutality, desiring sights of
pain and degradation, joys of apathy and indifference, and so on. Consider, for
instance, the art historian Griselda Pollock's description of the desensitizing
effect of the commodification of humanitarian images: "We want to see, but
from elsewhere, and so we send photographers into the most alarming and
dangerous places so that we might be able to see everything, the more extreme
the better, but at a protected and often aestheticizing second-hand. We hunger
for our daily doses of news reports, which must be filled with vivid images that
alone make us believe that this is reality" (Pollock 2007, 121). Pollock concludes
that the more we see, "the less we are able to respond affectively to what we are
shown. We have become inured to the pain of others in direct proportion to
our apparently insatiable need to be shown the horrors of the world and to be
exposed to the suffering of others" (2007, 121). I return to this discourse of "the
malady of spectating man" in chapter 6 (Rancière 2011b, 6).

5. "Sentimentality," Sontag notes, "notoriously, is entirely compatible with a taste
for brutality and worse" (Sontag 2003, 102).

6. Thus, I am leaving out of my picture important work on "humanitarian" visual
practices such as Weizman's (2009) discussions of the mediatized targeted
assassinations by remotely piloted drones in the Gaza Strip by the IDF (Israeli
Defense Forces) and Mark Duffield's (2018) analyses of the remote management of humanitarian crises by way of high-resolution satellite imagery.

7. See Fassin (2007) for a discussion of humanitarianism as biopolitics and "politics of life"; see Weizman (2009) for a discussion of Israeli "humanitarian" warfare as a kind of necropolitics; see Puar (2017) for a conceptualization of the biopolitical "right to maim."

CHAPTER 5. THE RACE TO HELP

1. In several publications, Tvedt has analyzed Norwegian self-images and Norway's images of the world based on its benevolent internationalism in the form of development aid. *Det internasjonale gjennembruddet* marks an innovation in his work by expanding the investigation of Norway's goodness regime to include immigration and asylum policy and the political rhetoric surrounding it. For other analyses of Norway's "goodness regime," see Loga (2002); Gullestad (2007); Witoszek (2011). See also the important experimental documentary and art project *The Goodness Regime* (2013) by the artists Jumana Manna and Sille Storihle. For criticism of *Det internasjonale gjennembruddet* from within the Norwegian academic community, see Gripsrud (2018); Brochmann (2018); Osland (2020).

2. "Når det gjaldt innflytelse over nasjonens kultur og dannelse og definisjonsmakt over den nasjonale samtalen om verden og landets plass i den."

3. "Norge fikk tusenvis, og etter hvert titusenvis og hundretusener, av innbyggere fra land i den ikke-vestlige kulturkredsen . . . fungerte ikke lenger den gamle nasjonalstatsideologien."

4. "I flere tiår promoterte staten selv og sentrale politiske miljøer systematisk multikulturalismen som samfunnsnorm og samfunnsideal."

5. "Semantikk og begrebsbruk på det innvandingspolitiske området."

6. "Mange af aktørerne innenfor dette godhetsregimet iscenesatte seg selv som 'det godes' forvalter."

7. "Som et politikkfelt over politikken og som repræsentant for det universelle, og for Det gode og for Det rettferdige."

8. See, for instance, NRK's interview with Listhaug (accessed March 2024), https://www.nrk.no/norge/frp-listhaug_-_-godhetstyranniet-rir-norge-som -en-mare-1.12633044.

9. "hvor jomfru Maria som sørger over sin sønn Jesus, ble erstattet av en minister eller en kjendis, gjerne på huk, men omgitt av afrikanske barn; helst mange barn, og åbenbart takknemlige barn."

10. "Etter hvert som det humanitær-politiske komplekset vokste og konkurransen mellom organisasjonene og aktørene om bistandsmarkedet tilspisset seg, økte fristelsen til å utnytte både egen moralsk kapital som en slags moderne samaritan og folks ønske om a vise empati med de fattige i Afrika."

11. Information on actors in the various Radi-Aid campaigns and videos is surprisingly sparse, but according to danmarkshistorien.dk, the roles were played by local artists from Durban: Samke Mkhize, Lungelo Ndlovo, Vivian Ncgobo, Nombulelo Ctili, Mthokozisi Biyela, Nandi Khumalo, Thandeka

Maqebula, Nontokozo M, Zuzile Skhakhane, Nombuso Dlamini, Philisiwe Ntintili. See https://danmarkshistorien.dk/vis/materiale/saih-radi-aid-africa -for-norway-2012 (accessed March 2023).

12. See Jefferess (2013) for a critique of the video's satirical reversals: "Once again black bodies perform roles created by and for white folks" (Jefferess 2013, 76).

13. SAIH is a student-driven advocacy organization whose work focuses on the right to education and academic freedom through collaboration with local partners in Asia, Latin America, and sub-Saharan Africa. Student organizations in Norway donate to SAIH's work, which is, however, predominantly funded by the Norwegian Agency for Development Cooperation under the Norwegian Ministry of Foreign Affairs. Domestically, SAIH has worked with the theme "Our image of the global South," through which SAIH engages with media representation of development, aid, and the global South. This is where the fictitious humanitarian organization Radi-Aid and its spoof campaign enter the picture. See "SAIH," n.d., accessed August 2022, https://saih .no/english/.

14. The SAIH website presents Radi-Aid as "a former awareness campaign created by the Norwegian Students' and Academics' International Assistance Fund (SAIH)." The aim "to challenge the perceptions around issues of poverty and development, to change the way fundraising campaigns communicate, and to break down dominating stereotypical representations" is further supported by the Radi-Aid Awards, which SAIH announced annually from 2013 to 2017. The Rusty Radiator Award went to an image or campaign deemed stereotypical and devoid of dignity, while the Golden Radiator Award was presented to campaigns that avoided white savior elements, graphic images of emaciated children, decontextualized suffering, and other forms of tired humanitarian iconography. The Radi-Aid work is closely related to other Scandinavian initiatives aimed at communicating a range of more uplifting facets of life on the African continent. One such initiative is Verdens Bedste Nyheder (The world's best news), a Danish news organization aimed at increasing awareness that the world is in fact moving toward the UN development goals, not away from them. "The world is better than you think" is a recurrent slogan on this media outlet, which currently has sister organizations in Norway and the Netherlands.

15. I am here referring not to the concept of Afro-pessimism developed by Frank B. Wilderson III (2020) but to the default depiction of the African continent in much humanitarian communication as a "disaster continent."

16. The research project was a collaboration with the British media scholar David Girling and a research team at University of East Anglia.

17. For my presentation of this study and its historical upshots, I am particularly relying on the discussions of it in Robin Bernstein's *Racial Innocence* (2011) and Anne Cheng's *The Melancholy of Race* (2000).

18. When brought as evidence of internalized racism in the landmark Supreme Court case *Brown v. Board of Education* (1954), the tests proved disturbing

enough to contribute to the ruling against segregation in public schools in the Unites States. In the years since *Brown v. Board of Education*, the doll tests have come to form a point of reference for the American imagination of race.

19. The research team does not specify the racialized identities of test subjects.

20. This performance of cultural and visual knowledge takes place despite a research design and an interpretative framework that highlight how some respondents "were slightly confused" by a specific question or that "respondents did not fully understand this question" (SAIH and Girling 2018, 24–27). The reader wonders if in a North European context divergent answers would be explained in the same way, as being caused by confusion and absence of comprehension.

21. "A class of saviors" is Miriam Ticktin's term for "those who care for the innocent" (2017, 583). Ticktin's critique of innocence would be the interlocutor of this chapter; as moral and political factor, Ticktin argues, "innocence demarcates human kinds according to their relationship to knowledge and action" (2017, 579). Thus, the others' innocence corroborates the class of saviors in their knowledge.

22. Gullestad is careful to emphasize the continuity between the Norwegian missionary organizations and Norwegian state-funded aid work institutionalized in the 1960s, suggesting that "the missions and the government's development aid have been related ideologically, economically, institutionally and socially." In this manner, Gullestad finds "not so much a profound break as a continuity—as goodness regimes—between the missions and the state-organized development aid and peace initiatives" (2007, 45–46). Gripsrud (2018) also emphasizes this continuity, while Tvedt (2018) posits the development of the Norwegian "humanitarian-political compleks" as beginning only in the 1960s.

23. During the last decades, "missionaries have launched several new initiatives that seriously attempt to be more sensitive to African interests and perspectives" (Gullestad 2007, 248).

24. "Organisert omkring meningspåvirkning eller oppdragende virksomhet, stortt sett på vegne av regjeringen gjennom Utenriksdepartementet—og beregnet på den norske befolkning."

25. "Statsfinansierte pedagoger," "oppdragerstatens pedagogiske entreprenører," og "sosial ingeniørkunst."

CHAPTER 6. VISUAL ECONOMIES

1. Notably, Bernstein and Wekker both analyze links between cherished material childhood culture and adult white innocence. Wekker describes, by way of example, how criticism of the Dutch figure of Zwarte Piet (Black Pete) "precipitates a strong reaction in the majority of Dutch people," who resolutely aver the cultural innocence of the figure. This dynamic is well-known in Scandinavian publics too.

2. Martens's film project has given rise to an extensive literature; see, for example, the readings and discussions assembled in Downey (2019).

3. Demos suggests we think of this atypical documentary form in Martens's project as "a kind of reverse photojournalism, or reverse documentarism, one that centers on the documentarian-artist-photojournalist, who is normally hidden in such projects" (Demos et al. 2013, 8).

4. Of his film, Martens says in an interview that "making this film is in itself a process analogous to making chocolate, coffee, coltan, or gold. The power equation between those who consume and those who supply the raw material in those industries is the same, regardless of what specific product is produced" (Martens qtd. in Demos 2013, 119). The materialism so central to Martens's interpretation of the economy of humanitarian images also comes to the fore in the film's interest in contracts. According to an interview, Martens entered into two contracts with his "protagonists," the local Congolese in Kinshasa and its environs. The first contract echoed current practice in central Africa, maintaining that any profit from a given image will not go to the persons depicted. Later, Martens signed a different contract that guaranteed those depicted a share of the profit, if any (Roelandt 2019, 54). The contracts are reprinted in Downey (2019). Martens has since established the Institute for Human Activities (IHA) in Western Congo, a center for aesthetic and critical practice, with an aim to channel profit from the institute into the local communities, rather than back into the capitals of the art world. See https://www.humanactivities.org/en/ (accessed April 2023).

5. I am referring to Jacques Rancière's description of a given distribution of the sensible as "an *a priori* distribution of the positions and capacities and incapacities attached to these positions" (2011a, 12).

6. Commenting on the divisive labor of "cosmopolitan photojournalists," Ariella Aïsha Azoulay notes that "photographers and artists are called upon to maintain the division between these worlds and contribute to its reproduction" (Azoulay 2019a, 291). Azoulay furthermore points to a more specific aspect of this maintenance work, suggesting that "it is this abundance of images of hopeless miserable people always from elsewhere—from 'developed countries,' that enables the perpetuation of the image of democratic regimes as bloodless" (2019a, 294).

7. In *Regarding the Pain of Others*, Sontag shifts back and forth between different positions in what she herself calls "the cosmopolitan discussion of images of atrocity" and their effects. One moment she seems to side, as she did in *On Photography*, with the suspicion that "flooded with images of the sort that once used to shock and arouse indignation, we are losing our capacity to react" (Sontag 2003, 108). Next, she finds this position to be a cliché (111). What does not seem to wither in Sontag's writing on images of violence, however, is her cautioning against passivity. More than the sheer quantity of images "dumped on people," passivity is what hardens their sensorium, she suggests; it is "passivity that dulls feeling" (Sontag 2003, 102).

8. Thus, I find Azoulay's depiction of the "imaginary distance" separating viewer from viewed more relevant to an understanding of late-humanitarian spectatorship than Sontag's depiction of an "imaginary proximity": "The imaginary

proximity to the suffering inflicted on others that is granted by images suggests a link between the faraway sufferers—seen close-up on the television screen—and the privileged viewer that is simply untrue, that is yet one more mystification of our real relations of power" (Sontag 2003, 102).

CHAPTER 7. DEBTORS

1. Fassin writes, "Each time a member of a humanitarian organization has been taken hostage in recent years, in Columbia or the Caucasus, the mission in question has been wholly diverted from its initial goals and has concentrated on a single aim—saving the abducted companion" (2007, 514).
2. Consider, for instance, the disparity between the humanitarian hospitality with which Ukrainian refugees were received in 2022 by state and civil society actors and the far more regulated and cool reception of, for instance, Syrian and Afghan war refugees from 2015 onward. The customary political explanation for this difference is that Ukraine is in the immediate vicinity of the Nordic countries, with no further explanation as to what "immediate vicinity" implies in an era of Nordic participation in humanitarian and military interventions well beyond European borders.
3. In a way, the so-called Nigerian email is also a privilege genre, albeit the circumstances in which it is dispatched and applied differ from the other privilege genres we are looking at in this study: Like humanitarian gifts and microloans, the advance fee scam is a genre of exchange registering and responding to global inequality and the affects of inequality.

CHAPTER 8. SENTIMENTAL ECONOMY

1. For a study of the coproduction of sentimental culture and (female) consumer subjectivity in the nineteenth-century United States, see Merish (2000).
2. *Verdensgaver* is UNICEF's term for third-party gifts in their Scandinavian online stores. I here use *world gifts* as a generic term for third-party gifts marketed by charitable organizations. See Kemp, Richardson, and Burt (2011) for a study of the marketability of the third-party gift.
3. Email correspondence with DanChurchAid. In fact, the Give-a-Goat concept is not a uniquely Scandinavian project; Oxfam's 2005 "A Goat for Christmas" campaign was, to the best of my knowledge, the first humanitarian goat-gift.
4. Certainly, the multiplication of the gift is typically subject to a degree of paternalistic control by the humanitarian organization involved. DanChurchAid, for example, specifies various terms to be met by any family in the South receiving a goat or other third-party gift; with reference to the goat, these include that "the first-born kid must be given to another vulnerable family, so even more people can benefit from the gift." ("Det førstefødte kid skal gives til en anden udsat familie, så endnu flere kan få glæde af gaven.") "Giv en ged," Folkekirkens Nødhjælp, accessed May 2025, https://www.noedhjaelp.dk/shop/giv-en-ged (in Danish).

5. To the benefactors the goat is a slightly comical rather than touching emblem. This humorous quality is significant for the popularity of the goat in skeptimental publics: The funny aspect helps neutralize the morally virtuous and intimately sentimental aspect that otherwise attaches to humanitarian gifts.

6. "Lad en underernæret tre-årig få dine venners julegave i år."

7. For an account of life technologies as a niche within humanitarian entrepreneurship, see Redfield (2012).

8. "Overlevelsespakke," UNICEF, accessed May 2025, https://www.unicef.no /verdensgaver/produkter/helse/overlevelsespakke?list_id=category%3A28.

9. See, in particular, Jacques Derrida's discussions in *Given Time* (1992) of the gift as something outside every kind of economy while also requiring the economy if it is to be something other than utopian abstraction. The literature on gift-giving and gift-economy is extensive; anthropology and philosophy, in particular, have given particular prominence to the cultural significances of the gift, from Marcel Mauss ([1925/1954] 2011) onward. Alan D. Schrift (1997) brings together a collection of seminal texts and contemporary interpretations of the subject. For an analysis of various forms of humanitarian aid as various forms of gift, see Erica Bornstein (2012).

10. On a different note, Benjamin Lee has proposed that gift exchange and the derivatives of finance capital have a number of structural similarities: "The gift and the derivative share the property that both take the volatilities and uncertainties of social life and transform them into manageable risks by equating things that are different" (Lee 2016, 2).

11. Some will consider the dominance mode of debt to be the most oppressive because it capitalizes on time itself and because its application of interest rates institutionalizes a mistrust between people. Others will consider the humanitarian gift to be most ethically problematic because it is nonreciprocal and thereby precludes the recipient from equality with the benefactor via a return gift (countergift). Thus, a familiar criticism of humanitarian gifts argues that if a gift does not necessitate a return gift it will engender guilt and shame in the recipient and ambivalence in the benefactor. Pierre Bourdieu has made a number of observations about the significance of gift-giving in a late-modern economy, identifying gift-giving as a rational strategy to accumulate social capital. Based on the assumption that generosity can in fact be a legitimate form of dominance, in *Le sens pratique* (1980) Bourdieu had already discussed gift-giving as a form of symbolic violence: Gift-giving implies a conversion of economic capital to symbolic capital, thus lending the gift a symbolic power, the basis of which might be economic but is hidden under a cloak of moral relations. In "Marginalia—Some Additional Notes on the Gift" (1997), Bourdieu pays particular attention to gift-giving in asymmetrical relationships: In asymmetrical power relations, he suggests, gifts often create a relation of dominance and dependence, because an active reciprocity is not possible (1997, 238). This description of gift-giving as a guilt-generating form of dominance

is highly reminiscent of Maurizio Lazzarato's description of the subjectivizing functions of debt.

12. The anthropologist Heath Cabot (2016) has discussed the relationship between humanitarian practices and solidarity initiatives in the response of Greek citizens to the increasing precarization and investigated the emergence of various solidarity networks in Greece. See also Cabot (2014).

13. For historical perspective, see legal scholar and sociologist Michele Landis Dauber's (2013) discussion of the relationship between economic crisis and humanitarian rhetoric in the United States of the 1930s, where a humanitarianizing rhetoric of calamity was central to validating the Roosevelt administration's recovery programs during and after the Great Depression. The Great Depression was talked about as a "disaster" and an "economic catastrophe," terminology based on the moral consensus that federal state resources could be channeled to alleviate suffering—if, that was, the suffering was "undeserved." Roosevelt's administration thus drew on a rhetoric and a moral economy that was to live on in the residual American welfare state: we help those whose situation seems to us to be no fault of their own.

14. See "IMF Survey: IMF Chief Calls for 'Marshall Plan' for Shattered Haiti," International Monetary Fund, January 20, 2010, https://www.imf.org/en/News /Articles/2015/09/28/04/53/sonew012010a.

15. See, for instance, the intermingling of humanitarian and debt relief vocabularies on the IDB website on Haiti 2010: https://www.iadb.org/en/news/webstories /2010-01-25/haiti-and-the-inter-american-development-bank%2C6464.html (accessed May 2023).

CHAPTER 9. THE ART OF GUILT-TRIPPING

1. According to available sources, the village was populated by Senegalese people, not Congolese, but the exhibition in 1914 was nevertheless referred to as "Kongolandsbyen"—the Congo village.

2. Baglo and Stien estimate, building on other such estimates, that twenty thousand to twenty-five thousand people were wholly or partially employed in this business in the period from 1870 to 1930 (2018, 168).

3. "Utstillingene var ikke bare disiplinerende maktdemonstrasjoner, [d]e var også steder for kulturmøter, identitetsbygging og for opplevelse."

4. "Bidro til å forflate historisk kompleksitet og følgelig videreførte oppfatningen av de opprinnelige beboerne i Kongolandsbyen og afrikanerer i samtiden som passive subjekter uten agens."

5. "Hva var omkostningen, for at dette hvite, norske 'vi'-et skulle få mulighet til å se seg selv i et nytt kritisk lys?"

6. Kristian von Hornsleth, "Idea," Hornsleth Village Project, accessed May 2025, https://www.hornslethvillageproject.dk/Uganda-Village-Project/Information /idea.

7. "Det foregår i dag en ideologisk kamp om hegemoni rettet mot spørgsmål om skyld og ansvar; hvis våre privilegier ikke er et resultat av vår fremragende innsats alene, men derimod et resultat av utbytting og asymmetriske maktforhold, så er privilegiene også delvis illegitime."

8. As the historian Mathias Danbolt and media scholar Tobias Raun emphasize in their analysis of *Hornsleth Village Project Uganda* and its "neocolonial ethnography" (*nykolonialistiske etnografi*), in the naming, or human branding, upon which the project is based, there is an implicit reference to Uganda's colonial history. From the identity cards that the inhabitants of Buteyongera hold up on their portrait photographs, we realize that *Hornsleth* is not the only "Western" name on their cards: "Several villagers bear forenames such as George, Rosemary, David—typical British names, which refer to Uganda's colonial history. By giving the villagers the name 'Hornsleth,' Hornsleth is thus framing himself as the white colonial master, and reiterates the cultural appropriation of the name of 'the racial other'—something that also happened in the era of colonialism and slavery" (Danbolt and Raun 2008, 30). ("Flere har fornavne som George, Rosemary, David—typiske britiske navne som henviser til Ugandas kolonihistorie. Når Hornsleth giver beboerne navnet 'Hornsleth' iscenesætter han sig altså som Den Hvide Koloniherre, og repeterer den kulturelle appropriation af 'den raciale Andens' navn—noget som også skete i koloni- og slavetiden.")

9. Cultural critic Stefan Jonsson notes the actually affirmative nature of Hornsleth's Uganda project, which to Jonsson is an example of a repertoire of cultural artifacts in which "attention is generated and careers created by overstepping boundaries and then calling a press conference" (Jonsson 2007). Danbolt and Raun similarly ask if the Uganda artwork is in fact not a case of "pure repetition" (*ren repetition*) rather than "critical playthrough" (*kritisk gennemspilning*) (2008, 30).

CHAPTER 11.HYPOCRISY LITERATURE

1. Lindholm's hypocrite trilogy comprises the poetry collections *Guld* (Gold, 2014), *No Hard Feelings* (2015), and *Resort* (2017).

2. *Oxford English Dictionary* (online edition, accessed May 2, 2025), under "hypocrite."

3. "Stankelbenet tager sig sikkert ikke af, at det bliver mast og druknet og kemisk angrebet. Men alligevel har Mette dårlig samvittighed. Hun er et svin. Sidder og spiser slik til billederne af krigen i Irak og får en mindre eksistentiel krise over at dræbe et stankelben. En ynk. Hykleri, hedder det vist."

4. "Sådan på verdensplan har Mette også klaret det godt. Okay, mere end godt: Født hvid, i 1960'erne i en forstand til Århus, Danmark, Europa, helt oppe hos de tidligere imperialister med kolonier nede ved de sorte. Dejlig billigt sukker og kaffe, for negrene var så gode til at arbejde uden løn."

5. "Mette ved ikke, hvad hun taler om, når hun siger, hun er lykkelig. Hun skulle tage og sige, at hun er glad for at være så skiderig og magtfuld, at hun kan stå og jokke på de fattige, mens hun slubrer sydamerikansk underbetalt appelsinjuice i sig og siger pyt til Sofie, fordi hun har tabt sit bib-bib-spil i børnehaven, 'så køber vi bare et nyt'. Det er jo dét, hun er glad for!"

6. "jeg trækker vejret via minerne i congo . . . jeg har microchipflashcardblodigtbørnearbejde i / kroppen / jeg har afrika som en struktur i øjet."

7. "some day world / vil jeg gerne sige undskyld på europas vegne / undskyld for den gode stemming."

8. Written in English in the original Danish edition.

9. "Politik er blevet et tic hos den unge generation, på hver tredje linje breakes nyheden om verdens uretfærdighed."

10. "undskyldninger for manglen på dybfølt, forpligtet indignation."

11. "Jeg har ikke talt med et menneske på flugt."

12. "Men så gør det da, digter, det er bare at tage bussen!"

13. For J. L. Austin, the performative speech act is not characterized by leading to a result over time. Rather, it is characterized by doing something at the very moment the speech is being uttered, by virtue of the utterance. With reference to Austin's *How to Do Things with Words* (1975), Ahmed emphasizes, "For an utterance to be performative, certain conditions have to be met. When these conditions are met, then the performative is happy. This model introduces a class of 'unhappy performatives': utterances that would 'do something' if the right conditions had been met, but which do not do that thing, as the conditions have not been met" (2004, para. 50). This strict sense of performative speech is not, I would argue, an expedient ideal for critique, nor, as I understand it, is it Ahmed's ideal, even though it might occasionally seem so. "The 'critical' in 'critical whiteness studies,'" Ahmed writes, "cannot guarantee that it will have effects that are critical, in the sense of challenging relations of power that remain concealed as institutional norms or givens" (2004, para. 10). But which critical discourse can act *felicitously in this sense?*

14. See also Ahmed's blog post on the functions of sympathy, "Becoming Unsympathetic" (2015).

15. "gamle, kloge mænd / 27 statsledere er ligeglade med en håndfuld intellektuelle, der kæfter op uden konsekvenser."

16. "Martin kan få hende til at tro på, hun er med i en bevægelse, selv om hun ingenting gør."

17. This latter image is even more prevalent in Hammann's later novel *Alene hjemme* (Home alone, 2015).

18. While a caustic portrait of privilege-aware hypocrisy, Glaffey's *To the Modern Man* ascribes hypocrisy exclusively to a specific male type. As I do not include in the category of hypocrisy literature works in which hypocrisy is an accusation directed toward others, I would categorize *To the Modern Man* more as a borderline case than as a paradigmatic example of this literary privilege genre.

19. "Jeg tror, at mange vil kunne genkende sig selv i bogen [*To the Modern Man*]— uanset køn—måske kan den få os til at stoppe op og tænke over, om det bliver en lille smule smagløst, når man går direkte fra demonstrationen på Rådhuspladsen til fordel for syriske flygtninge og så hen på hjørnet for at drikke et glas hvidvin, når man ikke orker at stå op mere. Sådan er livet i vores samfund, det er fyldt med hykleri og kontraster, og det er ikke kønt, men det er svært at give afkald på de privilegier, man har—det er det også for mig og alle mulige andre. Men derfor kan man jo i det mindste grine lidt af det—grine og se sit eget hykleri i øjnene. Det er i hvert fald minimalt mere spiseligt at have en form for selvironi end at være blottet for den."

20. "Tænk, hvis man skrev en roman om sådan en som Mette. Så ville mange af dem, der læste om hendes næstekærlige holdninger, superegoisme, drømme om forandring og ekstreme dovenskab, kunne læne sig endnu mere mageligt tilbage og føle sig både genkendt og forstået. 'Gud, det er jo lige sådan jeg har det,' kunne man sige. 'Jeg føler der er så meget forkert i verden, men jeg kan simpelthen ikke overskue, hvad jeg skal gøre ved det. Er vi virkelig så mange, der har det sådan? Vi mener det så godt, men vi er magtesløse.' Og så ikke mere. Bare genkendelse og så ned i Magasin."

21. In this category of "idealistic cynics" of political change, Robbins includes Samuel Moyn and Jacques Rancière, discussing their respective critiques of human rights in his article "'All of Us Without Exception': Sartre, Rancière, and the Cause of the Other," from which I am here citing (Robbins 2014).

CHAPTER 12. CRISIS AND COLLECTIVITY

1. See Rothstein (2020) for discussions of this archive.

2. "Vi har vel også kærlighed, siger Betty, ja, siger Linn, ja, det er heller ikke rigtigt, at der kun er ondskab, men vi er vidner til den; hver dag skal vi se børn, der lider og dør, uden at vi kan gøre noget ved det, og prøver man alligevel at gøre noget, opdager man, at der bag ved den første ulykke gemmer sig titusind andre. Det er overvældende, synes jeg, ikke at det er nogen undskyldning for at sidde med hænderne i skødet. Hermann var tre uger i Sydsudan med Læger Uden Grænser. Er han læge, siger Betty. Nej, tandlæge, siger Linn, *Tandlæger Uden Grænser*, så griner de lidt ad det, så sidder de bare lidt."

3. "Den strand, hvor jeg plejer at bade / nu kan jeg aldrig gå i vandet igen, stranden giver mig kvalme, havet får mig til at tænke på døden."

4. "Hvorfor gør de ikke noget, tænker Ib, hvorfor bader de og morer sig, når folk drukner i det samme vand. Spørgsmålet om, hvorfor han ikke selv gør noget, forsøger han at udskyde at svare på ved at betale et betragteligt beløb til en nødhjælpsorganisation en gang hver tredje måned, af og til oftere, når han overvældes af nyhedsstrømmen [. . .] og der er jo heller ingen, der får det bedre af, at vi går rundt og har det dårligt over verdens elendighed. Sådan noget siger han til sig selv uden rigtig at tro på det."

5. "og Wilma sagde, er fiskene så fulde af brød, når man hiver dem op, og Ernst sagde, ja, fiskene er fulde af brød og døde flygtninge."

6. "Al den væmmelige krig, der vælte ud af jeres skærme, børn, der bløder fra øjne og ører, børn med bortsprængte arme og ben, I kan ikke holde ud at se på det, så I skynder jer at give en hundredlap til en nødhjælpsorganisation og belønner jer selv med noget nyt tøj, fordi I er så dygtige, fordi I er sådan nogle menneskevenner, hvad I glemmer at tænke på er, at tøjet er syet af børneslaver, der sidder lænket til væggen på en eller anden uhumsk fabrik i den tredje verden, alt sammen, fordi det bedst kan betale sig, alt sammen, fordi I ikke vil betale det, tingene koster, men alligevel forventer I den allerfineste kvalitet til en billig penge."

7. "Jeg taler om det hele."

8. "Du flyder rundt i din latterlige badering med en drink, og folk drukner til højre og venstre, sagde han, og det er ikke, fordi de er uden for synsvidde, det er, fordi du har valgt ikke at se dem. Jeg har jo slet ikke nogen badering, sagde jeg. Vi er jo bare på ferie, sagde Ib."

9. One way in which to interpret this affective style could be via Ngai's description of the aesthetic category and emotional state she calls *stuplimity*. In *Ugly Feelings*, Ngai describes stuplimity as one of the dysphoric, noncathartic affects giving rise to a noncathartic aesthetic; stuplimity is a tension "that holds opposing affects together"—for instance, the opposing feelings of astonishment and exhaustion or shock and boredom (2005, 271). Unlike the sublime, stuplimity offers no "uplifting transcendence," no "serene, self-ennobling admiration for the colossal object in which Kant's sublime culminates," Ngai argues (2005, 267–69). Ngai employs the concept of stuplimity to characterize works of art that accumulate massive amounts of data and information and their effect on the reader or spectator. Stuplimity, she suggests, invites us to ask "what ways of responding our culture makes available to us, and under what conditions. [It prompts] us to look for new strategies of affective engagement and to extend the circumstances under which engagement becomes possible" (Ngai 2005, 262). Højrup's *Til stranden* is not a literary work that produces stuplime linguistic exhaustion in its readers. It does consider, however, the ways of responding our culture makes available to us and the conditions in which these responses occur. Hence, we could mobilize Ngai's concept not to characterize the overall form of *Til stranden* but more specifically to bring into focus its interpretation of the opportunities available for responding to the magnitude of "first-world complicity." In doing so, we would then be transposing a concept for responding to an immense linguistic network of signification onto a concept for responding to an immense geopolitical network of signification.

10. "oppustet og mæt af litterær samvittighed vil jeg skrive en tekst, der er fri for fiktioner og svulmende indsigt."

11. "og nu er forårssæsonen allerede begyndt og flygtningene drukner igen i Middelhavet."

12. "Jeg hader at hade så meget, og at man kan få pizza lavet på middelhavsvand nede i Kødbyen, situationen taget i betragtning."
13. "Jeg vil ikke leve højt på andres ulykke. Jeg vil ikke bruge lidelse til andet end det den er, men selv det at købe økologisk i Fakta, at gå til dyr yoga nede i Ryesgade føles som en brøde."
14. "At Ashkan dömer Filip och ser ned på hans borgerlighet, något Filip har förstått sedan länge, har han inga problem med. Tvärtom tycker han att det är rätt befriande att någon reagerer på hur han lever sitt liv och de store privilegier som betingar hans tillvaro. Det är skönt att bli påmind om det. Han glömmer det lätt."
15. "Hans grundinställning förblir att han är värd sina framgångar och sitt privilegierade liv" (182), "sin konsekventa vägran att låta sig övertygas om att agera i 'godhetens' tjänst" (183).
16. "mot Filips omedvetenhet om sin egen position": "Han framstod som oförmögen att ta in vilken makt han besitter."
17. "hans aningslösthet."
18. "fortæller og fortalt kan være der samtidig."
19. "almindeligt og fælles der taler igennem Mette der taler igennem fortælleren."
20. "Fulde idiot, tænkte jeg, tænker Linn."
21. "Hvorfor går du så meget op i mad, sagde han til mig, tænker Ib og ser på en gråspurv, der er landet på kagefadet. Hvorfor går du så meget op i vin og i biler og skjorter og latterlige jakkesæt til tusindvis af kroner, sagde Ernst og pegede på mig, tænker Hermann."
22. "Det var som sagt det afsindige efterår, da flygtningene kom vandrende op ad de syddanske motorveje, jeg var netop blevet løsladt fra psyk., forsøgte at få en hverdag op at stå, holde ængstelsen stangen, og en del af min nye rutine blev at gå."
23. "i et forfærdeligt humør, ka ikke tænke på andet end de brændende børn i Aleppo."
24. "50 mennesker i mørke og regn på et lille mørkt torv i regnvejr på en lille ø i Nordatlanten / de brændende børns skrig, raseri og afmægtighed."
25. "—Hvorfor gider du ikke tale om noget? / —Hvad mener du? / —Flygtninge. / —Jeg blir så træt. / —. . . / —Det var synd, du stod og græd i regnen. / — Hold op. / —Det var synd, det var mørkt, så ingen kunne se dine tårer. / —Pff. / —Men godt du skriver en bog om det så."

References

Abu-Lughod, Lila, Rema Hammami, and Nadera Shalhoub-Kevorkian, eds. 2023. *The Cunning of Gender Violence: Geopolitics and Feminism*. Duke University Press.

Aburas, Lone. 2017. *Det er et jeg der taler (Regnskabets time)*. Copenhagen: Gyldendal.

Adelman, Rebecca A., and Wendy Kozol. 2014. "Discordant Affects: Ambivalence, Banality, and the Ethics of Spectatorship." *Theory & Event* 17 (3). muse.jhu.edu /article/553380.

Adler-Nissen, Rebecca, and Ulrik Gad. 2014. "Introduction: Postimperial Sovereignty Games in the Nordic region." *Cooperation and Conflict* 49 (1): 3–32. https://doi.org/10.1177/0010836713514148.

Adorno, Theodor, and Max Horkheimer. (1947) 2002. "The Culture Industry: Enlightenment as Mass Deception." In *Dialectic of Enlightenment: Philosophical Fragments*. Translated by Edmund Jephcott. Stanford: Stanford University Press.

Ahmed, Sara. 2004. "Declarations of Whiteness: The Non-Performativity of Anti-Racism." *Borderlands* 3 (2).

Ahmed, Sara. 2005. "The Politics of Bad Feeling." *Australian Journal of Critical Race and Whiteness Studies* 1 (1). https://static1.squarespace.com/static /58ad660603596eec00ce71a3/t/58becd3de6f2e1086b36a265/1488899390367 /The+Politics+of+Bad+Feeling.pdf.

Ahmed, Sara. 2010. *The Promise of Happiness*. Durham: Duke University Press.

Ahmed, Sara. 2015. "Becoming Unsympathetic." *Feministkilljoys*, April 16. https:// feministkilljoys.com/2015/04/16/becoming-unsympathetic/.

Andersen, Bent Rold. 1986. "Rationality and Irrationality of the Nordic Welfare State." In *Norden: The Passion for Equality*, edited by Stephen Graubard, 112–43. Oslo: Norwegian University Press.

Andersson, Roy. 1970. *En kärlekshistoria* [A Swedish love story]. Stockholm: Europa Film AB.

Andersson, Roy. 1991. *Härlig är jorden* [World of glory]. Sverige.

Andersson, Roy. 2000. *Sånger från andra våningen* [Songs from the second floor]. Stockholm: Roy Anderson Filmproduktion.

Andersson, Roy. 2007. *Du levande* [You, the living]. Stockholm: Roy Anderson Filmproduktion.

Andersson, Roy. 2014. *En duva satt på en gren och funderade på tillvaron* [A pigeon sat on a branch reflecting on existence]. Stockholm: Roy Anderson Filmproduktion.

Andreassen, Rikke. 2015. *Human Exhibitions: Race, Gender and Sexuality in Ethnic Displays*. Farnham: Ashgate.

Andreassen, Rikke, and Anne Folke Henningsen. 2011. *Menneskeudstilling: Fremvisninger af eksotiske mennesker i Zoologisk Have og Tivoli*. Copenhagen: Tiderne Skifter.

Arping, Åsa. 2022. *Att göra klass: Nedslag i svensk samtidsprosa*. Gothenburg: Makadam Förlag.

Arter, David. 2016. *Scandinavian Politics Today*. Manchester: Manchester University Press.

Ashworth, John. 1992. "The Relationship Between Capitalism and Humanitarianism." In *The Antislavery Debate: Capitalism and Abolitionism as a Problem in Historical Interpretation*, edited by Thomas Bender, 180–99. Berkeley: University of California Press.

Azoulay, Ariella. 2008. *The Civil Contract of Photography*. New York: Zone Books.

Azoulay, Ariella. 2015. *Civil Imagination: A Political Ontology of Photography*. Translated by Louise Bethlehem. New York: Verso.

Azoulay, Ariella. 2019a. "The Double Gift Economy." In *Critique in Practice: Renzo Martens' Episode II: Enjoy Poverty*, edited by Anthony Downey, 285–95. Berlin: Sternberg Press.

Azoulay, Ariella. 2019b. *Potential History: Unlearning Imperialism*. London: Verso.

Badiou, Alain. 2001. *Ethics: An Essay on the Understanding of Evil*. Translated by Peter Hallward. London: Verso.

Baeré, Merle. 2018. "Har Grønland været en koloni?" *Information*, March 10. https://www.information.dk/moti/2018/03/groenland-vaeret-koloni.

Baglo, Cathrine, and Hanne Hammer Stien. 2018. "Alt eller ingenting: Annerledesgjøren og agens i to (post)koloniale kunstprojekter." *Kunst og Kultur* 101 (3): 166–85. https://doi.org/10.18261/issn.1504-3029-2018-03-04.

Baldwin, James. (1949) 1963. "Everybody's Protest Novel." In *Notes of a Native Son*. New York: Dial.

Baldwin, Peter. 1990. *The Politics of Social Solidarity: Class Bases of the European Welfare State, 1875–1975*. Cambridge: Cambridge University Press.

Barnett, Michael. 2011. *Empire of Humanity: A History of Humanitarianism*. Ithaca: Cornell University Press.

Bartky, Sandra Lee. 2002. "In Defense of Guilt." In *Sympathy and Solidarity: and Other Essays*, 131–51. Lanham: Rowman & Littlefield.

Bender, Thomas, ed. 1992. *The Antislavery Debate: Capitalism and Abolitionism as a Problem in Historical Interpretation*. Berkeley: University of California Press.

Bengy Puyvallée, Antoine de, and Kristian Bjørkdahl, eds. 2021. *Do-Gooders at the End of Aid: Scandinavian Humanitarianism in the Twenty-First Century*. Cambridge: Cambridge University Press.

Berggren, Henrik, and Lars Trägårdh. (2006) 2022. *The Swedish Theory of Love: Individualism and Social Trust in Modern Sweden*. Translated by Stephen Donovan. Seattle: University of Washington Press.

Berlant, Lauren. 1997. *The Queen of America Goes to Washington City: Essays on Sex and Citizenship*. Duke University Press.

Berlant, Lauren. 1999. "The Subject of True Feeling: Pain, Privacy, and Politics." In *Cultural Pluralism, Identity Politics, and the Law*, edited by Austin Sarat and Thomas Kearns, 49–84. Ann Arbor: University of Michigan Press.

Berlant, Lauren. 2004. "Compassion (and Withholding)." In *Compassion: The Culture and Politics of an Emotion*, edited by Lauren Berlant, 1–13. New York: Routledge.

Berlant, Lauren. 2008. *The Female Complaint: The Unfinished Business of Sentimentality in American Culture*. Durham, NC: Duke University Press.

Berlant, Lauren. 2011. *Cruel Optimism*. Durham, NC: Duke University Press.

Bernstein, Robin. 2011. *Racial Innocence: Performing American Childhood from Slavery to Civil Rights*. America and the Long 19th Century. New York: NYU Press.

Black, Hannah. 2017. "Open Letter," reproduced in Alex Greenberger, "'The Painting Must Go': Hannah Black Pens Open Letter to the Whitney About Controversial Biennial Work." *ARTnews*, March 21. https://www.artnews.com/artnews/news/the-painting-must-go-hannah-black-pens-open-letter-to-the-whitney-about-controversial-biennial-work-7992/.

Bornstein, Erica. 2012. *Disquieting Gifts: Humanitarianism in New Delhi*. Stanford: Stanford University Press.

Bourdieu, Pierre. 1980. *Le sens pratique*. Paris: Les Editions Minuit.

Bourdieu, Pierre. 1997. "Marginalia—Some Additional Notes on the Gift." In *The Logic of the Gift: Toward an Ethic of Generosity*, edited by Alan Schrift, 231–41. New York: Routledge.

Brochmann, Grete. 2018. "Du godeste, Terje Tvedt." *Morgenbladet*, May 18. https://www.morgenbladet.no/ideer/debatt/2018/05/18/du-godeste-terje-tvedt/.

Brochmann, Grete, Anniken Hagelund, Karin Borevi, Heidi Vad Jønsson, and Klaus Petersen. 2012. *Immigration Policy and the Scandinavian Welfare State 1945–2010*. London: Palgrave Macmillan.

Brodén, Daniel. 2014. "Something Happened, but What? On Roy Andersson's Cinematic Critique of the Development of the Welfare State." In *Culture, Health, and Religion at the Millennium: Sweden Unparadised*, edited by Marie Demker, Yvonne Leffler, and Ola Sigurdson. New York: Palgrave Macmillan.

Browning, Christopher. 2021. "Fantasy, Distinction, Shame: The Stickiness of the Nordic 'Good State' Brand." In *Do-Gooders at the End of Aid: Scandinavian Humanitarianism in the Twenty-First Century*, edited by Antoine de Bengy Puyvallée and Kristian Bjørkdahl, 14–38. Cambridge: Cambridge University Press.

Brügger, Mads. 2011. *Ambassadøren*. Director. Copenhagen: Zentropa Real.

Brysk, Alison. 2009. *Global Good Samaritans: Human Rights as Foreign Policy*. Oxford: Oxford University Press.

Buck-Morss, Susan. 2000. "Hegel and Haiti." *Critical Inquiry* 26 (4): 821–65.

Bukdahl, Lars. 2014. "Min IPhone er hvid som en hvid mand." *Weekendavisen*, November 21.

Butler, Judith. 2009. *Frames of War: When Is Life Grievable?* London: Verso.

Butler, Judith. 2013. "The Sensibility of Critique: Response to Asad and Mahmood." In *Is Critique Secular? Blasphemy, Injury, and Free Speech*, edited by Talal Asad, Wendy Brown, Judith Butler, and Saba Mahmood, 95–130. New York: Fordham University Press. https://doi.org/10.2307/j.ctt1c5cjtk.

Cabot, Heath. 2014. *On the Doorsted of Europe: Asylum and Citizenship in Greece.* Philadelphia: University of Pennsylvania Press.

Cabot, Heath. 2016. "'Contagious' Solidarity: Reconfiguring Care and Citizenship in Greece's Social Clinics." *Social Anthropology*, no. 24, 152–66.

Calhoun, Craig. 2010. "The Idea of Emergency: Humanitarian Action and Global (Dis)Order." In *Contemporary States of Emergency: The Politics of Military and Humanitarian Intervention*, edited by Didier Fassin and Mariella Pandolfi, 29–58. New York: Zone Books.

Carlsen, Jo. 2022. "Kristina Nya Glaffey: 'Mænd har eddermame talt meget de sidste 2000 år.'" *Jyllands-Posten*, April 21.

Cheng, Anne. 2000. *The Melancholy of Race: Psychoanalysis, Assimilation, and Hidden Grief.* Oxford: Oxford University Press.

Chouliaraki, Lilie. 2010. "Post-Humanitarianism: Humanitarian Communication Beyond a Politics of Pity." *International Journal of Cultural Studies* 13 (2): 107–26. http://dx.doi.org/10.1177/1367877909356720.

Chouliaraki, Lilie. 2013. *The Ironic Spectator: Solidarity in the Age of Post-Humanitarianism.* Cambridge: Polity.

Christiansen, L. B. 2015. "'Africa Is a National Cause': Race and Nation in Development Aid Communication—A Danish Case Study." *Critical Race and Whiteness Studies* 11 (1). https://rucforsk.ruc.dk/ws/portalfiles/portal/58204735/253Christiansen2015111.pdf.

Clark, K. B., and Mamie P. Clark. 1947. "Racial Identification and Preference in Negro Children." In *Readings in Social Psychology*, edited by T. M. Newcomb and E. L. Hartley. New York: Henry Holt.

Cohen, G. A. 2000. *If You're an Egalitarian, How Come You're So Rich?* Cambridge: Harvard University Press.

Cramer, Nina. 2025. "Embodied Practices by Black Contemporary Artists in Denmark, 1986–2023" (working title). PhD. diss., forthcoming at the University of Copenhagen.

Cuttitta, Paolo. 2019. "The Central Mediterranean Border as a Humanitarian Space." In *Global Perspectives on Humanitarianism*, edited by Ninna Nyberg Sørensen and Sine Plambech, 15–28. Copenhagen: DIIS.

Cuzner, Lars. n.d. "European Attraction Limited." Accessed May 19, 2024. https://larscuzner.com/european-attraction-limited-2/.

Cuzner, Lars, and Mohamed Ali Fadlabi. 2014. *European Attraction Limited*, artistic historical exhibition in Frognerparken. Oslo.

Dahl, Hans Frederik. 1986. "Those Equal People." In *Norden: The Passion for Equality*, edited by Stephen Graubard, 97–112. Oslo: Norwegian University Press.

Danbolt, Mathias. 2017. "Retro Racism: Colonial Ignorance and Racialized Affective Consumption in Danish Public Culture." *Nordic Journal of Migration Research* 7 (2): 105–13.

Danbolt, Mathias, and Tobias Raun. 2008. "Hornsleths un/fair trade—æstetisk evangelisme og nykolonialistisk etnografi i samtidskunsten." *Kvinder, Køn & Forskning*, no. 4, 23–32.

Dancus, Adriana Margareta, Mats Hyvönen, and Maria Karlsson, eds. 2020. *Vulnerability in Scandinavian Art and Culture*. London: Palgrave Macmillan.

Danmarks indsamling (DI). 2007–. Copenhagen: Danmarks Radio, DR1. https://danmarksindsamling.dk/.

Dauber, Michelle Landis. 2013. *The Sympathetic State*. Chicago: University of Chicago Press.

Davey, Eleanor. 2015. *Idealism Beyond Borders: The French Revolutionary Left and the Rise of Humanitarianism, 1954–1988*. Cambridge: Cambridge University Press.

DeChaine, Robert. 2022. "Corporate Social Responsibility and the Humanitarian Civic Imaginary." In *Routledge Handbook of Humanitarian Communication*, edited by Lilie Chouliaraki and Anne Vestergaard. London: Routledge.

Demos, T. J. 2011. "Poverty Pornography, Humanitarianism, and Neo-liberal Globalizations: Notes on Some Paradoxes in Contemporary Art." *Stedelijk Bureau Newsletter*, no, 121.

Demos, T. J. 2013. *Return to the Postcolony: Specters of Colonialism in Contemporary Art*. Berlin: Sternberg Press.

Demos, T. J., and Hilde Van Gelder, Carles Guerra, Thomas Keenan, Toma Muteba Luntumbue, and Renzo Martens. 2013. "Roundtable One: A Discussion of Renzo Martens' Episode III (Enjoy Poverty) (2009)." In *In and Out of Brussels*, edited by T. J. Demos and Hilde Van Gelder, 5–26. Leuven: Leuven University Press.

Derrida, Jacques. 1992. *Given Time: I. Counterfeit Money*. Translated by Peggy Kamuf. Chicago: University of Chicago Press.

Derrida, Jacques. 1997. *Limited Inc*. Translated by Samuel Weber. Evanston: Northwestern University Press.

Downey, Anthony, ed. 2019. *Critique in Practice: Renzo Martens' Episode II: Enjoy Poverty*. Berlin: Sternberg Press.

Duffield, Mark. 2018. *Post-Humanitarianism: Governing Precarity in the Digital World*. Newark: Polity

Edman, Lars, and William Johansson Kalén. 2010. *Blybarnen*. Stockholm: Laika Film & Television AB.

Edman, Lars, and William Johansson Kalén. 2020. *Arica*. Stockholm: Laika Film & Television AB.

Einhorn, Eric, Sherrill Harbison, and Markus Huss, eds. 2022. *Migration and Multiculturalism in Scandinavia*. Madison: University of Wisconsin Press.

Ejlerskov, Ditte. 2012. *My African Letters*. Aarhus: Siesta.

Ellison, Julie. 1999. *Cato's Tears and the Making of Anglo-American Emotion*. Chicago: University of Chicago Press.

Ellison, Julie. 2012. "Sensibility." In *A Handbook of Romanticism Studies*, edited by Joel Faflak and Julia M. Wright, 37–53. Oxford: Blackwell.

Ernst, Linea Maja. 2014. "Ikke alt guld glimrer." *Information*, December 5. https://www.information.dk/kultur/anmeldelse/2014/12/guld-glimrer.

Esping-Andersen, Gøsta. 1995. *The Three Worlds of Welfare Capitalism*. Cambridge: Polity.

Essed, Philomena. 2013. "Entitlement Racism: License to Humiliate." In *Recycling Hatred: Racism(s) in Europe Today: A Dialogue Between Academics, Equality Experts and Civil Society Activists*. Brussels: European Network Against Racism aisbl (ENAR).

Ezra, Elizabeth. 2020. "Out of Bounds: The Spatial Politics of Civility in *The Square* (Östlund, 2017) and *Happy End* (Haneke, 2017)." *Northern Lights*, no. 18, 103–13.

Fassin, Didier. 2007. "Humanitarianism as a Politics of Life." *Public Culture*, no. 19, 499–520.

Fassin, Didier. 2012. *Humanitarian Reason: A Moral History of the Present*. Berkeley: University of California Press.

Fassin, Didier. 2024. *Moral Abdication: How the World Failed to Stop the Destruction of Gaza*. Translated by Gregory Elliot. London: Verso.

Feldman, Ilana, and Miriam Ticktin, eds. 2010. *In the Name of Humanity: The Government of Threat and Care*. Durham, NC: Duke University Press.

Festa, Lynn. 2006. *Sentimental Figures of Empire in Eighteenth-Century Britain and France*. Baltimore: Johns Hopkins University Press.

Fleissner, Jennifer L. 2004. *Women, Compulsion, Modernity: The Moment of American Naturalism*. Chicago: University of Chicago Press.

Frantzen, Mikkel Krause. 2015. "Følelsen af ikke at føle noget." *Politiken*, December 6

Freeman, Elizabeth. 2019. *Beside You in Time*. Durham, NC: Duke University Press.

Friis, Elisabeth. 2015. "Gyldne tider—når poesien svarer finanslogikken igen." *Kritik* 214, (4): 52–62.

Gabrielsen, Stian. 2014. "A Congo Village as a Means to Make Amends." *Kunstkritik*, June 26. https://kunstkritikk.no/a-congo-village-as-a-means-to-make-amends/.

Gammeltoft-Hansen, Thomas. 2021. "The Do-Gooders' Dilemma: Scandinavian Asylum and Migration Policies in the Aftermath of 2015." In *Do-Gooders at the End of Aid: Scandinavian Humanitarianism in the Twenty-First Century*, edited by Antoine de Bengy Puyvallée and Kristian Bjørkdahl, 14–38. Cambridge: Cambridge University Press. https://doi.org/10.1017/9781108772129.003.

Gilroy, Paul. 2019. "Agonistic Belonging: The Banality of Good, the 'Alt Right' and the Need for Sympathy." *Open Cultural Studies*, no. 3, 1–14.

Gilroy, Paul, and Ruth Wilson Gilmore. 2020. "Transcript: In Conversation with Ruth Wilson Gilmore." UCL, Sara Parker Remond Centre, podcast, June 7, 2020. https://www.ucl.ac.uk/racism-racialisation/transcript-conversation-ruth-wilson-gilmore.

Glaffey, Kristina Nya. 2022. *To the Modern Man: Et portræt*. Copenhagen: Gyldendal.

Gormsen, Cecilie. 2015. "Støjbergs flygtninge-annoncer indrykket i Libanon." *Altinget*, September 7. https://www.altinget.dk/artikel/stoejbergs-flygtninge-annoncer -indrykket-i-libanon.

Gormsen, Cecilie. 2016. "Fredag træder smykkeloven i kraft: Se politiets vejledning her." *Altinget*, February 5. https://www.altinget.dk/artikel/fredag-traeder -smykkeloven-i-kraft-se-politiets-vejledning-her.

Graubard, Stephen. 1986a. "Introduction." In *Norden: The Passion for Equality*, edited by Stephen Graubard, 7–16. Oslo: Norwegian University Press.

Graubard, Stephen, ed. 1986b. *Norden: The Passion for Equality*. Oslo: Norwegian University Press.

Gripsrud, Jostein. 2018. *Norsk hamskifte?* Oslo: Vigmostad & Bjørke.

Grøndahl, Cathrine. 2008. *Jeg satte mitt håp til verden*. Oslo: Gyldendal.

Grønstad, Asbjørn. 2020. "Conditional Vulnerability in the Films of Ruben Östlund." In *Vulnerability in Scandinavian Art and Culture*, edited by A. M. Dancus, Mats Hyvönen, and Maria Karlsson. Palgrave Macmillan.

Gullestad, Marianne. 2007. *Picturing Pity*. Oxford: Berghahn Books.

Hammann, Kirsten. 2004. *Fra smørhullet*. Copenhagen: Gyldendal.

Hammann, Kirsten. 2008. *En dråbe i havet*. Copenhagen: Gyldendal.

Hartman, Saidiya V. 1997. *Scenes of Subjection: Terror, Slavery, and Self-Making in Nineteenth-Century America*. New York: Oxford University Press.

Haskell, Thomas L. 1992. "Capitalism and the Origins of the Humanitarian Sensibility." Parts 1 and 2. In *The Antislavery Debate: Capitalism and Abolitionism as a Problem in Historical Interpretation*, edited by Thomas Bender, 107–60. Berkeley: University of Berkeley Press.

Helland, Frode. 2016. "Agressiv skyldfrihet—hjernevask revisited." In *Skandinaviske fortellinger om skyld og privilegier i en globaliseringstid*, edited by Elisabeth Oxfeldt. 32–54. Oslo: Universitetsforlaget. DOI: 10.18261/9788215028095 -2016-02.

Hendler, Glenn. 2001. *Public Sentiments: Structures of Feeling in Nineteenth-Century American Literature*. Chapel Hill: University of North Carolina Press.

Hesford, Wendy. 2011. *Spectacular Rhetorics: Human Rights Visions, Recognitions, Feminisms*. Durham, NC: Duke University Press.

Hjort, Mette, and Ursula Lindqvist, eds. 2016. *A Companion to Nordic Cinema*. Hoboken: Wiley, 2016.

Højrup, Peter. 2017. *Til stranden*. Copenhagen: Gyldendal.

Hornsleth, Kristian von. n.d. Hornsleth Village Project Uganda. Accessed May 24, 2024. https://www.hornslethvillageproject.dk/.

Howard, June. 1999. "What Is Sentimentality?" *American Literary History* 11 (1): 63–81.

Howard, June. 2020. "Sentiment." In *Keywords for American Cultural Studies*. 3rd ed. Edited by Bruce Burgett and Glenn Hendler. New York: NYU Press. https:// keywords.nyupress.org/american-cultural-studies/about-this-site/.

Hunt, Lynn. 2007. *Inventing Human Rights: A History*. New York: W. W. Norton.

Huntford, Roland. 1972. *The New Totalitarians*. New York: Stein and Day.

Ingebritsen, Christine. 2006. *Scandinavia in World Politics*. Rowman and Littlefield.

Jackson, Peter. 2006. "Thinking Geographically." *Geography* 91 (3): 199–204. DOI: 10.1080/00167487.2006.12094167.

James, Aaron. 2014. *Assholes: A Theory*. New York: Anchor Books.

Jefferess, David. 2013. "Humanitarian Relations: Emotion and the Limits of Critique." *Critical Literacy: Theories and Practices* 7 (1): 73–83.

Jensen, Christina Nordvang. 2023. "I Ghana hedder det 'Orboni Wawu': Den døde, hvide mands tøj. Og der kommer stadig mere af det." *Information*, April 17. https://www.information.dk/udland/2023/04/ghana-hedder-obroni-wawu -doede-hvide-mands-toej-kommer-stadig-mere.

Jessen, Ida. 2018. *Telefon*. Copenhagen: Gyldendal.

Jonsson, Stefan. 2007. "Kunstfidus: Skandale som succeskalkyle." *Information*, September 22. https://www.information.dk/kultur/2007/09/skandale-succeskalkyle.

Jonsson, Stefan. 2011. "*Play* missar de andras perspektiv." *Dagens Nyheter*, December 5.

Karlsson, Helena. 2014. "Ruben Östlund's *Play* (2011): Race and Segregation in 'Good' Liberal Sweden." *Journal of Scandinavian Cinema* 4 (1): 43–60.

Kemp, S., J. Richardson, and C. D. B. Burt. "A Goat for Christmas: Exploring Third-Party Gifts." *Journal of Managerial Psychology* 26 (6): 453–64. https://doi .org/10.1108/02683941111154338.

Keskinen, Suvi, Unnur Dís Skaptadóttir, and Mari Toivanen, eds. 2019. *Undoing Homogeneity in the Nordic Region: Migration, Difference and the Politics of Solidarity*. Oxfordshire: Routledge.

Khemeri, Jonas Hassen. 2011. "47 anledningar till att jag grät när jag såg Ruben Östlunds film *Play*." *Dagens Nyheter*, November 18.

Kjældgaard, Lasse Horne. 2018. *Meningen med velfærdsstaten: Da litteraturen tog ordet—og politikerne lyttede*. Copenhagen: Gyldendal.

Klein, Naomi. 2010. "Haiti: A Creditor, Not a Debtor." *The Nation*, March 1.

Knight, Deborah. 1999. "Why We Enjoy Condemning Sentimentality: A Meta-Aesthetic Perspective." *The Journal of Aesthetics and Art Criticism* 57 (4): 411–20. https://doi.org/10.2307/432148.

Koivunen, Leila, Raita Merivirta, and Timo Särkkä, eds. 2021. *Finnish Colonial Encounter: From Anti-Imperialism to Cultural Colonialism and Complicity*. London: Palgrave Macmillan.

Körber, Lill-Ann. 2018. "*Gold Coast* (2015) and Danish Economies of Colonial Guilt." *Journal of Aesthetics & Culture* 10 (2): 25–37.

Krarup, Søren. 2009. *National værnepligt: Politisk ekskurs*. Copenhagen: Gyldendal.

Kurasawa, Fuyuki. 2013. "The Sentimentalist Paradox: On the Normative and Visual Foundations of Humanitarianism." *Journal of Global Ethics* 9 (2): 201–14. DOI: 10.1080/17449626.2013.818461.

Læger uden Grænser. 2014a. "Donor uden grænser" [Donor without borders]. YouTube. https://www.youtube.com/watch?v=s69lxnMD-uY.

Læger uden Grænser. 2014b. "Donor uden grænser—vores nye kampagne." November 24. https://msf.dk/fra-felten/donor-uden-graenser/?gclid=CjwKCAjwoIqhB hAGEiwArXT7K_GLLK97uvuF31ezru7Ht0V-QEc5Zlv3g3LURu1DyrMORY AqY2BN5BoCzLcQAvD_BwE.

Lanchester, John. 2018. "After the Fall." *London Review of Books* 40 (13).

Lazzarato, Maurizio. 2012. *The Making of the Indebted Man: An Essay on the Neoliberal Condition.* Translated by Joshua David Jordan. Amsterdam: Semiotexte.

Lazzarato, Maurizio. 2015. *Governing by Debt.* Translated by Joshua David Jordan. Amsterdam: Semiotexte.

Lee, Benjamin. 2016. "Introduction." In *Derivatives and the Wealth of Societies*, edited by Benjamin Lee and Randy Martin. University of Chicago Press. https://doi .org/10.7208/chicago/9780226392974.003.0001.

Liljegren, Bengt. 2018. *Krigarkungen: En biografi över Karl XII.* Lund: Historiska Media.

Lindholm, Victor Boy. 2014. *Guld.* Copenhagen: Kronstork.

Lindqvist, Ursula. 2016. "The Art of Not Telling Stories in Nordic Fiction Films." In *A Companion to Nordic Cinema*, edited by Mette Hjort and Ursula Lindqvist, 547–65. Hoboken: Wiley.

Linfield, Susie. 2010. *The Cruel Radiance: Photography and Political Violence.* Chicago: University of Chicago Press.

Linhart, Silje Hernæs. 2017. "Diktets surrogatmødre: Cathrine Grøndahls 'Prisen for et dikt.'" In *Åpne dører mot verden: Norske ungdommers møte med fortellinger om skyld og privilegier*, edited by Jonas Bakken and Elisabeth Oxfeldt, 128–45. Oslo: Universitetsforlaget.

Loftsdóttir, Kristín, and Lars Jensen, eds. 2012. *Whiteness and Postcolonialism in the Nordic Region: Exceptionalism, Migrant Others and National Identities.* London: Ashgate.

Loga, Jill. 2002. "Godhetens makt i den politiske offentlighet," *Kvinneforskning*, no. 4, 32–39.

Lousley, Cheryl. 2013. "'With Love from Band Aid': Sentimental Exchange, Affective Economies, and Popular Globalism." *Emotion, Space and Society*, no. 10, 7–17.

Lübecker, Nikolaj. 2015. *The Feel-Bad Film.* Edinburg: Edinburg University Press.

Lund, Anker Brink, and Gitte Meyer. 2016. "Civilsamfundets ABC: G for Godhedsindustri." *Altinget.dk.* October 4. https://www.altinget.dk/civilsamfund/artikel /civilsamfundets-abc-g-for-godhedsindustri.

Malkki, Liisa H. 2015. *The Need to Help: The Domestic Arts of International Humanitarianism.* Durham, NC: Duke University Press.

Manna, Jumana, and Sille Storihle. 2013. *The Goodness Regime*, video, 21 min.

Martens, Renzo. 2008. *Episode III: Enjoy Poverty.* Director and writer. Renzo Martens Menselijke Activiteiten, Peter Krüger for Inti Films.

Mauss, Marcel. (1925/1954) 2011. *The Gift: Forms and Functions of Exchange in Archaic Societies.* Translated by Ian Cunnison. Mansfield: Martino.

Merish, Lori. 2000. *Sentimental Materialism: Gender, Commodity Culture, and Nineteenth-Century American Literature*. Durham, NC: Duke University Press.

Merivirta, Raita, Leila Koivunen, and Timo Särkkä, eds. 2021. *Finnish Colonial Encounters: From Anti-Imperialism to Cultural Colonialism and Complicity*. Palgrave Macmillan.

Mitchell, W. J. T. 1994. *Picture Theory*. Chicago: University of Chicago Press.

Moyn, Samuel. 2012. *The Last Utopia: Human Rights in History*. Cambridge: Harvard University Press.

Mwesigire, Bwesigye bwa. 2014. "Exhibiting Africans Like Animals in Norway's Human Zoo." *This Is Africa*, April 25. https://thisisafrica.me/politics-and -society/exhibiting-africans-like-animals-norways-human-zoo/.

Myong, Lene. 2014. "Frihedens racistiske præmis." *Peculiar*, December 2. http:// peculiar.dk/frihedens-racistiske-praemis/.

Naseh, Negar. 2016. *De fördrivna*. Stockholm: Natur og kultur.

Naum, Magdalena, and Jonas Nordin, eds. 2013. *Scandinavian Colonialism and the Rise of Modernity: Small Time Agents in a Global Era*. New York: Springer.

Nestingen, Andrew. 2017. "Pessimism in Happy Times: A Global Economy of Guilt, Shame, and Happiness in Miika Nousiainen's Novels." *Scandinavian Studies* 89 (4): 616–34. https://doi.org/10.5406/scanstud.89.4.0616.

Ngai, Sianne. 2005. *Ugly Feelings*. Cambridge: Harvard University Press.

Nonbo Andersen, Astrid. 2017. *Ingen undskyldning: Erindringer om Dansk Vestindien og kravet om erstatninger for slaveriet*. Copenhagen: Gyldendal.

Nordenborg, Ragna, and Ola Trulsen. 2011. "*Vil lage ny 'Kongolandsby.'*" [Wants to create a new "Congo village"]. NRK, November 1. http://www.nrk.no/kultur /vil-lage-ny-_kongolandsby_-1.7858686.

Önnerfors, Andreas. 2022. "Folkhemmet: 'The People's Home' as an Expression of Retrotopian Longing for Sweden Before the Arrival of Mass Migration." In *Migration and Multiculturalism in Scandinavia*, edited by Eric Einhorn, Sherrill Harbison, and Markus Huss, 60–79. Madison: University of Wisconsin Press.

Osanloo, Arzoo, and Cabeiri deBergh Robinson. 2024. *Care in a Time of Humanitarianism: Stories of Refuge, Aid, and Repair in the Global South*. Berghahn Books.

Osland, Oddgeir. 2020. "Polemikkens pris." *Norsk sosiologisk tidsskrift* 4 (1): 42–50.

Östlund, Ruben. 2011. *Play*. Director and writer. Göteborg: Plattform Produktion.

Östlund, Ruben. 2017. *The Square*. Director and writer. Göteborg: Plattform Produktion.

Östlund, Ruben. 2022. *Triangle of Sadness*. Director and writer. Göteborg: Plattform Produktion.

Overgaard, Sidsel. 2014. "Artists Bring Back the Human Zoo to Teach a Lesson in History." NPR, *Code Switch*, May 4. https://www.npr.org/sections/codeswitch /2014/05/04/309021088/artists-bring-back-the-human-zoo-to-teach-a -lesson-in-history.

Oxfeldt, Elisabeth. 2016a. "Innledning." In *Skandinaviske fortellinger om skyld og privilegier i en globaliseringstid*, edited by Elisabeth Oxfeldt, 9–31. Oslo: Universitetsforlaget. https://doi.org/10.18261/9788215028095-2016.

Oxfeldt, Elisabeth, ed. 2016b. *Skandinaviske fortellinger om skyld og privilegier i en globaliseringstid*. Oslo: Universitetsforlaget.

Oxfeldt, Elisabeth. 2018. "White Guilt and Racial Imagery in Annette K. Olesen's *Little Soldier*." *Journal of Aesthetics & Culture* 10 (51): 15–24.

Oxfeldt, Elisabeth, and Jonas Bakken, eds. 2017. *Åpne dører mot verden: Norske ungdommers møte med fortellinger om skyld og privilegier*. Oslo: Universitetsforlaget.

Oxfeldt, Elisabeth, Andrew Nestingen, and Peter Simonsen, eds. 2017. "The Happiest People on Earth? Scandinavian Narratives of Guilt and Discontent." *Scandinavian Studies* 89 (4).

Oxfeldt, Elisabeth, and Devika Sharma, eds. 2018. *Skyld og skam i Skandinavien*. Special issue of *K&K* 46 (125).

Petersen, Beate. 2013. "Et ukomfortabelt prosjekt." *Kunstkritik*, March 4. https://kunstkritikk.no/et-ukomfortabelt-prosjekt/.

Piketty, Thomas. 2020. *Capital and Ideology*. Translated by Arthur Goldhammer. Cambridge: Harvard University Press.

Piketty, Thomas. 2022. *A Brief History of Equality*. Translated by Steven Rendall. Cambridge: Harvard University Press.

Pollock, Griselda. 2007. "Not-Forgetting Africa." In *Alfredo Jaar: La Politique des Images*, edited by Nicole Schweizer, 112–35. Geneva: JRP/Ringier.

Puar, Jasbir. 2017. *The Right to Maim: Debility, Capacity, Disability*. Durham, NC: Duke University Press.

Rai, Amit S. 2002. *Rule of Sympathy: Sentiment, Race, and Power 1750–1850*. London: Palgrave Macmillan.

Rancière, Jacques. 2011a. *The Emancipated Spectator*. London: Verso.

Rancière, Jacques. 2011b. "The Emancipated Spectator." In *The Emancipated Spectator*. London: Verso.

Rancière, Jacques. 2011c. "The Misadventures of Critical Thought." In *The Emancipated Spectator*. London: Verso.

Rasmussen, Mikkel Bolt, and Devika Sharma. 2017. "Critique's Persistence: An Interview with Sianne Ngai." *Politics/Letters*, February 27. http://quarterly.politicsslashletters.org/critiques-persistence/.

Ravn, Anna Raaby. 2018. "Hvis vor tids modkultur bliver ansvar og forpligtelser, så har 68'erne fået noget at tænke over." Interview with Theis Ørntoft. *Dagbladet Information*, March 23.

Redfield, Peter. 2012. "Bioexpectations: Life Technologies as Humanitarian Goods." *Public Culture*, no. 24, 157–84.

Reinhardt, Mark. 2007. "Picturing Violence: Aesthetics and the Anxiety of Critique." In *Beautiful Suffering: Photography and the Traffic in Pain*, edited by Mark Reinhardt, Holly Edwards, and Erina Duganne, 13–36. Chicago: University of Chicago Press.

Richey, Lisa Ann, and Stephano Ponte. 2011. *Brand Aid: Shopping Well to Save the World*. Minneapolis: University of Minnesota Press.

Ringgaard, Dan. 2009. "Hammanns hamskifte." *Kritik* 42 (191): 74–77.

Robbins, Bruce. 2014. "'All of Us Without Exception': Sartre, Rancière, and the Cause of the Other." In *The Meanings of Rights: The Philosophy and Social Theory of Human Rights*, edited by Costas Douzinas and Conor Gearty, 251–71. Cambridge: Cambridge University Press.

Robbins, Bruce. 2017. *The Beneficiary*. Durham, NC: Duke University Press.

Roelandt, Els. 2019. "Renzo Martens' Episode III: Analysis of a Film Process in Three Conversations." In *Critique in Practice: Renzo Martens' Episode II: Enjoy Poverty*, edited by Anthony Downey, 46–55. Berlin: Sternberg.

Rothstein, Klaus. 2020. *Den druknede dreng: Flygtningekrisen i litteratur og kunst*. Copenhagen: Forlaget Vandkunsten.

Roy, Ananya. 2010. *Poverty Capital: Microfinance and the Making of Development*. New York: Routledge.

Roy, Ananya. 2012. "Ethical Subjects: Market Rule in an Age of Poverty." *Public Culture* 24 (1): 105–8.

Rud, Søren, and Søren Ivarsson, eds. 2021. *Globale og postkoloniale perspektiver på dansk kolonihistorie*. Aarhus: Aarhus Universitetsforlag.

SAIH (Norwegian Students' and Academics' International Assistance Fund). 2012. "Radi-Aid: Africa for Norway." YouTube. https://www.youtube.com/watch?v=oJLqyuxm96k. https://www.youtube.com/watch?v=oJLqyuxm96k&t=37s

SAIH (Norwegian Students' and Academics' International Assistance Fund). 2013. "Let's Save Africa—Gone Wrong." YouTube. https://www.youtube.com/watch?v=xbqA6o8_WC0.

SAIH (Norwegian Students' and Academics' International Assistance Fund). 2014. "Who Wants to Be a Volunteer?" YouTube. https://www.youtube.com/watch?v=ymcflrj_rRc.

SAIH (Norwegian Students' and Academics' International Assistance Fund). 2016. "The Radi-Aid App: Change a Life with Just One Swipe." YouTube. https://www.youtube.com/watch?v=oBrNa-VoJfc.

SAIH and David Girling. 2018. *Radi-Aid Research: A Study of Visual Communication in Six African Countries*. https://www.radiaid.com/radiaid-research.

Sandemose, Aksel. (1933) 1994. *En flygtning krydser sit spor: Espen Arnakkes kommentarer til Janteloven*. Copenhagen: Gyldendal.

Schama, Simon. 1988. *The Embarrassment of Riches: An Interpretation of Dutch Culture in the Golden Age*. London: William Collins.

Schrift, Alan D. 1997. *The Logic of the Gift: Toward an Ethic of Generosity*. New York: Routledge.

Schuller, Kyla. 2013. "Avatar and the Movements of Neocolonial Sentimental Cinema." *Discourse* 35 (2): 177–93.

Schuller, Kyla. 2018. *The Biopolitics of Feeling: Race, Sex, and Science in the Nineteenth Century*. Durham, NC: Duke University Press.

Schwittay, Anke. 2015. *New Media and International Development: Representation and Affect in Microfinance*. Oxfordshire: Routledge.

Sharma, Devika. 2016. "The Predicament of Spectatorship: Renzo Martens and the Humanitarian Image." In *Discursive Framings of Human Rights: Negotiating Agency and Victimhood*, edited by Karen-Margrethe Simonsen and Jonas R. Kjærgård. Abingdon: Birkbeck Law Press.

Sharma, Devika. 2017. "Doing Good, Feeling Bad: Humanitarian Emotion in Crisis." *Journal of Aesthetics & Culture* 9 (1).

Sharma, Devika. 2019a. "Ny Feminisme I: Affekt og følelser." In *Ny kulturteori*, edited by Birgit Eriksson and Bjørn Schiermer Andersen, 519–48. Copenhagen: Hans Reitzels Forlag.

Sharma, Devika. 2019b. "Privileged, Hypocritical, and Complicit: Contemporary Scandinavian Literature and the Egalitarian Imagination." In *Comparative Literature Studies* 56 (4): 711–30.

Sharma, Devika. 2024. "Skeptimentality: *The Square* and the Aesthetics of Complicity." In *Nordic Journal of Aesthetics* 33 (68): 10–32.

Sharma, Devika. 2025 (Forthcoming). "The Art of Guilt-Tripping: A Transregional Genre of Exchange." In *Konsthistorisk tidskrift / Journal of Art History*.

Sliwinski, Sharon. 2011. *Human Rights in Camera*. Chicago: University of Chicago Press.

Sloterdijk, Peter. (1983) 2001. *Critique of Cynical Reason*. Translated by Michael Eldred. Minneapolis: University of Minnesota Press.

Solomon, Robert C. 2004. *In Defense of Sentimentality*. New York: Oxford University Press. DOI: 10.1093/019514550X.001.0001.

Sontag, Susan. 2003. *Regarding the Pain of Others*. London: Picador.

Stowe, Harriet Beecher. 1852. *Uncle Tom's Cabin; or, Life Among the Lowly*. John P. Jewett and Company.

Stubberud, Elisabeth, and Priscilla Ringrose. 2014. "Speaking Images, Race-less Words: *Play* and the Absence of Race in Contemporary Scandinavia." *Journal of Scandinavian Cinema* 4 (1): 61–76.

Taylor, Adam. 2014. "Norway's Infamous 'Human Zoo' Was a Travesty in 1914. Here's Why It Was Brought Back in 2014." *The Washington Post*, May 23. https://www.washingtonpost.com/news/worldviews/wp/2014/05/23/norways-infamous-human-zoo-was-a-travesty-in-1914-heres-why-it-was-brought-back-in-2014/.

Thomsen, Torsten Bøgh. 2016. "Lykke i ulykkens tid: Økosorg og klimamelankoli i Victor Boy Lindholms *Guld* og Theis Ørntofts *Digte 2014*." *K&K*, no. 121, 221–41.

Ticktin, Miriam. 2011. *Casualties of Care: Immigration and the Politics of Humanitarianism in France*. Berkeley: University of California Press.

Ticktin, Miriam. 2017. "A World Without Innocence." *American Ethnologist* 44 (4): 577–90.

Todd, Janet. 1986. *Sensibility: An Introduction*. London: Methuen.

Tvedt, Terje. 2002. *Verdensbilder og selvbilder: En humanitær stormakts intellektuelle historie*. Oslo: Universitetsforlaget.

Tvedt, Terje. 2018. *Det internasjonale gjennombruddet: Fra 'ettpartistat' til flerkulturell stat*. Oslo: Dreyers Forlag.

Utichi, Joe. 2017. "Meet Ruben Östlund." Deadline.com. May 29. https://deadline
.com/2017/05/ruben-ostlund-director-interview-square-palme-dor-cannes
-1202103984/.

Viemose, Hanne Højgaard. 2019. *HHV, Frshwn: dødsknaldet i Amazonas*. Copenhagen: Gyldendal.

Vik, Hanne Hagtvedt, Steven L. B. Jensen, Linde Lindkvist, and Johan Strang.
2018. "Histories of Human Rights in the Nordic Countries." *Nordic Journal of
Human Rights* 36 (3): 189–201. DOI: 10.1080/18918131.2018.1522750.

Weizman, Eyal. 2009. "Thanato-tactics." In *The Power of Inclusive Exclusion: Anatomy of Israeli Rule in the Occupied Palestinian Territories*, edited by Adi Ophir,
Michal Givoni, and Sari Hanafi, 543–66. New York: Zone Books.

Weizman, Eyal. 2011. *The Least of All Possible Evils: Humanitarian Violence from
Arendt to Gaza*. London: Verso.

Weizman, Eyal. 2017. *Forensic Architecture: Violence at the Threshold of Detectability*.
New York: Zone Books.

Wekker, Gloria. 2016. *White Innocence: Paradoxes of Colonialism and Race*. Durham,
NC: Duke University Press.

Wexler, Laura. 2000. *Tender Violence: Domestic Visions in an Age of U.S. Imperialism*.
Chapel Hill: University of North Carolina Press.

Wilderson, Frank B. 2020. *Afropessimism*. New York: W. W. Norton.

Williams, Raymond. 1977. *Marxism and Literature*. Oxford: Oxford University
Press.

Witoszek, Nina. 2011. *The Origins of the "Regime of Goodness": Remapping the Cultural
History of Norway*. Oslo: Universitetsforlaget.

Yang, Julianne Q. M. 2017. "Filming Guilt About the Past Through Anachronistic
Aesthetics: Roy Andersson's *A Pigeon Sat on a Branch Reflecting on Existence*."
Scandinavian Studies 89 (4): 573–96.

Index

Page numbers in *italics* refer to illustrations

individual autonomy, 59–60
inegalitarianism, 193, 199–200, 203n1
inequality: global, and egalitarian imaginary, 157–58; racial, 108, 149. *See also* economic inequality
injustice, and Scandinavian public culture, 3, 5, 23
innocence: black African, 120–21; childlike, 88, 122, 182; false sense of, 85–86, 117; guilt and, 120, 157; loss of, 26, 38, 182; racial, 26, 49–51, 88, 97–107, 111, 116, 120–22; Scandinavian colonialism and, 206n24; sympathy and, 215n4; Ticktin's critique of, 218n21; white, 108, 110–11, 218n1
innocent colonialism, 22
intelligence, equality of, 118
Det internasjonale gjennembruddet (The international breakthrough) (Tvedt), 90–93
internationalism, 2, 17–22, 109, 199, 216n1
International Monetary Fund (IMF), 138, 144
interplay of opposites, 79

Jackson, Peter, 134
James, Aaron, 26
Jessen, Ida, 83–84, 86–88, 121
Jubilee Debt Campaign, 144
justice, distributive, 169, 199–201

Kalén, William Johansson, 57
En kärlekhistoria (A Swedish love story) (dir. Andersson, 1970), 53
Krarup, Søren, 44
Kundera, Milan, 34

Læger uden Grænser, 27–28
Lanchester, John, 179–80, 198–99
The Last Utopia (Moyn), 9
late capitalism, 50, 61, 146, 162
late humanitarianism: capitalism and, 130; collective sensibility, 71; communication and, 75; embarrassment of riches, 112; historical sensorium and, 87; imaginary distance, 219n8; introduc-

tion to, 8–12, 16, 28; privilege montage and, 78–80; skeptimentality and, 104; sympathy and, 196
Lazzarato, Maurizio, 29, 137–41, 144–45
Les damnés de la terre (Fanon), 176
Leth, Jørgen, 155
Lindholm, Victor Boy, 166, 168–70
Lindqvist, Ursula, 53–54
Listhaug, Sylvi, 44, 92
literary privilege genre, 169, 174, 224n18
Live Aid initiative, 132
living reality, 118–21
Lousley, Cheryl, 132, 133
love, theory of, 19, 44, 59–62
Lübecker, Nikolaj, 54

The Making of the Indebted Man (Lazzarato), 137–39
Malkki, Liisa H., 16
marginalization, 41, 46, 50
Martens, Renzo, 29, 108–9, 111–12, 146, 155
Meckseper, Josephine, 66–67
microfinance, 131, 140–42
middle class, Nordic. *See* Nordic middle class
Milanović, Branko, 198
"The Misadventures of Critical Thought" (Rancière), 65
Mitchell, W. J. T., 114
Moderata Samlingsparti (Moderate Party), 45
moral-affective disposition, 117–18
morally embarrassing, 14, 33–38, 44, 59, 134, 191, 194
moral sentiments: compassion as, 6–17, 33, 39, 196–97, 208n3; complicity and, 14–15, 25, 36; embarrassment as, 14, 33–44, 59, 134, 191–94; immoral sentiments and, 15; as Scandinavian public culture, 42; sensibility of privilege and, 44–45; Solomon on, 33
moral solution, 126
moral superiority: goodness and, 147; humanitarianism and, 111, 122, 206n21; introduction to, 1, 16; Radi-Aid and, 106–8; skeptimentality and, 126

moral superpowers, 18
Moyn, Samuel, 9
multiculturalism, 90–91
Munfocol, Muauke B., 148
My African Letters (Ejlerskov), 125–27, 146, 157, 168
Myong, Lene, 26
Myrdal, Gunnar, 17

Naseh, Negar, 186
The Need to Help (Malkki), 16
neocolonialism, 3, 57, 72, 98, 115, 156, 223n8
neoliberalism, 3, 9, 53, 128, 137–42, 184, 212n1
The New Totalitarians (Huntford), 52
Ngai, Sianne, 15, 35, 161–62, 179, 194
Nigerian email scam, 125
Nordic exceptionalism, 21, 206n23
Nordic interpretations of privilege, 17–23
Nordic middle class: collectivity and, 179–81, 187; democracy and, 207n25; global privilege and, 198; humanitarianism and, 94; hypocrisy literature and, 169; introduction to, 1–2, 12, 19–20; moral sentiments and, 193; refugees and, 84; sentimentality and, 41–42, 130
Nordic welfare model: global privilege and, 199–200; humanitarianism and, 68, 84; hypocrisy literature and, 180; introduction to, 2, 7, 18–23, 28; sentimentality and, 43, 50; skeptimentality and, 47, 54–64; social democracy and, 207n25; subordination of indigenous peoples, 207n27
Norwegian Agency for Development Cooperation, 106
Norwegian Missionary Society (NMS), 105

On the Genealogy of Morals (Nietzsche), 137
Open Casket (Schutz), 150
Operation Day's Work (Operasjon Dagsverk), 93
opposites, interplay of, 79
optimism, 93–98
Ørntoft, Theis, 50–51, 59
Östlund, Ruben, 28, 42, 45–51, 58–59, 61–63, 187

Oxfeldt, Elisabeth, 22–23

passive spectators, 120
performance of not-noticing, 88, 101–2
Picturing Pity (Gullestad), 104–5
A Pigeon Sat on a Branch Reflecting on Existence (dir. Andersson, 2014), 55–57, 59, 61–62
Piketty, Thomas, 193, 197, 200
Play (dir. Östlund, 2011), 45, 51, 54
politics of life, 127
The Politics of Social Solidarity (Baldwin), 19–20
Politisk roman (Political novel) (Aburas), 184
Ponte, Stefano, 152
Potential History (Azoulay), 195–96
Poverty Capital (Roy), 140
"Prisen for et dikt" (The price of a poem) (Grøndahl), 6–7, 150, 185
privilege: Bartky on, 2–3; capitalism and, 3; Nordic interpretations of, 17–23; racism and, 3; resignation and, 3; sadness over, 3; socioeconomic, 2, 18; unearned, 2–3, 8, 169–71, 195, 209n8. *See also* sensibility of privilege
privileged observers, 7, 114
privilege genres: artistic, 7–8; fee scams and, 220n3; guilt and, 23, 149–57, 169; hypocrisy literature as, 165, 174, 177, 224n18; literary, 169, 174, 224n18; overview of, 5–8, 23, 28–29, 36, 42, 79; sensibility of privilege and, 128; sentimental economy and, 128, 131–33
privilege-guilt, 162–64
privilege montage, 7, 73–79, *74*
privilege sensibility. *See* sensibility of privilege
Progress Party (Fremskrittspartiet), 44, 92
proximate proximity, 120

racial inequality, 108, 149
racial innocence, 26, 49–51, 88, 97–107, 111, 116, 120–22
racial noninnocence, 103–4
racism: abolitionism and, 25–26, 41, 102,

110, 130–32, 206n18, 210n13; entitlement, 26; privilege and, 3; stereotypes, 51, 94, 97–100, 106, 212n14; whiteness and, 15, 72, 101–2, 111, 148, 170–73, 224n13. *See also* slavery

Radi-Aid: benefactors and, 103–4; defined, 217n14; goodness regime and, 149; optimism and, 93–98, *95*; overview, 29, 89; racial innocence and, 98–107, 111, 122; research study, 98–100, 104–5

Rancière, Jacques, 65–67, 79, 118

Ravn, Olga, 170

recipient mentality, 154

reciprocal vulnerability, 63

recognizability, 174, 188

refugee crisis, 1, 83–84, 180, 185

Regarding the Pain of Others (Sontag), 6

regime of goodness. *See* goodness regime

Reinfeldt, Fredrik, 45

Richey, Lisa Ann, 152

Ringgaard, Dan, 188–89

Robbins, Bruce, 80, 162–64, 175–78

Rosler, Martha, 65–67, 78, 86

Roy, Ananya, 29, 140, 144–45

SAIH. *See* Students' and Academics' International Assistance Fund (SAIH)

Sartre, Jean-Paul, 176

Scandinavian public culture: aesthetic of sympathy, 62; defined, 22; egalitarianism and, 20, 196; guilt trips and, 7–8; humanitarianism and, 80; hypocrisy literature and, 174, 180; injustice and, 3, 5, 23; moral sentiments as, 42; privilege montage in, 65; skeptimentality and, 43–44, 92; slave labor and, 206n24

Scandinavian sensibility. *See* sensibility of privilege

ScanGuilt project, 22–23

Schama, Simon, 109–10

Schuller, Kyla, 41–42, 51

Schutz, Dana, 150

seeing, in spectatorship, 5–6, 28–29

sensibility, collective, 4–5, 24, 26, 36, 71, 196

sensibility of privilege: aesthetic of complicity, 8; defined, 4, 33; exploita-

tion and, 127–28; gift and debt logics, 128; humanitarianism and, 5, 11–12, 85–89, 109, 122; inegalitarianism and, 199–200; innate sensitivity, 4; literary privilege and, 174–75; moral sentiments and, 44–45; precondition for, 2–3, 22; privilege-guilt and, 162; racism and, 149; skeptimentality and, 16, 29–34, 65–67, 107, 195–96; third-party gifts and, 136

sentimental economy: debt economy, 128–29, 136–39, 141–45, 146; "Give-a-Goat" (Given ged), 133–35; Haitian earthquake, 142–45; late-humanitarianism and, 130–36; overview of, 29, 130–36; privilege genres and, 128, 131–33

Sentimental Figures of Empire in Eighteenth-Century Britain and France (Festa), 40

sentimental humanitarianism, 13–17, 39, 73, 96–97, 200

sentimentality: aesthetic of sympathy and, 8, 79, 87, 165; humanitarianism, 13–17, 39, 73, 96–97, 200; intimacy of, 41; politics and, 39–42; skeptimentality and, 13–17, 33–36

sentimental publics, 15, 40–41, 46, 79, 102, 108, 197

shame: debt economy and, 137, 139–40; feelings of, 35, 37–38, 67; in hypocrisy literature, 185–86, 190; moral sentiments and, 153; national, 25; white, 150–51, 155, 170–71

Singer, Peter, 3

skeptimental beneficiaries, 6, 173–78

skeptimental gaze, 56, 86–88, 183

skeptimentality: ambivalence and, 37–39; defined, 14; economic inequality and, 36, 65–67; importance of, 194; sensibility of privilege and, 16, 29–34, 65–67, 107, 195–96; sentimentality and, 13–17, 33–36; whiteness and, 15

skeptimental logic, 13–15, 50–51

skeptimental mutation: complicity and, 165; guilt-tripping and, 152–57; in hypocrisy literature, 183–84; introduction to, 8, 15; sentimentality and, 35, 48, 135

skeptimental publics, 28, 42, 83–89